The Michael Handbook

DI013762

by
Jose Stevens, Ph.D.
&
Simon Warwick-Smith

"This system of knowledge is a way of living your life that makes perfect sense and is fun. It is a way of knowing the truth and the reasons for existence."

- Michael

Warwick Press

The Michael Handbook

Published by:

Warwick Press
P.O. Box 2023
Orinda, CA 94563

We are interested in your views and any further information. Write to the above address.

Cover Illustration Courtesy of "The Exploratorium"
Cover Design by Robert Pawlak

LCCN: 86-40578
ISBN 0-941109-00-3

Simon's Dedication

For Kate with all my heart.

Jose's Dedication

For Lena, Anna, and Carlos

Acknowledgements

A book is not the effort of its authors buy a group effort from friends, colleagues, spouses and so forth. We would like to acknowledge and thank more people than there is space to list. To all of you, our sincere thanks.

We want to acknowledge the special contribution to this body of knowledge by J.P. Van Hulle and Aaron Christeaan.

We are fortunate in having secured the artistic services of Lenore Schuh, with her gift for capturing abstract feeling states in sketch form. Also, thanks are due to Naomi Steinfeld for writing assistance.

We would like to thank Joy Perasso for their love and support.

The origins of the information as presented here lie in years of study and volumes of channeled information, for whom we acknowledge Michael.

A Brief Overview

This teaching exists to assist the planetary shift toward older soul age evolution.

The ultimate goal of existence on the planet is to unite, and in everyday terms this means cooperation instead of competition. That is why self-acceptance and acceptance of others is important, and why unconditional love is the highest goal within this teaching.

This body of knowledge describes personality in terms of "overleaves", a set of characteristics that overlay your essence or soul. With the knowledge of this system, you can choose whether you operate from the positive or negative parts of your personality. When you come from the positive parts, you are acting out of true personality, and that is how your essence or inner being can grow and express itself.

Many modern schools of philosophy and psychology represent facets of this system. Readers of Maslow, Jung, Eric Erikson and Freud, as well as others, will find a ring of familiarity here.

Elements of this system were being taught in the 1920's by Gurdjieff, Ouspensky, and later Rodney Collin. Readers will discover that many of the underlying tenets resonate with Eastern philosophies, especially Sufism.

This teaching, as presented here, surfaced in the early 1970's in the San Francisco Bay Area through different mediums and channels. The information is channeled from the being called Michael and is named after him.

Michael is a non-physical being who once lived many lifetimes on the earth. He completed his experience and moved on to other realms of existence from where he teaches.

Contents

Preface

We wrote this book to take those with little or no knowledge of this teaching up to a basic level of understanding. Our approach has been to teach by analogy, analogy that will draw on your everyday experience.

This book is not a body of facts but a way of seeing the world, a language, a medium, a perspective. It contains one interpretation of how the universe works and is broad in that it speaks of the universe, and focused in that it explains the workings of everyday personality.

Some of the terms expressed here differ from the way this system is presented elsewhere. This is a result of the expansion of understanding about the system and the process of self-confirmation that goes with it. Different things are true for different people, experiences and cultures. The terms are intended only as a transitory vehicle toward seeing the world with wider perception.

The book has been designed both to entertain and to educate. The written word becomes carved in stone. Please do not "believe" what we have written here but check it out for yourself. And once you have mastered it, let it go.

Introduction

This book is a map, a long lost map, that reveals the contours of a rugged and exotic terrain and a trail through it. Here, you will find the essential elements that make up your personality: the role you play, the goal of your life, your basic attitude, and the stumbling blocks that exist. Here, you also will discover how you can shift gears to accelerate your self-understanding and move toward unconditional acceptance of others.

This book is about a spiritual teaching. "Spiritual" because it examines the context of our existence, "teaching" because that's what it does. Many teachings advance mankind, this is one.

Two thousand years ago, at the beginning of the age of Pisces, a great teacher (one of many who came at different times), Jesus Christ introduced a spiritual teaching. It flourished and flowed down through the centuries like a river of truth. Wherever you were or whoever you were, peasant or nobleman, there was generally a monastery or church in your area where you could strive with coming to terms with your existence. For the last two thousand years the opportunity for spiritual growth has been available to all men and women, albeit with the blemishes and distortions that mankind placed upon it.

The age of Pisces is coming to an end, taking with it the symbol of the fish which is also the symbol of Christianity. A new age approaches: the age of Aquarius, with new teachers and new concepts about our existence. The ideas contained in this book filter out from small groups who live them in their lives. These concepts include that the universe and life itself is a rational system, not random chaos, with describable elements such as essence, false personality, reincarnation, our underlying oneness, and so on.

These notions can help to set the context for the growth of the planet as the major civilizations of the world continue their rapid integration after thousands of years of separateness. With this integration can come awareness of our actions on a personal scale and on a world wide scale.

For example, the concept of reincarnation means that we cannot exhaust the world's supply of oxygen nor contaminate the oceans without coming back to experience the consequences; nor can we deplete world forests and animal populations.

We will live with our decisions.

The nations of the world do not generally recognize these concepts. For example there is no general understanding of the notion of false personality and of the underlying essence. It takes wider perception than the present average soul age of the world population to understand this. Recognizing the distinction between false personality and essence would facilitate better decision making world-wide and improve international relations, not to mention reducing the chance of nuclear war.

This book is presented not as just another school of thought but as a genuine transformational text.

"The philosophy of one century is the common sense of the next."
                                                           - I Ching

"The greatest thing you can do with this teaching is share it."
                                                           - Michael

Chapter One

The Grand Scheme

The Tao (or God) thinking aloud:
"I've been bored lately. Being "all that is" is, of course, wonderful, but I feel that it's time for a new game. I feel totally creative today and I'm in the mood for something quite unusual.

Wouldn't it be interesting and fun to play hide and seek with myself! I'll pretend that a part of myself has forgotten that it is part of me. The game will be for that part to remember that it truly is a part of me.

I'll create some mazes and diversions to make the journey a real adventure. Aha! I'll fragment this part of me up into millions of parts and let them interact with one another. I'll concoct some fancy distractions and paradoxes so they'll never know. That'll keep them, er, me, busy for a long time trying to sort it all out.

I'll leave them clues and little signs along the way to keep them on the trail if they get too far off course. Naturally, there will be an underlying structure to the game to give it a semblance of awesome order. I'll even arrange for the parts to have free choice so that they, uh, we can really get into trouble. But that will make winning even more delicious. Well, let's get started."

And that's exactly what the Tao did and here we are.

How do we read the clues and signs and unravel the mystery to find our way back to the Tao or ourselves? That is what this book is about.

Read on and discover.

The Grand Scheme

How has the Tao set up the original and cosmic scale hide and seek game?

The Tao - All That Is

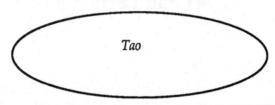

The Tao (or God), being infinitely creative, evolves into higher levels of consciousness by knowing itself in rich and varied play. Within this play, the Tao casts off sparks of itself. These sparks forget their origin, and pursue a course leading to remembering themselves again through a colorful and creative journey.

Cast from the Tao - Sparks of Consciousness

By dividing itself up, the Tao has created the illusion of separateness within wholeness. That is, the purpose is defeated if there is not the sense of separateness to be creatively overcome.

That is why human beings have separate bodies and separate identities, compete for limited resources and so on. This separateness makes the game possible.

To accomplish the goal of self-knowledge, the Tao has divided itself into seven stages (planes) of existence, the structure that provides the awesome order.

The Seven Planes - Separateness Within Wholeness

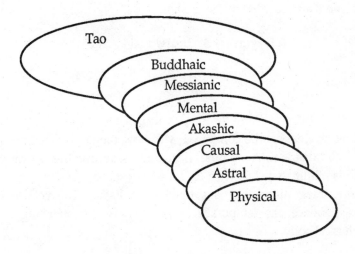

The physical plane is the most isolated one, by virtue of its properties of time. On the physical plane energy vibrates so slowly that it appears to be solid matter. Bumping into things is a good reminder that you and the object are separate. On higher planes, energies can merge and separate at will.

The game begins on the physical plane. The Tao has hidden cleverly and we, the cast off sparks, finish counting and start to look for it. However at first we do not even know we are looking.

As the plane most characterizing separateness, the physical plane represents the cutting edge of new experience for the Tao. The individuals participating in it may be seen as adventurous pioneers, each one advancing by venturing into frontiers of experience that are unique.

Sentient beings are created by the Tao out of itself, and many of these entities venture out to play and learn in the physical world. The entities separate temporarily into hundreds of individual essences called fragments in order to get the most varied and complete experience possible.

With each incarnation, a fragment essence takes on a temporary personality. This physical personality dies with the body each lifetime but the lessons learned and the situations experienced are recorded by the essence.

A Fragment - An Individual Essence

This process can be compared with how the body digests food. Some food that is eaten becomes flesh and tissue, and the unwanted waste is eliminated. Likewise essence "digests" the experience of a lifetime, integrating what is valuable into itself. The vehicle for that experience, the temporary personality, is cast off along with the physical body.

An Entity - A Collection of Essences

The fragment or essence evolves this way until upon the completion of many lifetimes it ultimately fulfills its purpose and completes its experience. At that time it reunites with its fellow fragments on the astral plane, one dimension above the physical plane.

A less spiritual analogy is to say that life is a game of pinball. Your essence is learning how to operate the pinball machine. It pulls the spring-loaded plunger and fires the first ball up and around into the top of the maze. The ball rolls, bumps and rebounds its way down. As the ball approaches a hole in the course, essence strives to use the contrivances available to save it. Not knowing the rules, it learns by its experiences. The ball drops down a hole, end of game. It is then time for a new ball and a new lifetime.

Essence decides how it is going to play this next one in view of what it learned last time. It fires the ball (sets up the life) so as to learn as much as possible. After a few hundred shots it has mastered the game and moves on to a new one.

One cycle for an individual essence may take from about 49 to 400 physical lives. There is an unconscious thread of knowing from one lifetime to the next - which, under certain circumstances, can become conscious. This is the stored essence experience, "forgotten" by the body personality.

Apparently unfounded feelings of familiarity with a complete stranger can be the vague stirrings of deeper emotions.

For example you can see a strange face across a room and get a strong rush of feeling. That can be essence recognition of a past life connection; a husband, wife, or child from long ago.

The law of karma facilitates essence to learn what life is about. Briefly, this is the law of consequences or payback. What you do to someone else, he or she will do back to you, sooner or later, with the same intensity.

To accomplish the learning, essence neither avoids nor seeks pain or pleasure. It desires to experience intensity (i.e. karma) through the vehicle of a body and a personality.

Much of the focus of this book is about the body personality and the ways we can learn to recognize and master it.

The Grand Scheme

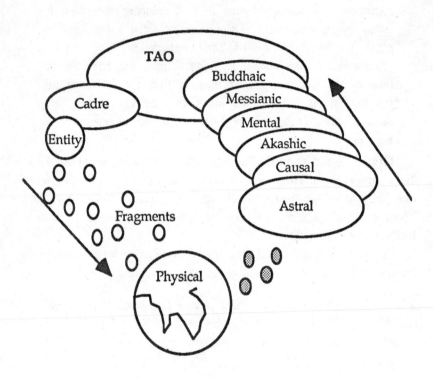

Life is like going to the movies. Your essence likes action, intensity and living on the edge. It strives and encourages you to become immersed in as much drama as possible. Death and injury are just as if you were watching someone else's. The personality alone believes that the world ends with death.

The accumulation of experience by essence increases the essence's knowledge of the Tao and results in remembering one's origins and connectedness. As remembering occurs with increasing number of lifetimes, a greater harmony between essence and the physical personality is displayed. The false personality plays an increasingly small part, leaving only essence to direct activities. The game of hide and seek gets hot.

Essence Collecting Experience

It seems the very fabric of the barrier or filter that prevents remembering grows thinner and thinner as you accumulate lifetimes of experience. Increasingly you become able to perceive more, to see objectively about yourself and others, and to truly understand the wider context. This ability is like a muscle that grows stronger with exercise.

The progression of experience is not random but structured. A single essence moves through five major stages on the physical plane: infant, baby, young, mature, and old. Each stage requires many lifetimes to complete and has peculiar characteristics that are readily identified and an important part of this system.

Each lifetime essence selects a set of personality traits and a life purpose for mastery. These traits are called "overleaves" because they overlay the essence and distort its purer energy in a way that makes for a lively and enriching experience.

An analogy might be that in a given sport a player assumes a certain position on the field such as goalkeeper, providing for a range of individual and team experiences. In each game the player may assume a different position and eventually masters all of them.

Each overleaf or personality trait has a positive and a negative pole. Acting from the negative pole creates disharmony and neurosis and acting from the positive pole creates satisfaction and health. (Refer to the Overleaf Chart on p. 326)

As a soul accumulates experience, so one can increasingly recognize the impulses of the body personality and develop and broaden the ability to act from essence.

The older the soul the more one has the facility of moving towards the positive poles via understanding and self awareness. This can enable a transformation in one's life, and when recognized on a large scale, in the behavior of countries toward one another, and a transformation of the planet.

The overall goal is for each fragment to experience all that life has to offer, and to progress towards wholeness, integration and balance. The model for this is self-acceptance and acceptance of others. Thus the game of hide and seek leads to a major discovery. "Me" discovers "we" and "we" discover "I". The game is finished. The Tao has been caught.

Chapter Two

Essence and Personality

This section describes the differences among the terms essence (higher self), true   personality, and false personality. The term "personality" is generic and includes both true and false personality.

Essence

Essence or soul is eternal and is the stream of consciousness from lifetime to lifetime. The essence develops its own unique flavor after a certain number of lifetimes and experiences on the various planes of consciousness.

Essence may be described as a being without the boundaries of time or space. It is the consciousness of all past, present and future lives, and the spirit that exists between lives - an integrated energetic being without a body.

Essence and Personality

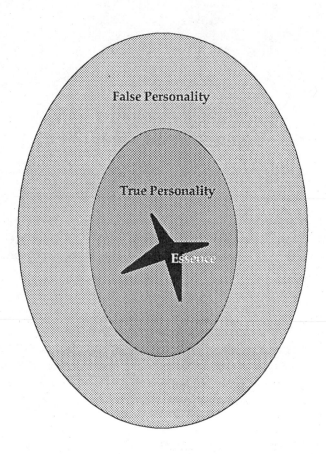

With each successive lifetime, the fragment essence records the experience of the individual personalities and begins to develop characteristics of its own. It adds a new layer to itself, rather like the growth rings on a tree. At the core is pure essence and around it are layers of memory of different experiences of different lifetimes. Eventually the essence has a wrapping made up of many, many different lifetimes. This accumulated essence wisdom is quite different from an individual personality of any one lifetime.

In the first few lifetimes the personality is dominant since so few lives have been recorded. After many lifetimes the individual personality becomes less important because it goes into the memory bank of a multitude of experiences: souls with more experience are less governed by their personalities. In younger souls the personality is more controlling.

You can develop the skill of looking into a person's eyes and gauging how many lifetimes their essence has had. Younger souls eyes have a kind of fresh, clear energetic look whereas older souls eyes look deeper, and there is almost a worn, experienced look. In souls who are ready to complete you can see acceptance and love.

Another analogy is that essence is surrounded by fifty film screens and is watching fifty films simultaneously. Each one is one of its lives, with a unique theme and plot. It learns and grows constantly from each of them.

Personality

True Personality

Each essence decides what experiences it will seek for a particular lifetime. At the time of birth it chooses a set of parameters (the overleaves) to set the scene, so to speak. These parameters make up the true personality.

The moment of birth determines the pattern of magnetic and gravitational influences upon certain glands of the body. The position of the planets from the time you take your first breath sets the clock running, so to speak. Your astrological birth chart is a general map of trends and challenges that will affect you throughout your life.

The essence selects the bodytype, a product of the parental gene pool, carefully chosen by the essence for its traits (see Bodytypes). In addition, essence selects the set of permanent personality characteristics called overleaves.

The true personality is composed of the set of overleaves minus the chief feature (covered later). More specifically the true personality is manifest when you are acting from the positive poles of the overleaves.

This true personality is essential to survival in a body and dies when the body dies each lifetime.

So-called "negative" karma cannot be created when acting from positive poles, but only from negative pole behaviour.

Generally essence chooses conditions and events in childhood that promote the development of the overleaves chosen. So that if you chose to be an intellectual and say academically gifted, then you would generally give yourself the right conditions for intellectual stimulation. There are no accidents, so you can see with your own upbringing what the elements were that then became an enabling influence for you as an adult.

The term personality parallels the concept of ego in the Buddhist tradition. The ego describes the boundary of the personality. The ego experiences itself as separate and unique in relation to other egos. This facilitates the experience of separateness on the physical plane. Without this ego or separateness it would not be possible to experience the kind of relationships that are part of the physical existence.

The relationship between essence and true personality can be likened to a rider and a horse. The rider is the essence and the horse is the true personality. The rider can thus direct the horse in the general direction that it wants to pursue. However, the horse is of course left with the choice of where it wishes to place its feet.

Occasionally the horse will choose a particular path because it knows best on the smaller scale.

In comparing the horse with the rider, the true personality similarly is limited in its sense of vision. The personality lives the life of a horse, with limited knowledge of who the rider is.

Essence, the rider, uses the body and its set of overleaves to express itself in the physical plane. The true personality gives it some limitations and a focus to manifest within. When the horse and rider ride together in harmony we can say that essence manifests clearly through the true personality.

Imagine if you were to live in the jungles of east Africa 800 years ago. To survive in that setting you would be adapting yourself to a primitive environment. Similarly the essence with its richness and variation and power is adapting to be on the earth in a body. The true personality is quite a crude vehicle for it, but one well adapted to the physical environment.

False Personality

False personality is the offspring of the true personality. It is the illusory vehicle that is made up of parental and cultural imprinting, the activities of the chief negative feature, and the negative poles of all the other overleaves. It is easy to see how it is illusory. Imprinting (or conditioning) is what you learn from others - in other words it is someone else's way of handling a situation. You gradually shed this and learn your own way.

False personality is blind to itself and runs the show a great deal during each lifetime. It tends to be tenacious, unrelenting, and becomes more subtle the older the soul becomes.

The false personality is purely physical and as mentioned is based on conditioning and imprinting. Its mechanical nature performs in terms of stimulus and response, and is simply reactive. The false personality consistently performs on a cause and effect basis, and is generally at the effect of the overleaves. It is particularly subject to illusion and fantasy, and is not at all necessary to survival.

False personality suffers from the illusion that it alone is important and must survive at any costs.

The false personality believes that it is real, and all there is to the self, and that it makes ultimate decisions. However, the essence actually makes major choices and uses the false personality to experience and learn lessons.

The false personality is governed chiefly by fear. In the analogy of the horse and rider, fear (false personality) sometimes takes over the horse (true personality). When the horse becomes frightened it may seek to secure itself at the expense of the rider (essence) and attempt to unseat the rider. The rider may be thrown off temporarily while the horse runs independently. However essence prevails and eventually establishes rapport with the horse once again.

The chief negative feature is the root of the underlying fearfulness of the personality. Acting out of the negative poles is a product of fearfulness and the tendancy to make false assumptions. Acting from the positive poles reflects seeking to clarify what is true, and acting in a caring way (love).

Many spiritual practices and exercises are geared toward eliminating the false personality so that essence may be expressed freely through the true personality. Although it is a mammoth task, false personality can be extinguished in a given lifetime, however this does not usually take place until the old soul age.

Much of the false personality may be sloughed off during the late teens and early thirties so that essence can manifest in the mid-thirties; however, during many lifetimes this does not occur at all.

Note that true personality cannot be eliminated because without it you could not be in a physical body.

The term "ego" (such as "having a big ego") relates not to the false personality as a whole but concerns how we see ourselves and how we think others see us. Wanting to feel important for example is that unconscious fearful part of ourselves that is afraid we are not lovable the way we are. We believe we might feel more loved if we were more important.

On a global scale both individuals and governments do not generally recognize the distinctions between true personality, false personality and essence. Countries operate as if individuals were solely personality and their policies reflect this. This book provides some of the tools and information to distinguish between true personality, false personality, and essence. Recognizing essence expression brings new-found freedom and a higher level of consciousness. Personal recognition comes first, and global recognition follows. This will become clearer as you read on.

Karma

Karma is the law of consequences, or balance. If someone causes you a broken leg in one lifetime, you may cause him or her a similar injury in another. The law requires that the emotional upset is redressed and experienced equally on both sides.

Karma occurs when one person interferes with the free choice of another. Of course, "good" karma occurs when a person increases anothers ability to choose.

What facilitates karma is imbalance. Imbalance is one of the functions of the personality. If all persons on this planet were in nodding agreement with one another there would be little learned from existence. The levels of soul perceptivity combined with the personality ensure differences and a wide variety of encounters. Generally in the early lifetimes karma is created, and in the later ones karma is re-paid, ensuring balance in the long run.

The universe itself is in imbalance. It comprises two elements - beingness and growth. The universe is growing toward higher levels of consciousness and the imbalance enables growth. The personality provides one mechanism for the imbalance and one path for man's evolution to higher consciousness.

> *Energy is intensity and intensity is karma. You set out to fulfill certain karmic needs each lifetime. It can look like a little board that you poke holes in every time you create a karma. You fill those holes with little pegs everytime you complete a karma. Each lifetime you set out to fill a certain amount of those holes. When all the holes are filled (i.e. your karmas completed) then you die. They are the karmas that you needed to complete this lifetime. Sometimes you ram an extra large peg into a smaller hole. This means you completed a much larger karma than you planned on completing this lifetime.*
>
> *Another way of putting this is that you are always seeking to reduce your sense of separateness through experiencing your differences with others.*
>
> *When you are no longer chasing differences you are back in the Tao. So you leave the Tao with a large empty peg board and it takes many lifetimes, and even many cycles as different roles to complete it.*

Maya

Maya is a term common to many Eastern religions and means "illusion". The physical plane has itself been created by the Tao and so it can be described as maya.

The false personality is one complex illusion, and the purpose of this volume is to offer tools to perceive that it is only a construct and has describable limits.

Similarly each soul age has its own maya, and maya abounds for those pursuing the spiritual path. For example sometimes a spiritual guru accumulates the trappings of wealth and then gets caught up in the consequences - buying land, handling taxation and insurance - far, far away from the original high spiritual aspirations that attracted the followers in the first place. Likewise a spiritually developed person can, for example, become enmeshed in maya by believing that his rigorous practices and observances make him somehow better than another.

A form of maya in this system is that the only way to be is an old soul, and to those who give it credence it carries illusory status. Casting aspersions on baby souls is another. Beginning students tend to feel that "because I am a priest I will act like a priest." This is a misuse of this system. Your role and overleaves describe your inner urges. Only you decide how you will be in the world, it is not pre-ordained by this system or anything else.

It is true that this system describes how our essences often arrange karma as a basis for gaining experience. But we hasten to add that the concept of karma is a limitation, and this system of knowledge is a description of limitations. You are what you believe, so if you believe you transcend these limitations then you do.

This should be sufficient to give you an indication of the size and slippery nature of maya.

Planes of Existence

Essence directs the activities of the personality from the astral plane. The astral plane is one of seven planes of existence that comprise our universe.

All of these are contained within the Tao itself. The developmental progression throughout these planes leads from the most physical to the least physical.

Any one fragment's essence exists on all the planes simultaneously. Access to one's experience on the other planes can be attained for example in the dream state, but the gross limitations of the personality make it difficult to comprehend the experience.

The Seven Planes of Existence

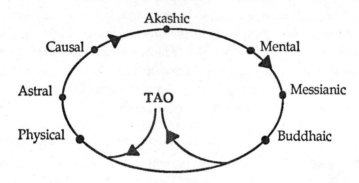

People often have difficulty understanding how the different planes exist when you can't see them, touch them, hear them or smell them.

Imagine a science project that somebody works out. A flea circus is set up in a box. You can see in but the fleas can't see out because the walls are mirrored on the inside.

The fleas believe the whole world is inside that box as they hop around and do what they do. You can see all the fleas because the box is not very big and you are outside of it. You may be controlling the science project or you may be an observer who is just watching the fleas, but likes them and feels warm toward them, because of the feeling that we're all in this bigger game together anyway.

You watch all the fleas do their numbers. They are not going to be aware of you. They can't see, touch, smell or know that you exist but they are there and you can observe them at any time.

It would be a better analogy to think of them not as fleas but as say little tiny sentient people just like us.

People feel the other dimensions are difficult to believe in because they cannot be perceived by the bodily senses. Yet we believe in our beliefs which cannot be seen by anyone. Who has seen an emotion or touched it? What does the image of the wind look like? And who has seen, touched or smelled time?

Chapter Three

Soul Ages

"Desire to live again, because that will be your lot in any case."

-Nietzsche

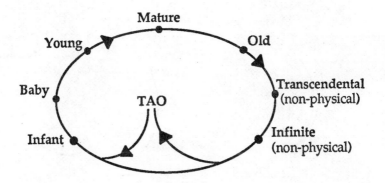

As a spark of light, the soul leaves the Tao. For with the birth of its separation begins the journey home. This is the soul's infancy, a beginning that parallels the infancy of a single human lifetime.

The essence develops and grows through lifetimes ranging from high drama to benign tranquility - playing every kind of part that can be experienced in society, from king to peasant, over thousands of years.

The Seven Soul Ages

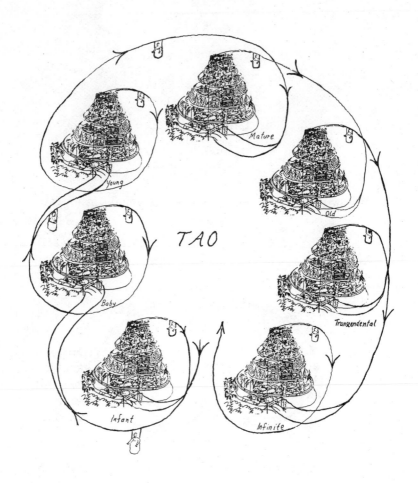

The School of Life

We shall see in this chapter how a person's perceptions develop, change, and broaden over a succession of lifetimes. A teenager sees the world differently from a forty year old - this reflects an evolution of perception.

We call the soul's developmental process the "school of life". In each separate stage each person sees the world in a strikingly different way. The stages are like grades, beginning with kindergarten, leading finally to graduation from college. We shall explore these stages and the levels within them. We will gain a sense of the orderliness and completeness of our journey and our underlying purpose on these travels.

As an aside, the perspective of calling our lives a game means that we have chosen to be here, to be responsible for how we play and what we make of our chosen roles. Seeing ourselves as players in a game gives a clear mandate for success, however we define it.

The Grand Purpose

What is the purpose of this developmental sequence that all of us have embarked upon? What are we developing towards and what are we developing from?

The experiences that essence (soul) sets up for the personality (persona) are called lessons. However people don't really learn; they remember what they already know.

Like a diamond in the rough, essence is encased in the jagged edges of the personality. Lifetimes of experience are the honing and faceting process that produce the brilliant diamond. Gradually the superimposed layer of the personality is buffed away so that each lifetime essence becomes increasingly revealed - as it always was but with sparkling facets won from many lifetimes.

> *People practised in meditation are able to travel inwardly and visit the depths of their essence. At the core of each essence is the Tao (or God).*

When people say they learned from an experience they are saying that they gained some remembering, taking them one miniscule step closer to oneness with all that is. The purpose of the rhythm of successive lives is to return to the completeness of the Tao - a movement from maximum separateness, loneliness and fear to oneness, emotional connectedness and love.

Yet how did we become so separate in the first place?

Casting Off

The Tao is driven to seek new experiences, to know itself in increasing depth through its evolution to higher and higher forms of consciousness. As a part of the Tao we are integrated partners in that creative dance, including the physical plane with all its planets and lifeforms - intricate, timeless and challenging!

> *Sentient (ensouled) life assumes a multitude of guises throughout the physical plane. Sentients on this planet are upright bipeds, whales and dolphins. Other forms in the universe include for example, gaseous beings existing as molecules. There are also other creatures, many of whom are well described in science fiction novels where the authors remember earlier experiences. The kinds of readers attracted most to these novels are of course those who were there.*

The Entity - A Family of Fragments

We have learned that the Tao casts out fragments of itself in the form of bright pure energy, as a crackling fire releases sparks into the air.

Cast from the Tao - Sparks of Consciousness

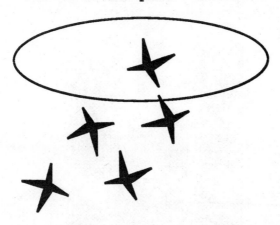

Each fragment goes through separation processes that make it distinct, colorful and different both from the Tao and from its fellow fragments.

The fragments wishing to go to the physical plane stay in what we could call a holding zone (waiting "in limbo" if you will). There they form an entity or oversoul with 800 to 1200 other fragments who wish to have similar experiences. Each fragment chooses a role, an essence twin (if any), and maps out what it seeks to accomplish during the cycle. The entire entity then chooses the appropriate planet to begin the cycle. The entity or oversoul is ready to play.

An Entity - A Collection of Essences

A Representation of the Michael Entity - 1050 Essences
(Primarily Warriors and Kings)

THE MICHAEL ENTITY

Grasping this picture calls for a long view of time. How fascinating to see society develop and change over successive lifetimes! You may live in one civilization such as ancient Greece, return to participate in say the Roman empire, and return to Greece at a much later date and witness the changes that have taken place. With the sizzling pace of new technology, returning in one hundred years time is a tantalizing prospect and you in essence choose the part you wish to play. (Past life regression is a tool you can use to bring these aspects into conscious memory.)

On leaving the Tao and this holding zone, the group of fragments (entity) is too intense and too powerful to incarnate in a single body so it separates back into its 800 to 1200 fragments.

Each fragment incarnates on earth as a unique individual with the entity as its reference point and "cosmic family".

Starting the Cycle

In general not all fragments begin their cycle on earth at the same time. Like birds in migration a few jump ahead at the chance to start the new cycle, the majority of the entity follow and a few fragments lag behind.

Each fragment progresses through five soul stages on the physical plane. The fragment begins as an infant soul, moves through the baby, young, mature, and old stages, and then cycles off to re-unify with the rest of the entity on the astral plane.

Each soul age incorporates a higher and more evolved perceptivity level such that a person within that stage experiences himself and the world around him in a new and different fashion.

Countries tend to reflect the predominant soul age of their population and act out the characteristics of that soul age. They reveal their particular level of perception in how they conduct their affairs.

The Soul Ages

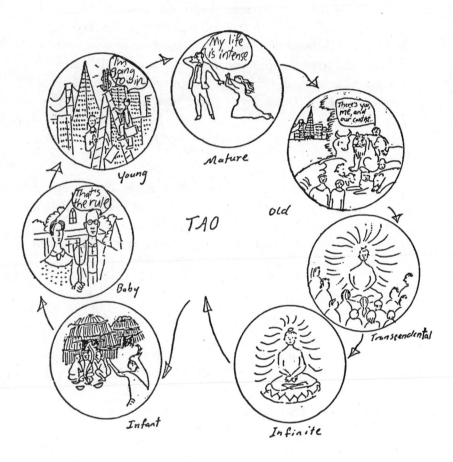

Comparing Soul Age With Chronological Age

Soul Age *(Many lifetimes)*	Comparable Physical Age *(One lifetime)*
Infant Soul	Newborn (to 18 mos)
Baby Soul	Toddler (18 mos-5 yrs)
Young Soul	Child (6-12 yrs)
Mature Soul	Adolescent (12 +)
Old Soul	Adult

At the time of writing, the Russians are attempting to subdue the population in Afghanistan. The Russian Governments' aspirations are control and dominance - very much young soul values of wanting to win. The Afghani's are in a struggle for survival - this is part of the baby soul's learning stage. In a way each is facilitating the other in their learning. This system does not make a value judgement as to whether the war is right or wrong, but provides the tools for insight and can show alternatives.

To recap, an entire cycle from leaving the Tao until returning to it comprises the seven soul ages (five on earth) and seven levels within each soul age.

Having completed the overview of soul ages we shall now look at each one in detail.

The Seven Stages of Perception

Soul Age	Description
Infant	Being here and coping.
Baby	Creates structure of civilization.
Young	Power issues; fame, money.
Mature	Emotional lessons, relationships and self karma.
Old	Detached from the drama of everyday life. Intellectual expression. Gifted in teaching.
Transcendental	Connectedness on a higher level.
Infinite	Conscious of everything.

INFANT SOULS

Focus:
"Where am I? And who are you?"
"I'm working out the rules by trial and error in primitive experiences".
"Let the game begin! Where can I tangle with experience?".
"I'm not up to the demands of society, it's too complex".

The fragment just cast from the Tao is raw, without experience and struggling for physical survival. Key words are primitive, fearful and helpless.

Neanderthal man fits the description of the fledgeling soul. Even in today's society he is still as primitive, only the environment has changed.

As tribal peoples, they can appear mystical. They are able to resonate closely with the Tao and with nature, and are untainted so to speak by life experience. They can demonstrate special powers such as psychic abilities about nature and the movement of animals.

When discovered by Europeans in the late 1700's, the native Australian aboriginals were the least developed of any primitive people in the world. For example, they had no written language. They were predominantly infant souls at that time with some older souls to guide them. Aboriginal art and mythology as handed down by generations is elaborate and conveys an intense emotional connectedness to the land. Only a rare few of the so-called more developed newcomers were able to understand and respect this intensity.

Infant souls often live on the fringes of society. They prefer living in the back woods or in isolated parts of the world where they can cope with survival issues without the complexity of technological society. In a highly complex society the early level infant souls may be overwhelmed and end up in institutions.

The introduction of diseases, alcohol or guns can wreak havoc with their simple symbiosis and lifestyle. Early explorers, missionaries, traders and the like had a well-documented impact on, for example, Pacific Islanders. These natives weren't necessarily all infant souls, but their lifestyle had many of the characteristics.

Analogous to young babies, infant souls focus on the body - how to use it, how to care for it. They learn how to exist in their environment at a rudimentary level of understanding. They experience the world as "me and not me" and this means everything that is not their body is "other". (This is identical to psychological Object Relations theory for babies).

You can see how the infant soul has similar priorities as an infant up to 18 months old.   Their needs are for raw and intense experiences, such as famine, plagues, battle, being oppressed, floods and so forth. The essence is integrating the characteristics of this planet and can only improve in its understanding and competence.

Infant souls generally do not persevere with sexual relationships. Even though they may reproduce, their experience of sexuality is animalistic. Only in the later part of the cycle they may explore "how can I get this person to like me?" and feel the beginnings of attachment to a sibling or parent. They are learning and experimenting with forming relationships.

The infant soul has to be taught what is right and what is wrong. Unfamiliar situations may cause them to be bewildered and perhaps even hostile. They usually do not seek employment except for the simplest tasks - they may appear dull even if they are intelligent.

They are inexperienced and unsophisticated in potentially creative endeavors - cooking and eating is strictly an exercise in survival.

Tribal infant souls are usually superstitious.   They create myths, legends and rituals to allay their fears and gain a sense of protection.

During World War II the United States Air Force built landing strips on remote islands in the Pacific. Some were inhabited by primitive tribes made up of mostly infant souls. The tribal people believed that the aircraft and the men in them were gods. They made images of the aircraft, honored them, and created a mythology that persisted many years after the airplanes had left.

There are no countries that are primarily made up of infant souls because they simply could not exist and maintain a society without the assistance of older souls. Infant souls do tend to cluster around the equator because survival is easier in that constant climate.

Individual infant souls do not become famous or well known because they do not have the sophistication nor the experience.

> *There is the famous case of the infant soul who as a child had been raised by wolves in India.   He was discovered and removed from his natural environment to civilization where people tried unsuccessfully to educate and change him.   The object of great scientific interest, scientists flocked from around the world   to study him.   He was overwhelmed by the attention   and died a short time later.*

The overall developmental pattern of the planet is   such that no more infant souls will be cast off from the Tao once the planet reaches predominantly mature soul perceptivity (about 2,000 A.D.).

There will no longer be the opportunity for raw infant soul experiences such as famine on a mass scale. Also the speed of growth of the older soul ages quickens as they learn how to learn, creating a gulf that   widens exponentially. As in a class of bright students mixed with slow learners, the slow learners get left increasingly far behind. The influx of "beginners" is visibly declining.

Positive Aspects
   Simple, earthy, child-like, naive, intuitive, living in the moment, unquestioning, Garden of Eden, mystical, work with symbols.

Negative Aspects
   Animalistic, helpless, frightened, ignorant, can be intensely gripped by the negative poles of the false personality as extremes are experienced early on, aggressive.

BABY SOULS

> **Focus:**
> "That's the rule and that's what we'll do."
> "I need someone to tell me where I fit in and what I should do."
> "If you don't fit in, unbelievably nasty things could happen to you." (totalitarian societies)

The baby soul has more experience of life on earth - a little more sophistication and slightly less fear.

In one example of a typical baby soul community, life works like clockwork. Everything has its place: church on Sunday, softball for the men, quilting for the women, long traditional work hours for the men, childrearing for the women, and so on. Many small communities in mid-America operate this way, one good example being the Amish towns of Pennsylvania.

The baby soul age is characterized by the perception that there is "me and other me's". This stage has similar precepts to a two-to-four year old, and is more mobile and able to explore the world with more dexterity. However, he still finds the environment a scary place and seeks guidance from more developed souls.

Baby souls seek out higher authorities who can lay out firm clear rules. They like structure just as young children like structure, and find comfort in knowing what to expect from their parents and from their environment. Tradition, rituals, and law and order provide an underlying sense of security.

The baby soul rituals are still carried forward on an archetypal level within our own society. As an example, the early origins of marriage lie with the man capturing a woman to take as his wife. This marriage by capture is still symbolized by the proud husband carrying his wife over the threshold of their new home.

Baby souls tend to be unshakeable in their beliefs and if opposed with another point of view they may be confused and even hostile. They can fight and kill for their beliefs if they have been taught that this is acceptable by the culture. Historically, baby soul activities include the crusades, the Inquisition, religious campaigns, and missionary work.

Baby souls like to be solid citizens and community leaders - seen as righteous and as models, such as a highly orthodox minister or preacher, sheriff or mayor. They may zealously follow the rules and seek to force other members of society to do likewise. They are the guardians of society and civilization, and oppose anything that seems to threaten the existing structure - even change itself! Having graduated from the infant stage they want to make sure that there are some standards to live by. Some mainstream religions serve this function and operate to watch-dog and care for those with the baby soul need for authority.

Christianity is a good case in point. Jesus Christ did not seek to leave behind any written teaching. In the centuries that followed the predominantly baby soul society imposed a structure, rites and rituals that Christ himself did not create. The principle of recurrence (reincarnation), for example, was an integral part of Christianity until the leaders decided it made them more powerful to change the doctrine to threaten miscreant followers with hell and damnation in the hereafter. But the Bible and Book of Common Prayer retain the references to "eternal life".

Baby souls want to be good so they like to be the good student. They prefer smaller, traditional institutions that give them structure and guidance. As authorities are the final word, there is an absence of original thought.

Baby souls have a strong belief in dichotomy - including for example the belief in good and evil or that god is a male authority opposed by a wicked devil. They seek punishment for non-conformists - hence the origin of the notion that God will strike you down as punishment for a "bad" deed.

Of course baby souls flourish and blossom in bureaucracies such as government because they are interested in organizing and developing the fabric of society with laws, regulations, and lines of authority.

The baby soul focus is "Do it right or not at all", or "That's the rule and that's what we'll do". There is only one way.

Around sexual matters there is often an uneasiness, with some degree of shame and guilt. At times the baby soul will decry sex altogether or simply tolerate it for procreation only. This correlates with the experience of young children who are not yet sophisticated enough to understand sexuality in its wider sense.

Food is purely functional to the baby soul. Codliver oil is a classic baby soul phenomenon - you take it because it is good for you, and despite the vile taste. Overall, their preferred diet is marked by sameness and habit.

Baby souls have few insights into their own lives. They do not perceive that their thoughts, feelings or attitudes cause psychological problems. If they experience emotional difficulties they have a tendency to somatize, such as forming gall stones in the place of experiencing angry emotions. In approaching help they would rather have medication or surgery to cut out the problem than to look at possible causes or pursue alternative, gentler remedies.

Baby souls tend to be obssessive about germs and cleanliness - the environment or "not-me" is dangerous and must be controlled.

Within the U.S. most advertisements on radio and television concerning cleansers, antiseptics and deodorizers are pitched to a population that has many baby soul attitudes or imprinting in these areas.

At times baby souls can demonstrate a fairly brutal mentality, including beatings, physical abuse and violence. This occurs in baby soul police states or where baby souls hold a pocket of power in any country, such as the Army or Police. Hence the phenomemon where young souls investigate some atrocity committed by zealous baby souls. The Klu Klux Klan is a baby soul organization. The Mafia is a young soul organization with the goals of power and wealth, using baby soul enforcement tactics to terrorize the baby soul rank and file.

This malicious behavior is a crude method of learning how to survive in the world and a vehicle for creating karma.

Baby souls generally speaking do not gain reknown or prominence in the world. However, in the later levels they are capable of it. An example of a well known baby soul is Idi Amin who was dictator of Uganda until deposed in 1979 after a reign of terror. Colonel Kaddafy of Libya is a seventh level baby soul, as is President Botha of South Africa.

There is a large baby soul population in middle America. India has a great number of late-level baby souls, and baby souls are common in Ireland, Argentina, and most countries in South America.

The soul ages of countries may change over time depending on who wishes to incarnate there. For example the soul age of India has dramatically shifted over the centuries from an old soul area to a primarily infant and baby soul nation. As India pushes for technological growth the souls incarnating there will increasingly be young souls and some older souls.

The population of North America at one time contained numbers of old souls such as the Indian Iriquois Nation. In fact the United States constitution is founded on the Iriquois Nation's governmental principles. Some of this country's founding fathers were old souls who had the perception to recognize their value.

Positive Aspects

Good citizen, conscientious, concerned, loyal, family minded, can be relied on to do the "right thing", creates rules, tends to see things simply; sense of security is important; structure the chaos of the infant souls.

Negative Aspects

Unbending, dogmatic, petty bureaucratic, may aggressively defend what is "right", rigid, operates more from emotion than reason, can be brutal and violent, unquestioning of authority.

YOUNG SOULS

> **Focus:**
>   "There's you and there's me - and I'm going to win."
>   "The world is my oyster."
>   "I can have it all."

Having mastered the baby soul issues of survival the essence is looking to discover how powerful it can become. Think of the underlying motivation of a child between five and thirteen - when children begin to move away from parents and form peer groups, and test their abilities in the outside world. They like to refer back to their parents (older souls) from time to time for guidance and reassurance as they venture forth.

Independence is a key issue, the ability to go and get what they want out of life.

Powerfully driven, young souls strive for positions of prominence and wealth: movie stars, politicians, religious leaders and the like.

Young souls do not always pursue what they like. They pursue what they believe will create success. They want to know where successful people live. If the right people live in the hills they will buy a house in the hills. They buy to project an image of how they want to be seen. This may include an anti-establishment stance, not because they feel that way but because it's the way to be.

Young souls flock to well known universities so they can get degrees of prominence. They gravitate to those Ivy League exclusive universities that produce corporate winners. Popular television programs (soap operas) about the rich and famous are caricatures of the lives and perceptivity of young souls.

Young soul perceptivity revolves around the concept "There is you and me, and I am going to win." There is an acknowledgement of the other person, yet it is competitive in nature. Young souls can be good at what they do, but they tend to pursue fame, wealth or power at any price. This attitude breeds competition and a love of contest. We are all familiar with the "politics" of working in a young soul office where the sense of contest and competition permeates the air.

Young souls are their bodies. They are heavily identified with their physicality and not at all sure that their consciousness survives it. They will take extreme measures to preserve youth from the avid consumption of beauty products through to plastic surgery. They block out matters around death and regard it with recalcitrance bordering on terror.

> *Several companies have taken to deep freezing people's bodies upon their death in hopes that they can be revived in the future as medical technology advances. Hope lives forever in man's breast - albeit frozen.*

In the United States the phobia surrounding the physical body and its welfare manifests in the extreme size of the medical profession and the cost of hospital care. The disproportionate size of this industry reflects the young souls' fear of death.

Believing that they are not coming back gives them great drive and motivation to become wealthy and famous - life is a one-shot deal.

Young souls do not often question their motives. They have difficulty having insights into their own or other people's behaviour. When they do run into personal problems such as marital breakup or drug abuse they may go for help briefly until the crisis is over. Contrast this with the older soul who might see his therapist weekly as part of his inner preoccupations. The older soul might examine the personal crisis and pull it apart to draw as many lessons from it as possible. Each is valid in its own way.

The young soul interest in appearances carries over into many areas - for example cleanliness. They may give an appearance of order and neatness but if you were to look in their closet it might be a mess.

Young souls give lip service to philosophy and the arts and in the final level begin to show some interest in alternate religions. This helps them to prepare for the mature stage. The majority of the Earth's population is late level young and this viewpoint comprises the consensus on the planet.

There are a great many examples of famous young souls: Alexander the Great, John F. Kennedy, Mao Tse Tung, Augustus Caesar, Marie Antoinette, Margaret Thatcher, Ferdinand Marcos and his wife Imelda, Jacquelyne Onassis and Aristotle Onassis, James Cagney, Jack Benny, Bing Crosby.

Many of the powerful countries of the world are in the young soul stage. They are characterized by material wealth and military power and impact other regions of the world. Some examples of predominantly young soul countries are the United States, Germany, Israel, Singapore, Hongkong, Korea - all lead world economic rates of growth and are major players in world trade.

Young soul countries are frequently involved in international conflicts over baby soul countries. These baby soul countries such as El Salvador, wishing to advance and grow, draw attention to themselves with their internal conflicts, and enlist the aid of young soul nations such as the United States. The baby soul nation hopes to advance; the young soul nation hopes to gain power and advantage in the world theatre. The Vietnam war was a case in point.

Positive Aspects
Productive, industrious, authoritative, create new structures that are more efficient than the old, create wealth, foster "progress", lead the way; they are the most comfortable globally as they enjoy a majority.

Negative Aspects
Competitive, pushy, self-righteous, find out what is "in" and then do it more than anyone else, excessively materialistic, lacking insight as to own motivations, "I win, you lose" and winner takes all, fond of machinations for their own sake, vying for advantage, exploit now for there is no tomorrow; seeing situations as only "I'm right and you're wrong."

MATURE SOULS

> Focus:
>   "My life is intense, real and dramatic."
>   "There is something missing from my life."
>   "I have started exploring for meaning."
>   "It seems you are exactly the same as me."

The mature soul stage corresponds to the ages from 13-19 or the period of adolescence. This is the time in the cycle when the soul age is, to continue the analogy, shifting from the perceptions of a child to those of an adult.

The younger soul ages are outward-looking and karma creating. The essence has conquered survival and accomplished fame, wealth and power. But the person senses an uneasiness, an emptiness that something is missing.

The mature soul challenges and questions the young soul's bumper sticker, "He who dies with the most toys wins." He asks - Who am I? Why am I here? In short, mature souls begin to seek the Truth.

The personality does not ask these questions. They come from essence. The center of beingness is changing from power (the third chakra) to relationships (the fourth or heart chakra).

The mature soul stage is the introduction to spiritual openness and this never comes easily. It is the stage of maximum stress on the personality. During the mature stage there is an infusion of new psychic energy that the personality is not always equipped to handle. The personality sometimes breaks down under the strain, resulting in schizoprenia, psychosis and a higher suicide rate than the other soul ages.

Schizophrenics often display remarkable insight, perceptivity, and wisdom. It is not uncommon for these troubled people to have intense visions of a spiritual nature. However, they are mostly treated according to a baby and young soul medical model, with all its inherent limitations.

Mature souls become deeply immersed in relationship issues. They experience another person as that other person experiences themselves. The boundaries that separate people begin to breakdown. Not only does the mature soul know how the other person is feeling, but he knows how the other person feels about himself.

This perceptivity can breed confusion. Sometimes the person literally does not know who is feeling what, when. The difficulties are with boundaries, identification, symbiosis, and role identity. Boundary problems are characteristic in people who are having great emotional turmoil.

The mature soul focus is, "Do it anywhere but here" or, "My life is intense, real, and dramatic." This means the mature soul has his own priorities and sense of direction. He doesn't expect others to necessarily agree with him and wants to be left alone to pursue his own interests.

> *Often this is reflected in the lives of troubled artists such as Vincent Van Gogh or Ernest Hemingway - mature souls who sought to express their visions in their own unique way.*

Whereas baby souls prefer a house like everyone else has and young souls crave a mansion in the hills, a mature soul might prefer to live in a home he might have physically built himself. He might choose an area carefully chosen for its beauty and serenity that he feels uplifted by. Achieving inner self-determined standards is important.

> *The mature soul stage is a time of creative flowering, extending to artistic brilliance. Albert Einstein and Galileo were two who rose to prominence through their major contributions to scientific knowledge. Typical of the mature soul, their discoveries had great impact on man's understanding of the universe and his place in it.*

During the mature soul cycle the unused portions of the brain that have been latent during the earlier stages of development come into use. Some of this potential is actualized in the mature and old stages and further capacity is awaiting the further evolution of human consciousness.

Mature souls do not have the young soul essence-level drive for fame but none the less may achieve it, such as with Marilyn

Monroe, to learn mature soul lesssons from the perspective of a high-profile lifetime.

Sometimes they will turn away from recognition or a high status position to the bewilderment of the young souls around them. This might be the case with for a prominent attorney who changes careers to become a wildlife photographer with a much lower income.

Mature souls often seek a mate or a relationship that they can maintain for their entire lifetime. Because the mature soul stage is characterized by the development of personal relationships, lifelong marriages are a more common occurrence. This is in contrast to the young soul whose interest lies in power and, to some degree, power within a relationship.

Whole cities and communities are havens for mature souls: some examples are Amsterdam, Holland; Berkeley, Calififornia; and Cambridge, Massachusets.

Mature soul populations include Egypt, Greece, Italy, and Poland. The emphasis once again is on the development of relationships, social interaction and preoccupation with the arts and philosophy, rather than on the development of material goods.

> *Travelers will attest hat these nations have, for example, telephone services and public transport that result more in emotional intensity than efficiency.*

Prominent mature souls include: Marilyn Monroe, Marlon Brando, William Shakespeare, Ernest Hemmingway, Aristotle, Indira Gandhi, Vincent Van Gogh, Mozart, Moshe Dayan, Jimi Hendrix, Galileo. Carlos Casteneda and Albert Einstein are examples of final level mature souls who moved into the first level old stage. Also Clint Eastwood, Christopher Reeves, Richard Burton; many fine actors and actresses are mature souls doing what they do best - emotional intensity.

Positive Aspects

Emotionally open, relationship-oriented, "I care about you", "I belong to ... and everyone should" (inclusive), perceptive, open to spiritual growth, aware of inner meanings, in touch with both young soul and old soul perspectives and thus the most balanced soul age.

Negative Aspects

Identified, intense, soap opera dramatics, emotionally explosive, neurotic, can create successive crises and be a victim of them, "you are exactly the same as me," internal battlefield, "I see how you see me, and I don't know whether to respond to that or to my needs instead " (This is not negative but neutral.)

OLD SOULS

Focus:
"You do your thing and I'll do mine."
"I'm getting tired of this game."
"I grasp the big picture and like to live by it."
"The material game just isn't what it used to be".

Having mastered the mature soul lessons on the complexities of personal relationships, the old soul embarks on mastering the next dimension - the context of existence, otherwise called spirituality.

A teaching cycle, the soul perceptivity corresponds to adulthood in any individual lifetime. They ask, "What is my purpose in the greater scheme of things?"

Old souls perceive themselves and others as part of something greater and part of an integral whole. The old soul realizes a deep interrelatedness, and the connection existing among all people. When he looks at another person, he sees in that other person an aspect of himself.

As people interact in their day to day lives, they are merely interacting with themselves. All the while they are talking to the grocer, their friends and collegues they are talking to themselves. God is everyone and everything, and it is God talking to himself, one part to another.

The typical old soul is individualistic, easygoing, and one who seldom does anything he doesn't want to. He's fond of good food, wine and company and generally isn't motivated to pursue a career to get ahead. Despite his apparent lack of focus and intention he often has a surprisingly good grasp of what makes society tick and has keen insights into people.

They are often unusual within their own societies with their distaste for the 9 to 5 job. They would rather be poor and struggling to pay the bills than don a coat and tie, and compete in the corporate world. Nonetheless, some will attain wealth and success, as happens in any soul age.

Old souls are not averse to hard physical labor. They enjoy placing it in a spiritual context. A carpenter might derive satisfaction from doing a good job while aware of all the nuances and apparently unrelated things that happen in the course of the day that provide food for inner observation and growth. The quality of inner satisfaction is an important criterion, albeit with a spiritual flavour.

Self-employment or working in a small business where they can design their own schedule to meet their own particular needs are favored forms of occupation. Old souls are attracted to the freedom this offers. On the other hand mature souls who run their own businesses enjoy intense and stimulating relationships, and young souls who see this form of business as the best way to get rich.

Unique, personal and unorthodox spiritual practices are preferred by old souls. They like creating private rituals such as gathering on a hilltop with a circle of friends to chant, dance and meditate in commemoration of a time of personal importance. Upon moving to a new house, they may create a ritual to cleanse the house of the energy of the former occupants to clear a new space for themselves to occupy.

Old soul practices may seem odd to a younger soul population; however old souls are usually discreet with these practices and know how to pass in society without detection. An old soul may wear a business suit and drive an expensive car, but scratch the surface and you usually find an eccentric.

Old souls gravitate towards gardening, wine making, teaching, counseling. They tend towards philosophy and art, and find solace in natural surroundings.

Some Characteristics of Old Souls

- May appear sloppy or lazy.
- Avoid higher education and learn from enquiry, experience and on-the -job exposure.
- May master a skill just to remember it, and then drop it. This may be puzzling behavior to others.
- Travel may be part of the search for truth, the sense that there might be something out there.
- Medicine tends to be alternative and holistic.
- Not identified with being either male or female as they have done so many past lives as each.
- Tend to be sensual, hedonistic, compared with younger souls who feel bound by what you can and can't do.
- May appear eccentric as they follow inner perceptions and needs that may transcend what is perceivable by the five senses and linear time.
- Focus directly in searching for spiritual truth.
- Have a finer sense in knowing what is true than any other soul level.
- Before cycling off must teach everything they know to at least one other person (e.g. Don Juan Matus with Carlos Casteneda).

Self Esteem

Mature and old souls tend to have more difficulty with poor self-esteem than any other soul level. Why is this so?

Generally younger souls are not troubled by poor self esteem because they are more oriented toward gathering experience of the outer world. Where younger souls tend to gain experience by creating karma with others, older souls are interested in completing karma because they are not coming back.

One of the tasks of old souls is to meet this challenge and to realize their own worth as human beings. The final lesson is unconditional self-acceptance and unconditional acceptance of others. This requires mastery of self esteem issues. The key to acceptance is forgiveness and self-love.

The False Personality

Old souls know the false personality creates problems as a function of its structure, and these can be resolved through insight and the perception of what is true.

The personality is less important in an old soul because it is one of many personalities that have been experienced over numerous incarnations. The current false personality of a younger soul figures more prominently in the present lifetime because there have been less incarnations to influence it.

The extraordinary richness and strength of the essence has several important consequences. One of them is that the old soul is able to be more aware of himself and his personality, thus choosing how he presents himself. He can choose which particular overleaves to manifest in certain situations and he can determine whether he is operating out of essence or false personality. This makes the mature and old soul uniquely flexible in their attitudes whereas the infant, baby and young souls are the product of and constrained by their false personalities.

This means older souls (i.e. mature and old) can go to a meeting and choose what overleaves they will act out of (e.g. "To hell with caution mode, I'm going to play with power mode and carry myself as an authority. I shall be certain of what is true and express it convincingly.") By placing their intention on it, they start to experience it. With practise they can develop and use the skill of choosing overleaves at will.

Those fragments that have experienced a large number of lifetimes find that the barrier between essence and personality is weaker and therefore memory of past lives is stronger. The older soul will tend to remember skills and talents he has mastered in former lives as well as the unfinished karma with specific individuals he comes across. Mature and old souls will often exhibit knowledge or wisdom way beyond their immediate experiences of the current lifetime.

Old souls sometimes take difficult overleaves as a self- karmic challenge. Because of these abrasive overleaves they can be obnoxious to extremes in a way that is more penetrating and difficult to handle than any of the earlier stages. Not all older souls are automatically mellow and easy to get along with!

Some examples of old souls are John Muir, Carl Jung, Thomas Merton, William Blake, James Joyce, Walt Whitman, Abraham Lincoln, Don Juan Matus, Mark Twain, Gurdjieff, and a wide variety of spiritual teachers; also Robert Redford, George Burns.

Old soul countries are Czechoslovakia, Iceland, Holland, a good deal of the rural population of Switzerland, and of Russia. Russia, however, is governed by predominantly young souls.

Old soul nations prefer neutrality in international conflicts. If this becomes impossible they prefer to be subjugated than suffer violence and bloodshed. They then teach their captors about harmony and humaneness. This was the case in Alexander the Great's conquest of Persia and parts of what is now modern India.

Positive Aspects
Easygoing, caring, laid back, let's do it tomorrow, harmlessly eccentric, kindly, spiritually aware, intensely perceptive, gentle, accepting, philosophical, sense of love for everyone, good teachers, searching for the truth, worldly.

Negative Aspects
"I'm no good at ...," difficult personalities (intense self-karma around liking self), impoverished, weird, "If we disagree then I must be wrong", struggling, lazy, unmotivated.

The Focus of Each Soul Age

Infant Souls	"Where am I? - And who are you?"
Baby Souls	"This is the rule and it must be followed."
Young Souls	"I can have it all."
Mature Souls	"My life and relationships are intense, real and dramatic."
Old Souls	"You do your thing and I'll do mine".

We have examined five main stages of the soul's growth: infant, baby, mature, and old soul stages. We shall briefly compare them before discussing the last two, the transcendental soul and the infinite soul ages.

● The philosophies and writings of younger souls are complex and difficult to read. The philosophies and writings of older souls are simple and easy to read - e.g., simple statements such as "love yourself".

● Younger souls don't understand older souls, but older souls are able to understand young souls.

● The activities of each soul age are totally appropriate to that age. You wouldn't expect a two year old to act like a forty year old, each is fine for their age.

TRANSCENDENTAL SOULS

The name transcendental refers to the ability to see beyond the overleaves that overlay our essences and our perceptions. Transcendental souls are able to transcend the personality and the illusion that comprises the physical plane.

The transcendental soul stage follows the old soul stage however the transcendental soul historically rarely incarnates on the earth. It appears that with the shift of the planet from young to mature soul that the numbers of transcendental souls is increasing.

If the old soul cycles off the physical plane then how does the transcendental soul manifest?

At the seventh level of the old soul age each fragment cycles off to the astral plane to join its entity and to await the other fragments. Once the fragments have all completed their reincarnational process on the earth they are reunited into one entity to pursue experiences and lessons on the higher planes of existence.

Occasionally one of these reunited entities will reincarnate again on the earth as a transcendental soul.

Often the transcendental soul manifests during the life of the final fragment to leave the earth. When this final level old soul has completed all karma and all personal lessons the entity then joins him for the remaining years of the body's life. The single fragment in the body now can interchange at will with other fragments and has access to the total knowledge of the entity and the experience of all completed lifetimes. The Indian leader of the 1940's, Mahatma Gandhi, is a prime example.

Historically, the importance of a transcendental soul has been as a teacher who comes for a specific purpose. In the Buddhist tradition he is known as the Bodhisattva or great soul who returns to earth in order to help others gain enlightenment. The work of the transcendental soul prepares the way for an infinite soul to come thereafter.

Transcendental souls experience others as themselves and have great wisdom of their own. Usually they have no religious affiliation and pursue no formal education yet others immediately recognize them as teachers and spiritual leaders.

THE INFINITE SOUL

The infinite soul is a representation of the Tao itself. The infinite soul comes to the earth, say, every two thousand years, although historically, for example, Christ and the Buddha came within six hundred years of each other because each impacted separate and distinct regions and civilizations.

These avatars have world impact for literally thousands of years. There are often magical and mystical events surrounding the birth of these exalted beings and their presence is felt and prophesied long before their arrival.

The infinite soul, like the transcendental soul, manifests through the body of a seventh level old soul. The seventh level old soul cycles off and allows the infinite soul to occupy the body.

The man Jesus, a seventh level old king, gave his body to the Christ form of the infinite soul. The man Siddhartha Gautama, a seventh level old priest, gave his body over to the Buddha form of the infinite soul.

The form of teaching manifests as one of the three exalted planes of existence:

Plane	Example Teacher	Teaching
Physical	-	-
Astral	-	-
Causal	-	-
Akashic	-	-
Mental	Lao Tsu	Truth
Messianic	Christ	Love
Buddhaic	Buddha	Oneness

What this means is that the infinite soul chooses to manifest one of the exalted planes of consciousness to give the teaching a particular flavor. Nevertheless, the teaching is all from the Tao itself.

Some examples of infinite souls are Krishna, Buddha, Jesus Christ, Lao Tsu and Ra.

In sum, there are five soul ages physically manifest on the earth. They are described as being like the ages of man as a simple introduction. As you use this information and practice perceiving peoples' soul ages you will grasp more of what they actually are.

Dimensions of the Soul Stages

Age	Orientation	Dimensions
Infant Baby	me and not me *"Me"* me and other me's	*One*
Young Mature	me versus you *"You and Me"* me and you	*Two*
Old	you and me are we *"You, me and our context"*	*Three*

Learning of the Soul Stages

Infant souls learn through suffering

Baby souls learn through pain

Young souls learn through losing

Mature souls learn through anguish

Old souls learn through terror

Within each of these ages are seven levels. Each level is a way of seeing the world. The next chapter describes how these steps of successive expansion and contraction lead you further along the ever-widening path of perceptivity.

Chapter Four

Soul Levels

In this chapter we embark on a voyage of experience through the seven soul levels. Let us take a magnifying glass and scrutinize the path of the soul more closely.

Each of the seven perceptivity stages has seven levels within itself. One level takes approximately three lifetimes to complete or some 200 life years, depending on how rapidly a fragment progresses through the lessons and experiences of that level.

Some fragments choose to move through the soul stages quickly and take only one lifetime to complete one level within one stage. Most fragments choose to develop at a more leisurely pace, some taking up to 300 or more lifetimes to go through the entire process or cycle.

The designations "fifth level mature" or "second level baby" for example are relatively superficial ones. Most people have completed a number of cycles, have lived many life forms and journeyed back to the Tao time and time again. These levels simply refer to the kinds of lessons/experiences that people have set up for themselves at this time.

The Seven Soul Levels within Each Soul Age

The Seven Soul Ages

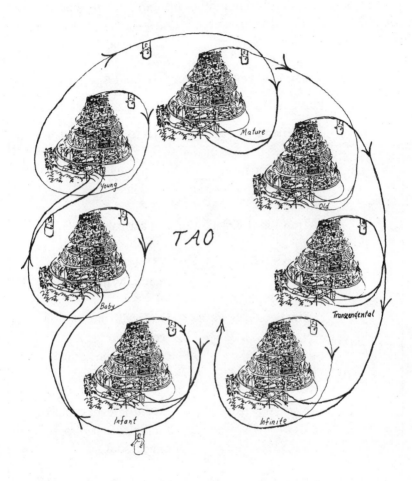

Each level has a definite flavor and characteristic. Every person lives the level differently, bringing to it their unique combination of role and overleaves.

Seven Soul Levels Within Each Soul Age

Level	Theme	Characteristics
1	Examine new soul age	Frequently slips back to previous stage.
2	Transition/ Creation	Self karma.
3	Introspection	Adapts to the change internally; fixed values.
4	Emotions	Deals with outside world. Works constantly on karma. Exemplifies stage.
5	New knowledge	Eccentric level, explores for limits; first glimpse of next soul age.
6	Karmic completion	Hectic and fast moving; pre-planned by essence.
7	Teaching	Share experience with others; self karma.

Positive and Negative Poles of Soul Levels

These exist and can be identified however their value is limited because the inference is that the negative poles are undesirable. For soul levels this is untrue - you seek to experience absolutely everything that relates to your soul level.

So the approach here is to describe the level in its entirety without using the polarities that might mislead people into discriminating about what is and is not appropriate for them.

The Inner Dynamic - What the Levels Are

The First Level

The first level is an introduction to the overall level whether it be infant, baby, young, mature, or old. The person experiencing the first level usually manifests about one third of the new level and two thirds the previous level. For example a first level mature soul will appear mature about one third of the time and will appear young about two thirds of the time. So the first level becomes a taste of the kinds of experiences to come.

Example - Prince Charles of England

The Second Level

The quality of the new soul age manifests with some intensity. Emotional centering helps people to "get it" on an emotional level. Often people are at war within themselves, choosing exalted goals with ordinal modes or vice versa. The dilemma amplifies the nature of the soul age. Part of the person pushes to go outward, part pushes to go inward. This creates conflict that can make for a difficult lifetime.

The essence pushes to evolve and often the goal is growth. That is, you can attain what you want by using the new perceptivity. Using the former perceptivity keeps you stuck and frustrated. For example old souls will sometimes find themselves wanting to slip back to the mature level and yet also wanting to strive for the old soul perspective.

Examples - Princess Diana, Beverley Sills, Brigitte Bardot, Elizabeth Taylor

The Third Level

Largely introspective, this person will often be timid, self-conscious and hermit-like. He or she manifests the soul level. So a baby soul at third level will act as a classic baby soul.

Intellectual center helps the inward examination - scholars like to bury themselves in this. The exalted roles that enjoy being outward-going in the world find this level hard going and try to complete it as quickly as possible. The intensity of it leads many to choose the goal of re-evaluation. The spiritualist attitude facilitates the inward looking process.

Examples - Howard Hughes, Laurence Olivier, Greta Garbo, Clark Gable

The Fourth Level

The fourth level is the grounding for the particular stage. It is consolidation and application. The person feels comfortably a baby soul or comfortably a young soul. An extroverted level, this soul is oriented toward the formation of karma.

(The mature stage shows up the confusion and difficulty of the fourth level. The person is heavily identified. He or she doesn't say "I have a problem", but "I am the problem". This is identification, not distinguishing yourself from what you are dealing with. Often in the mature stage we find personality disintegration in this level, such as psychosis or severe mental disorder; not all mental disorders belong in fourth level mature however.)

Example - Robert Redford

The Fifth Level

During the fifth level integration begins. The understanding of the overall level starts to come together. The fifth level is a time of producing. More karma is created here and so stability goes out the window. The limits of the entire stage are tested and there is much exploration and experimentation to see what is possible to experience.

Commonly discrimination is the goal and aggression the mode. Whereas the fourth level represents the status quo for the stage, during the fifth level one appears to be the eccentric. The more solid roles like the warrior and king find this eccentricity uncomfortable, however the creative roles such as artisans delight in it. Sometimes we see people here who have chosen to be eccentric through extraordinary intelligence. They select intellectual center as the vehicle for eccentricity.

Example - Salvador Dali

The Sixth Level

During the sixth level a person pieces the experiences of previous levels together, continuing what was started at the fifth level. Essences at this level generally like to choose the goal of growth. The obligations of the entire stage must be dealt with and most of the karma must be handled. The sixth level of the mature stage is perhaps the most demanding of all because of the difficulty inherent in both. As an old soul the sixth level can also be a most challenging level and often takes many lifetimes to complete because all karma of the entire cycle must be completed preparatory to cycling off.

Examples - Charles Manson and John Hinckley (intense karma for each), Pope John-Paul II, Mother Theresa

The Seventh Level

The seventh level is the end of one soul age and preparation for the next. This is a comfort zone and usually enjoyed in a laid back fashion. During this level life unfolds without undue difficulty.

The seventh level soul makes the best teacher for those in the soul age he has just completed. For example a seventh level baby soul is a helpful teacher for those in the baby soul cycle. A seventh level old soul level teaches all younger soul levels and feels the need to teach everything he has learned through the process of all his lifetimes. Old souls will often take on a disciple, or an understudy so to speak, and teach everything they know to that person. This prepares them for cycling off and joining their entity. One example of this is Don Juan Matus who taught Carlos Casteneda his own unique understanding of reality before cycling off.

Examples - Martin Luther King, Shirley Maclaine, Anwar Sadat and Lady Godiva (strange bedfellows indeed)

A Glimpse Into Each Level

First	Oh no! What am I coming into? Perhaps I'll just taste it. Oops no! I preferred where I was. But...
Second	I'm going to play with this and find out about it.
Third	I'm going to sit quietly in a corner and pull it to bits so I really know it.
Fourth	Ho Ho! I understand it and I'm *doing* it!
Fifth	Where are its limits? I'll experiment and find them. This could be wild.
Sixth	I know its limits. I'm now doing my life intensely and paying back karma.
Seventh	I'm taking a break and teaching (But what's ahead?)

Typical Number of Lifetimes Per Level

Each soul age and each level has a typical number of lifetimes. These are not meant as accurate but merely to give the reader a feel for the size of the wheel of experience that comprises one essence cycle.

Soul Age	Soul Level	Lifetimes per Level
Infant	1 through 7	5 to 10 per level
Baby	1 through 5	5 to 6 per level
	6	8 to 10
	7	2 to 3
Young	1 through 5	2 to 3 per level
	6	4 to 5
	7	1 or 2
Mature	1 through 5	3 per level
	6	8 or 9
	7	1 or 2
Old		A matter of choice for the individual essence, from 4 to 5 lifetimes for the entire soul age to 30 to 40 lifetimes. This soul age is hallmarked by great flexibility.

The average number of lifetimes for the entire cycle is 180, but can range from as low as 35 to as high as 400.

Manifesting Soul Level

When an old soul is physically three years old, he is not behaving like the old soul he is. He acts like a three year old, and this corresponds with infant/baby soul perceptivity and behaviour. He wants to know the rules, and engages in temper tantrums like any three year old.

As he grows older in an individual lifetime, he moves through and acts out older and older soul levels and stages. By the age of 35 to 42 he may start operating at his true old soul perceptivity level. Only one in three lifetimes on average does a person reach and act from his true perceptivity level. This is because a person often has priorities other than spiritual growth per se. For example being the father of young soul daughter who becomes a celebrity means the man might manifest as a young soul for his entire lifetime to fulfill his life task agreement with his daughter.

Also, familial and societal imprinting act as a kind of strong hypnosis or drug retarding the manifestation of one's true identity. This is especially the case for a mature or old soul who is brought up in a predominantly younger soul society such as Japan or the United States.

When a person acts like someone from a younger stage we say he is *manifesting* that younger stage. If a fifth level young soul is acting like a second level baby soul he is manifesting as a baby soul. He may in fact move on to act his true soul age however he will not ever manifest as older than that.

Manifesting Perceptivity and Life Issues

Within each lifetime a person reacts with different levels of perception around different issues. So that an old soul may act in a controlling and survival oriented way around money (baby soul), achievement-oriented around the success of his business (young soul) and carry a sense of the greater context of things in his marriage, accepting the daily ups and downs with innate wisdom (old soul).

In other words you handle issues in your life from different levels of perceptivity. Uncovering which issues you handle at what level can be quite illuminating.

Consequences of Manifesting

The concept of manifesting is a biological phenomenon. When the human egg (ovum) is fertilized in the mother's womb, the subsequent growth for nine months parallels the whole path of evolution.

The nineteenth century German biologist Ernst Haeckel came up with a law as to why embryos look like primitive animals. "Ontogeny recapitulates phylogeny" he said, meaning that to reach the adult state, embryos must retrace their species past and go through all its previous evolutionary forms, from slime to slug to fish to frog to shrew to ape.

This system says that manifesting does not stop here, in the physical form but extends similarly to consciousness - in our case, soul perceptivity.

There is a strong case to be made that evolution on this planet is currently along the path of consciousness (a new octave) where it was formerly following a physical developmental path. The consciousness cycle is much faster than the physiological cycle loosely described as Darwinian evolution. (The take-off point for the growth of consciousness was the arrival of sentience, i.e. ensoulment.)

Similarly civilizations (or series of civilizations) manifest until they reach the level of the previous civilization. Then the growth begins. The planet at this juncture (the last 100 years and the next) is seeing the integration of all the major civilizations that have been emerging on separate and isolated growth paths for thousands of years. This is but one more indicator of the significance of this period for the planet - planetary integration and the birth of the global village.

Level	Infant	Baby
1	Often psychic; attuned to planet but not people; close to instinctive center; no intell. center; guarded; feral.	Starts to care about what people think of them. Love from others is an issue. How to get it is a mystery.
2	Less scared; uses thought; can pass in society; tests society's rules for limits.	1st level issue becomes burning; I'll hurt myself if you don't love me.
3	Quieter; no sex in 1st 3 stages; has decided can make peace with others so not so often locked up; can live on edge of towns.	Gives up 1st and 2nd behavior, goes inward. Looks to authority (outward) as to how life might work.
4	Starts sex animalistically; no conscience; is friendly as it works better.	Solid members of society; wants to belong to religions, clubs, to find out who they should be. Feels attached to others.
5	Does nefarious things; wants to be different; tries everything.	Quiet; can be perverse; may have weird fetishes or really bizarre behaviour, e.g. water plants with maple syrup.
6	Paying back massive amounts of karma. May take many lifetimes.	Very karmic; pronounces that people should follow authority.
7	Sly, naturally clever; passes in society, is not in personal relationships; may start to open emotionally and begin caring for someone else, e.g. mate or parent.	Complacent; discovers about caring, being cared for. Looking at trying to be authority.

Young	Mature	Old
Expresses anger; cautious but can be domineering.	Uneasy; starting to recognize importance of emotional attachments, but buries it.	Confident, still mature; in no rush to improve.
Dogmatic. Fearful, covers it with dogma. Likes being authority.	Inner conflict between success & relationships. Agonising.	Hovers between drama and objectivity; internal warfare.
Quiet, often gets away from it all, hermit; not too much conscience; doesn't like people much.	Quiet, intense, probably not too materially successful; very agonising.	Quiet, very knowledgeable; quiet daily life. Drawn to teach.
Friendly successful; your average yuppie; often authority, wealth and power.	Friendly, passionate, relationships more important than anything. Soap opera life.	Extroverted; teaching oriented. Authoritative, almost like power mode.
Wealth and power through unusual means. Still outgoing, friendly.	Emotional drama; unusual dresser; solid roles uncomfortable being bizarre; fluid roles love it.	Unusual, spiritual looking. Almost not-of-this-planet at times.
Busy karmic, competent; this gets them to extreme power; sees something lacking but can't identify it; very set in ways.	Very agonising; most difficult of any level; most karma, very emotional; expressive roles may go crazy; nervous breakdowns.	Extremely busy; hard worker, spirituality very important, no rest. Heavy teaching. Trust issues.
Absolute authorities, calm born to money or gifted for career. Authoritative manner; looking at mature; may do EST as experiment. Wants to do what's popular.	Complacent, emotionally attached; teaching; not too interested in old soul detachment; almost stagnation, it's easy.	Almost only self karma left. Lazy. Teaching - but only one or two people. Acceptance issues.

What It All Means

We have seen that the experience of life on earth takes a great many lifetimes to complete and that there is a specific developmental sequence to these lifetimes.

Within this overall structure there is much room for creativity and a unique approach to how this is accomplished. Just as in any individual lifetime you must progress through certain developmental stages without exception; in the big picture the same structure exists. Nevertheless no two human beings are exactly alike nor are their experiences exactly duplicated.

The next chapter describes how we select a single essence role to master throughout the entire developmental process. Then we design each lifetime to provide certain lessons, experiences, and karma, through the selection of personality traits called overleaves.

The overleaves are the vehicle for experiencing separateness. They set us up for challenges time and time again. The paths we choose to solve life's dilemmas reflect our undertanding of the universe. Each solution is unique to each person and reflects the degree of his or her advancement along the path of perceptivity outlined in these pages.

Chapter Five

Roles

Earlier chapters set the scene for the "school of life" - the accretion of experience from a series of lifetimes. We saw how perceptions change in a similar way to a child growing up into an adult. The experiences gained at every age stretch the perceptivity and encourage further growth.

The major constant through all those lifetimes is the essence role.

Introducing Roles

Each human being, although uniquely different, is one of seven possible essential roles: server, artisan, warrior, priest, sage, king, or scholar. These terms refer to a way of perceiving the world, not to the usual career definitions.

A scholar doesn't necessarily work in a library - scholars may be writers, scientists, actors, or any profession that allows them to study the subject of their greatest interest. A warrior doesn't necessarily make a career in the military - they can be businesspeople, therapists, school teachers, or any profession that lets them structure the environment so that things get done. The same is true of all the roles.

Let's see the seven roles in action. Suppose a party of settlers made up of the seven roles is planning a settlement on the frontier. The following is the stereotype of what each role might say.

Warrior: Tonight we'll need a roof over our heads, and food and water. Let's find a cave or make a shelter, and light a fire. I'll reconnoitre for signs of natives and see if it's safe.

Scholar: I've been studying the rock type and the ridge up there is limestone and might have caves. Also this plant species is a variety of sweet potato that we can bake in the fire.

Priest: Once we're settled for the night I want you all to gather so as we can give thanks to God for our safety and good fortune.

King: Those are all sensible suggestions. You two go and examine the ridge and report back. You fellows find more of that edible root and bake some up. When we gather after dinner I'll explain our progress and spell out where we shall settle and how best to do it.

Artisan: I have designed a device for drawing water out of a well. Although it's a new invention I think it will work and save us the long trek to the river.

Server: Those of you who are cold can come around the fire I've built over here. Hot drinks will be ready in a few minutes. Does anybody need a bite to eat before we start?

Sage: This is going to be fun! We need to get word back to the folks in the home country about where we are and that we're okay We've got some great stories to tell them!

This simplistic vignette shows the basic social functions or complementary nature of the seven roles.

The Seven Essence Roles

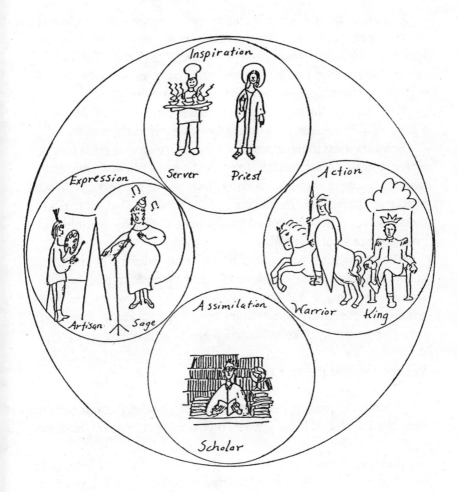

Purpose of Knowing Our Roles

Just as an actor gives a far better performance when he knows his character, so we can live our lives more effectively when we know our roles and those of others. Knowledge of the roles also can bring about a larger degree of self-acceptance in a way that self-examination from a purely personal perspective may not.

Each role has its own particular characteristics that show up in a person's life no matter what their upbringing, culture, and so on.

Scholars must inquire, artisans must create, priests must inspire, warriors must do, servers must give, sages must tell, and kings must master. These characteristics are so intrinsic to the role that when people are prevented from living out the inherent characteristics of their role (external or internal inhibitions), they may feel blocked, even to the point of falling ill.

The old dictum, "know thyself", proves true here. The more you know about your role - what it is, what its positive and negative aspects are, how it interacts with other roles, how to use it as wisely and effectively as possible - the more you know about your part, and the more you know about yourself as an enabling actor.

Where Do the Roles Come From?

When pure essence, the spark or soul of consciousness, is cast out from the Tao so that it can have its own unique experience, it adopts a role.

Essence leaves the Tao like pure white light. White light traveling through a prism is refracted into the seven colors of the spectrum (frequencies). In a similar way the essence, as white light, is refracted into one of seven frequencies or roles upon leaving the Tao.

Note For Advanced Students

As you master this system of knowledge and gain a deeper understanding of the roles, you will perceive them literally as frequencies or rates of vibration, because as energies, that is what they are.

In other words, the roles did not come first. The Tao created the categories "exalted inspiration", "ordinal action" etc., and what we call the roles is simply the essence giving form to one catagory of beingness.

In summary, the roles are created by the Tao to introduce variety in experience and to offer specific vehicles or forms for consciousness.

The Cycle of the Role

The role is adopted for a complete series of lifetimes. This sequence constitutes one cycle. The same role is carried through lifetime after lifetime until the cycle is complete.

Just as an actor plays a role on stage, so the essence acts out the role during a particular cycle. Once the role is played out (fully mastered), it is discarded--just as as an actor who has mastered a particular role will want to move on to a new, more challenging role. Over an infinite period of time the essence experiences all the roles in the many different forms of the physical plane.

How To Find Out Your Role

This chapter will make the most sense to you if you read with the intention of locating your own role, checking the information out internally for accurate fit, just as you might try on different pieces of clothing for fit and suitability.

For some, the "aha" will come quickly - enough characteristics of a particular role will resonate with your own self knowledge and illuminate the whys and wherefores of your life. For others however the "aha" will come more slowly. This is because some people have forgone the faint but steady light of their inner being for the immediacies of earning an income, handling motherhood, or what you will. Also, it may be difficult to distinguish the role of priest, say, from the societal occupation of minister.

Mostly, however, the difficulty of recognizing your own role is due to the heavy imprinting (conditioning) to think, feel, and act like another role. Within a particular family, indeed, within an entire culture, there are inducements for people to take on the characteristics of certain roles, and to avoid the characteristics of other roles.

For example, in the United States, women have been taught to act like servers, whether this is their true role or not. Consequently, a woman reading this material may recognize server qualities in herself, yet actually be a scholar who has been conditioned with the imprinting appropriate to the server role.

Men in the western world are taught to be warrior-like, and in reading this material will doubtless find moments of recognition in the description of the warrior role. Yet a man may be an artisan, struggling against his true nature to appear "manly" in the macho sense due to prevalent cultural standards.

So you may have been taught to act in one way, yet in actuality be an entirely different way. This inner way becomes apparent and recognizable from time to time by the deep satisfaction and richness you experience when you act out of your essence role.

Discovering your role enables you to resonate with the sense of it, and you may find your life becomes easier and more enjoyable. The effort required to act contrary to your essence role is greater compared with the ease of a "go with the flow" approach of your innate inclinations.

The Threefold Focus: Ordinal, Neutral and Exalted

All the overleaves are divided into three types of energy: ordinal, neutral, or exalted. These categories help you to identify the roles and spot them in the population.

Look at the Overleaf Chart to clarify any references to roles and overleaves, and also the Glossary for terms. The Overleaf Chart lies at the heart of this book, and reveals the basic structure of the personality.

The Seven Essence Roles

Axis	Ordinal	Neutral	Exalted
Inspiration	Server		Priest
Expression	Artisan		Sage
Action	Warrior		King
Assimilation		Scholar	

Ordinal

If you refer to the Overleaf Chart you will see that the ordinal roles comprise server, artisan, and warrior. They are narrow focused, and oriented to more immediate tasks. They have a distinctly practical, down-to-earth approach. The ordinal roles outnumber the exalted roles in the population.

They like one-on-one interactions rather than standing up and addressing the masses.

Neutral

The neutral category stands alone and for the roles it is the scholar who is neutral. The neutral quality here allows for the ability to step back and be able to interact with all the other types and even assist them to understand one another.

Exalted

The exalted roles (priest, sage, and king), are wide focused, and oriented toward the big picture. They provide the leadership by their ability to deal with large groups of people. In general they prefer larger, more stage-like appearances and stand out more. There are fewer exalted roles because less are needed.

ESSENCE VIBRATION

Each role has a vibrational rate of its essence. That primary vibrational rate accounts for the differences in roles.

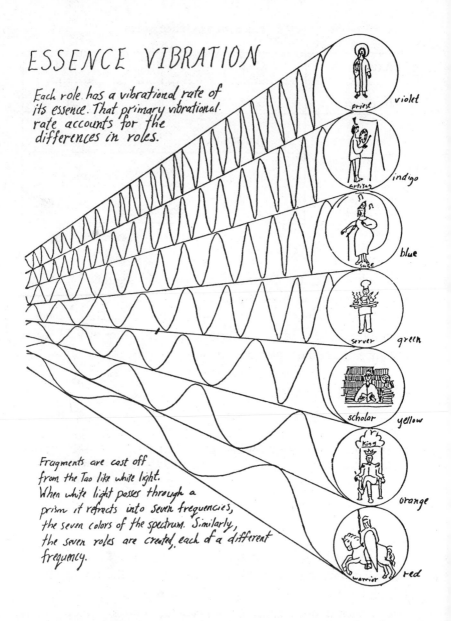

priest — violet

artisan — indigo

sage — blue

server — green

scholar — yellow

King — orange

warrior — red

Fragments are cast off from the Tao like white light. When white light passes through a prism it refracts into seven frequencies, the seven colors of the spectrum. Similarly, the seven roles are created, each of a different frequency.

The exalted overleaves in general affect others more and the self less. They are always paired with an ordinal overleaf (see Overleaf Chart).

Characteristics of . . .	
Ordinal Overleaves	**Exalted Overleaves**
Passive	Active
Inner process	Outer process
One on one	One to many
Introverted	Extroverted
Homing in	Broadening out
Examples	
Caution mode	Power mode
Goal of submission	Goal of dominance

The Four Axis

The roles and all the overleaves are also categorized under four axes that determine the essential flavor or unique specialty of the character. The four axes are inspiration, expression, action, and assimilation.

Inspiration

The inspiration axis includes the roles of server (ordinal) and priest (exalted). These roles experience their primary beingness by being inspired by life. They urge and motivate people to new heights, whether it be career, love or inner revelations. Inspiration axis overleaves such as passion are related especially to feeling and the senses.

Expresssion

The expression axis includes the roles of artisan (ordinal) and sage (exalted). These roles are gifted at communicating ideas or feelings through signs, symbols, gestures, speech, color, and form. These creative roles bring beauty and drama, passion and color, into our lives. The overleaves in the expression axis such as skepticism, are just that - more expressive.

Action

Warrior (ordinal) and king (exalted) are the action axis roles. They are characterized by groundedness, physicalness, and a love of getting things done. All the action axis overleaves such as aggression, are characterized by doing, rather than expressing or inspiring.

Assimilation

The neutral role of scholar falls under the assimilation axis. This means that the scholar experiences life primarily by absorbing information, organizing it, and storing it. All the assimilation axis overleaves such as observation, have a neutral quality and are oriented toward absorption of one kind or another.

As you master the notion of roles you may see historical comparisons. The Romans were a society of warriors, the ancient Greeks were scholars, the ancient Egyptians priests, and so on.

The Positive and Negative Poles of the Overleaves

All essence roles and all overleaves (personality) have a positive and a negative pole. They also have a neutral or balancing position that lies between both poles. Look at the Overleaf Chart at the end of the book.

Positive does not mean "good" and negative does not mean "bad". One is more conscious, the other less conscious. The aim of this system is to promote consciousness. You can observe when you are acting from a negative pole and then choose whether to stay there or move to the positive.

The positive pole enhances essence communication. The negative pole retards it and generally comes from fear and illusion. Positive poles are expansive and feel good whereas negative pole activity is divisive and usually feels bad to self and others.

	+ Creation
Example:	ARTISAN
	- Self-deception

An artisan in the positive pole will feel and be constructively creative. In the negative pole the artisan will still be creative however it will be oriented toward self deception such as engaging in wishful thinking or some illusion that has nothing to do with reality. In other words, they can create their own reality and do it so convincingly that they are out of touch without knowing it.

You always have the choice of coming from the positive or the negative poles of your overleaves, including your role. This is one of the major thrusts of this teaching.

This book expands and describes what those choices are, going into all forty nine overleaves and describing in detail the positive and negative poles of each.

From that you can evolve to be a higher person, operating from your true personality, which is how essence manifests.

Usually when people operate out of the negative poles of their overleaves it is a product of imprinting, rather than a natural tendency. The imprinting comes in and pulls you into your negative poles a lot of the time. It is useful for karmic purposes for you to get pulled into your negative poles.

This places imprinting in an unduly negative light which is not so. The other side of the coin is that imprinting is how you first learn how to be a human being. As you grow older it is your base wherefrom you are able then to question and refine who you are.

There is a tendency among students of this system to feel a victim of their essence. In other words " My life is tough - I am impoverished/don't have a good relationship (or whatever) and my essence set it up that way so there's nothing I can do about it". This is a delusion, using this knowledge as a means to feel helpless. You cannot blame things on your essence, despite its hidden qualities, that you as a personality do not want to do.

Your true personality is you being in the positive poles of your overleaves. The upper layers of your essence manifest this way. The negative poles of your overleaves comprise your false personality. Your true personality of this lifetime will be the newest layer of your essence after the lifetime is done.

To recap, the purpose of the overleaves is to enable you to recognize and operate from true personality, which is the vehicle for your essence to express itself.

The Seven Roles in Action

The essence of *server* is service, to work for the best interest of others and assist them in a physical sense with their needs and wants.

The essence of *priest* is compassion, to work for what they perceive to be the higher good in a spiritual sense. The essence of *artisan* is creation, to invent new ways of seeing, doing, and feeling, altering the environment so that it is ever new, ever different. This means creating new fashions, styles, forms, structures such as buildings, roads, and landscapes, and extends to the creation of atmosphere.

The essence of *sage* is expression or wisdom, and the ability to communicate. It includes play and how to have fun.

The essence of *warrior* is persuasion, that talent for organizing people with plans and strategy. The essence of *king* is mastery, the ability to produce the best outcome by directing and supervising everyone. The essence of *scholar* is assimilation or knowledge, the ability to amass, study, and organize information in a comprehensive and useful way.

The essence of a role can sometimes be better expressed through a saying that characterizes it the most. Here are some examples.

Server: "What can I do to make you feel nurtured?"

Priest: "How can I support you in your spiritual growth?"

Artisan: "If it hasn't happened yet then let me create it."
             "Let me create it for you."

Sage: "If it is worth knowing you'll get it here."
             "Let me show you how life can be fun."

Warrior: "To hell with meaning - give me results!"

King: "The buck stops here."

Scholar: "I'll go anywhere for knowledge."

Summary of the Roles	
Server - Service	Priest - Compassion
Artisan - Creation	Sage - Expression
Warrior - Persuasion	King - Mastery
Scholar - Assimilation	

Inspiration Roles: Server and Priest

+ Service	+ Compassion
SERVER	PRIEST
- Bondage	- Zeal

The inspiration roles are server and priest. They are related to one another through inspiration but they do not slide back and forth. In other words, a server does not become a priest at times or vice versa. They usually feel a strong affinity for each other and depending on other overleaves they get along well together. Both the server and the priest are inspired by life and generate inspiration in others but they do it in different ways.

SERVER   *(+Service, -Bondage)*

What is a server and how can you tell if you are one? The most important thing to know about servers is that they truly like to help out and will do almost anything for anyone. They usually have a friendly, approachable look. The typical server might think like this:

"I will generally say 'yes' to any request if it is reasonable. I like to provide the impetus so things get done. I'm practical and tend to think of the little things that are vital but people forget. If we go camping I'm the one who remembers the matches and the can-opener.

Sometimes I think I know what is best for people and set it up so that it happens. I like having things done my way and people rarely notice it happening. Most people feel fairly unloved so I open my heart in caring for others - looking after people who are sick, or buying birthday presents. Caring is an important thing and I value it highly."

Server: Relating to Self

Servers are generally modest, self-effacing people. They get a lot done and don't seek awards or effusive praise. They carry an innate sense of being reliable, practical and productive.

The secret to their power and value to all the other roles is that they make it happen - quietly and efficiently.

Servers can be difficult to spot because they can be imprinted by their culture and by their parents who may be other roles.

In any one lifetime the other overleaves such as dominance or power can color the style of their service. For example, the server with a goal of dominance will be a leader in service of those he leads while a server in submission will be devoted to a cause or leader he wishes to follow.

The fastest means of spiritual growth is service to others, putting others needs before your own. The other roles (excepting priests) readily distance themselves from performing this function. This is because of the struggle the ego has in learning to surrender itself to others and serve them. The struggle for surrender for the server manifests as the negative pole of manipulation. They haven't really surrendered but are setting up the situation so that they have hidden or overt control.

The server is a mid-frequency role signifying that in relation to the other roles he is in the mid range of about 50%. What does this mean? This term has not been used up until now so here is a brief explanation.

An Aside on Frequency...

Back in Chapter One we saw how fragments were cast off from the Tao like white light. When white light passes through a prism it refracts into seven frequencies, the seven colors of the spectrum. Similarly the seven roles are created, each of a different frequency - literally.

Each role has a vibrational rate of its essence. That primary vibrational rate accounts for the differences in the roles.

A high frequency role tends to be visionary and far sighted. The essence leaves the body often and for lengthy periods ("the lights are on but nobody's home"). They are good at remembering dreams and astral experiences, they tend not to handle practical matters well, and so on. Priests and artisans are high frequency roles.

The low frequency roles take one day at a time, they are "solid" as opposed to "fluid", and tend to say - "I'll believe it when I see it." The essences of solid roles are not comfortable being out of the body. Warriors, scholars and kings are low frequency and called the "solid roles." Servers and sages occupy the mid-range.

Server: Relating to Others

Servers put other peoples' needs before their own, and so facilitate their own spiritual growth. They help with the smooth running of society by making sure everyone is offered assistance. In short, servers nurture and love.

They are excellent at covert control, liking to be behind the scene making sure that situations unfold according to what they judge most appropriate. The converse is that servers avoid confronting people, preferring to be indirect and oblique, and leaving things unsaid.

Servers have an eye for detail and a sense of timing. When they are not in control of the situation they feel uncomfortable and frustrated, and trapped or enslaved. They can become overcommitted and taken advantage of by others because of their willingness to be of service.

Servers gravitate to such professions as medical doctors, nurses, psychotherapists, waiters, butlers and similar service people. Servers make it possible for all other roles to do their work by being the support. They heal them when they are hurt, provide food when they are hungry, shelter them when they are in need.

Servers are an ordinal role so they prefer to work one-to-one with people and aren't usually comfortable serving masses of people through leadership positions. Occasionally, a server sees his or her path as more exalted - such as Queen Elizabeth II.

Server: Relating to the Environment

Servers comprise about 30% of the global population and are the most numerous of any role.

Some might ask "Why would anyone want to be a server? It sounds like so much work." The answer is that servers are both inspired by service and are inspirational to others. They know that service to others is true humility and the shortest path to enlightenment.

The role of server used to be called "slave" in this system because of their historical function as slaves or servants. However society has transcended the need for slavery and the role of server has evolved to that of facilitators. The word slave is misleading in that it holds a negative connotation for the role that most puts into effect the concept of love for others.

Servers like to stay in the background so they do not become as prominent as the other roles. Kings and Queens may be servers who are thrust into power, albeit with recalcitrance. Even though servers are in the majority of all the roles, a preponderance of servers can be found in India and China. Both countries are embarking on a massive labor-intensive thrust toward productivity as they surge toward early level young perceptivity.

Countries like the United States currently have relatively few - maybe 10% of the population. Of the servers in the U.S. the bulk are over forty years old, pre-dating the surge of servers to India and China.

Famous Servers

Mother Teresa, Pearl Buck, Alice B. Toklas and Gustav Adolf; Queen Elizabeth II, Queen Victoria, Anna Pavlova, Albert Schweitzer, biblically - Mary and Joseph; Peter Lorre, Florence Nightingale, Queen Victoria.

Positive Pole: Service
Caring, warm, loving, inspiring, capable, other-directed, competent, trustworthy, friendly, nurturing, devoted, caretaker, achieving spiritual growth through service to others, subtle.

Negative Pole: Bondage
Victimized, enslaved, martyred and self-sacrificing, manipulating, mushy, frustrated, domineering, covert, underhanded, subservient, over-extended, doormat, unable to act, feeling tied down, inability to see appropriate service and therefore pushing people into inappropriate activities and places.

PRIEST   (+ Compassion, - Zeal)

How is a priest like and yet unlike a server? How would you be able to spot one in a crowd? The priest is the server exalted. The essence of priest is compassion and the ability to serve others by inspiring them to take on challenges and grow. The priest can make others melt with emotion or, by contrast, galvanize them to fight to the death in battle.

Priests feel driven to strive for what they perceive to be the higher good. They may even feel that others are blind and ignorant to the urgency of it. Those others, on the other hand, may feel that life is fine and that the higher good can wait.

Let's take an example which might best illustrate how a priest might respond compared to other roles:

A small business has just changed hands and everyone is wondering what will be expected of them by the new owners. A priest comes in as head of the new company. The first approach would be to look at the large picture. Where do they want to lead the company, in what direction, for what purpose. They must come up with a vision that combines the talents and skills of the people working for them. Then they will attempt to inspire their employees, get them to see the merits of the vision and how each person can make a significant contribution. Combining the large inspirational vision which gives people a sense of purpose and letting each person know how their efforts fit into this important goal would be the challenge to the priest.

Priest: Relating to Self

The priest is an exceptionally high frequency role - the most fluid of all the roles. Less concerned with physical things including their own bodies, they tend to be visionaries. Priests usually have high energy and zip along at speed. Retiring late at night and rising very early, they may be involved in numbers of projects with an intensity that would daunt lesser mortals. Question a priest closely and you'll find a sense of mission and purpose. Followers flock to them for guidance on personal and spiritual matters.

Priests like to move quickly through their life experiences and push others to move quickly as well. As a result they may thrust themselves through their cycle of lifetimes much more rapidly than the other roles.

They prefer emotional centering and enjoy moving into higher emotional states. Others with intellectual centering may accuse priests of being flaky or ungrounded because they are operating more from emotion than reason.

The role of priest is one of the most difficult to handle appropriately and is often not mastered until the old soul stage. One way to understand this is to think of a violin. Compared with other instruments the fine tuning of a violin is critical to produce a good sound. The slightest thing can send it out of tune, however when in tune, it elicits intense emotional responses from others.

Priest: Relating to Others

Priests are sometimes so obsessed with inspiring others that they are not interested in whether their information is accurate or not. This can alarm people of other roles who are more exacting as to the facts of the situation. Being impulsive and visionary their impracticality has lead, in times gone by, to them being killed.

Priests are often political creatures and can be fanatical about what they are striving for.

Historically, warriors have developed a distrust of priests. Over the centuries priests have inspired warriors to go into battle, - and the warriors have often gone to their death because the facts of the situation were not ascertained. Scratch a warrior and you find they harbor an innate cynicism about priestly zeal.

Priests in general get along well with their complement - servers and with scholars who can understand them better than other roles. Priests are sometimes mistaken for artisans because they are both high frequency roles.

Priest: Relating to the Environment

Unlike servers, there are a very small percentage of priests (about 7%) and they are distributed far and wide in the population.

As powerful inspirers and facilitators of spiritual growth, priests are in high demand. They serve by helping or goading others to self-examination. Because they are exalted, priests are capable and skilled at communicating with large groups of people. They often gravitate to ministry or positions of military leadership where they can uplift large congregations or legions of troops. Priests also make excellent radio and television personalities, and similar high profile positions but are also found in a more modest settings such as the helping professions.

Priests make excellent healers; using deep compassion they are able to assist others emotionally and spiritually. Tribally, they are often the healers, medicine men and shamans.

Primitive tribes needed strong leadership. The leadership evolved from controling the tribe in one of two forms - either by outright coercion and force (a common characteristic of warriors and kings), or exploitation of inner superstition into fear.

This second method gave rise to the priesthood and organized religions. Especially in the younger soul stages, priests in primitive societies tended to prey on peoples' superstitions for political purposes. Priests are the most political of any role, so often priests are the first in a baby soul society to rise to prominence. One example is Colonel Kaddafy of Libya.

Famous Priests

Most famous evangelists are priests. Other examples of well-known priests are: Thomas Aquinus, Thomas Merton, Rasputin, Allen Ginsberg, Princess Diana, Hitler, Constantine, Napoleon, Idi Amin, Julius Caesar, Nero, J.S. Bach, Kohmeini, Jesse Jackson, King Arthur's Guinevere and Nancy Reagan.

Positive Pole: Compassion

Compassionate, inspirational, caring, enthusiastic, healing, warm, guiding, emotionally connected, nurturing, visionary, sense of mission, humanitarian, aware of the planet as a whole or a country as a whole, oriented to breaking people through their inertias or their ruts (natural goads).

Negative Pole: Zeal

Zealous, fanatical, feverish, unworldly, evangelical, flaky, prosletizing, irrational, unthinking in their vision, non- practical, tendency to want to fix you whether or not there is anything right or wrong with you, tend to be reactionary, bigoted, over-extended.

The Expression Roles: Artisan and Sage

+ Creation   + Dissemination

ARTISAN   SAGE

- Self-deception   - Verbosity

The expression axis roles, artisan and sage, are gifted at communication. They each communicate different areas of experience. Sages are creative with words, and artisans are creative with things.

They bring beauty and fun to the world as well as a fresh perspective. They like to team up and may work together on creative projects such as film, drama, music, and so on.

ARTISAN   *(+ Creation, - Self-deception)*

The essence of the artisan is creativity, the desire to bring to life that which has never been done before. How is this achieved? The answer is primarily through inventiveness and engineering. The artisan is the ordinal expression role who applies his inventiveness to create new forms and atmospheres. For the artisan, all of life is a canvas upon which to paint something new, something different.

If you could peek inside an artisan's head this is what you might discover:

> *"This color scheme is too uninteresting, it expresses nothing. Just let me get my hands on it. I'll transform the place. Here, let's try these colors, they'll create a feeling of coziness while those decorations will lend a touch of class to the atmosphere. That's good for now, tomorrow I'll change the place entirely again to create a different effect. I really want to do something entirely new here, something that will get people to notice. As it is I'll have to shop for a new outfit that will go with these colors..."*

Artisan: Relating to Self

Artisans specialize in expression through creativity and invention. One of their forms of creativity is that they create the atmosphere in a group situation. Sometimes the mere presence of an artisan is enough to influence a shift, and transform the quality of expression in a room. In other words, an artisan need not necessarily do anything to create an influence, simply being is enough.

For those readers who are justifiably skeptical we recommend some empirical investigation. If an artisan in a group is unhappy or dissatisfied, our experience is that the whole group becomes blocked and held back. Checking in with artisan group members about how they feel can bring noticeable results.

The artisan is a high frequency role and this allows them to be fluid and flexible in their approach to life. They are capable of handling a number of different projects at the same time. Artisans create a multitude of possibilities to draw on that may bewilder other roles.

In business they may raise a vast number of matters and tackle them all at once - finance, taxation, production scheduling, marketing, etc., all in an apparently semi-random fashion. They then may not have the impetus to follow through.

Artisans are expressively creative at every level. They approach the world as if it were a canvas on which they can wax creative. Many feel that their skin is itself a canvas, and the appeal of tattoos is well nigh irrisistible. Artisans are the kind of people that, if they cannot be creative, they feel frustrated, blocked and upset. For them creativity is a way of remaining healthy.

Michelangelo is a good example of an artisan. In his last lifetime he sought to achieve perfection in his works of art as the culmination of all his lifetimes of creativity. He achieved that goal of perfected creativity and cycled off.

Artisans relish creative dressing and may be distinguished by the extrordinary costumes they wear. They come up with new and different hair styles and inventive ways of dressing that border on the bizarre. Artisans are creative not only in the creative arts but also creating ideas, moods, emotional milieus, or new conceptual schemes.

In the younger cycles the artisan is more likely to be creative on a purely physical level; however in the later cycles the older artisan works also with the abstractions - i.e., ideas and atmospheres.

The creative juices may flow so thick and fast that they do not want to take the time to wait for what they have mentally created to manifest into physical reality. The absence of follow-through means they may leave a trail of unfinished projects behind them.

Artisan: Relating to Others

Artisans are chameleons and adept at appearing like any other role, making them difficult to spot. This makes them good actors and indeed they often love the theatre. They may not be able to sustain the acting however, get bored and shift to another appearance. This is a telling trait.

Artisans get along well with sages. Artisans are similar to priests and both tend to remember out-of-body experiences. Artisans can feel intimidated by warriors, who represent an opposite way of being. Artisans hold an instinctive fear of the warrior's way of being as solid, focused and confrontive. This fear can be related to historical situations where the artisan was no match for the warrior on the attack with his sword.

As described later, artisans generally resonate well with kings. The king employs the creativity and artistry of the artisan. The artisan enjoys the mastery and power associated with the king. They are common partners in business or marriage.

Artisans find the day-to-day routine dull and boring and will create novelty simply to alleviate the boredom. Because of their inventiveness they become deceptive and distort information simply because of their drive to be creative.   The proverbial creation of a rumor is a good example of artisan influence.

The least comfortable role on the physical plane, artisans often appear to be spaced out, impractical or flaky relative to the more solid roles.

As an ordinal role artisans prefer working one-to-one or in small groups. They are more intimidated by large crowds where their creativity gets dispersed. There are exceptions to this, such as artisan actors.

Artisan: Relating to the Environment

Artisans comprise about 18% of the population globally and an even higher percentage of Americans are artisans (30%). Artisans are so quick with ideas that they are frequently pioneers and ahead of their time. Sometimes by the time society at large adopts their ideas such as high fashion, they have become bored and go on to something new and different. Because they are so far ahead, of all the roles they may feel the most alone or misunderstood. And indeed they are! They frequently gather together in artistic support groups, or artists communities where they can find a measure of fellowship and understanding. However, artisans are not necessarily good at understanding other artisans.

Artisans are often drawn to the arts or to the crafts; carpentry, interior decoration, architecture, fashion, make up, hairdressing. They represent the innovative aspect of any industry, and industries need to be innovative to survive.

Artisans are the architects of civilization in that they create the ideas that society and culture are built around. For example, ideas such as democracy and socialism, or the substitution of money for bartering, were invented by artisans.

In recent times in Western culture artisans tend to be more comfortable in their female lives because Western culture allows females more freedom in areas of creativity. Male artisans struggle more with their sexual identities and may feel led into acting macho to be accepted by other males.

We are seeing a trend of artisans being commonly male, bringing softness and creativity to our understanding of masculinity. When we discuss warriors we shall see that they are presently more often than not women, paving the way for acceptance of women as being more direct and focused - i.e. masculine qualities.

●

Famous Artisans

Some examples of famous artisans are Sir Walter Raleigh, Frank Lloyd Wright, William Blake, Vincent Van Gogh, Walt Whitman, Raffael, Michelangelo, George Lucas, Goethe, Thomas Jefferson, Mozart, Edgar Allen Poe, and of course Leonardo da Vinci.

Positive Pole: Creativity

Spontaneous, innovative, original, eccentric, imaginative, visionary, inventive, gamesters, mood creators, different, larger essence than others, reaching out for what is new, chaos-producing (which warriors then organize) and paternal (whether male or female).

Negative Pole: Self Deception

Completely confused, deceptive of others, irresponsible, moody, self-indulgent, false, impulsive, bizarre, more emotional than other roles and so subject to heavy depressions; soft, weak-willed, allowing others to control situations and so abdicating their own power.

In the negative pole (self deception) artisans simply create their own reality. They can create their own understanding of situations that has no bearing on the facts, and live in a cloud of fantasy. This means they may deceive themselves, and other people without being aware of it. Because of this artisans can appear the most disturbed of the mentally ill.

SAGE   *(+ Dissemination, - Verbosity)*

How is a sage different in expression from an artisan? How can you pick out a sage from a crowd of people? The answer to the latter question is usually "with ease". Sages stand out from the crowd. They are the exalted expressive role and born attention-getters. They can be dramatic, witty, hilarious, long winded, and demonstrate great wisdom.

How does a sage think? This is one exaggerated possibility:

> *"No, I'm afraid you have misinterpreted me. What I meant to say exactly was that the hamster's condition is grim, not grave. Listen, you simply must understand. In fact I better put it in print for all to hear. The hamster has suffered before and will suffer again but he will withstand the crises just as we all have these last few moments. Let's see, I still don't think you quite get it. How can I put it a different way? It's terribly important to me that you get what I am trying to tell you. Maybe if I said it more humorously or, perhaps, I should understate it a bit and catch you off-guard. No, I believe a dramatic portrayal would be best. Hang on while I go get my hamster costume on. Maybe if I tell you about the plight of hamsters you'll feel a little better about your own."*

Sage: Relating to Self

Like the artisan, sages are highly creative. They are skilled at the creative use of words and their expression. Unlike the artisan they are most comfortable in large groups or crowds calling attention to themselves at every opportunity. They are the most fun loving of the roles, given to wit and the ability to entertain publicly. Sages are so fun loving, that they are slow to mature. They are oriented more to fun than to the more serious aspects of adult life.

The sage is gifted at expressing and creatively using words, putting language together in an unique and unusual way. A sage will be the first to correct misuse of English or a misinterpretation of meaning.

Sage: Relating to Others

They have a tendency to declare their own ethics and are excellent at manipulating words in a way that might be construed as deceitful by others. Sages play with the truth. They are skilled at perceiving the truth and then may wax creative with it.

Sages are capable of being masters of deceit and trickery and this makes them excellent actors, hucksters, and sellers of snake oil. Sages expect the attention of their audience and can become quite annoyed if ignored. However, unlike priests, they do not expect their listeners to spiritually grow from what they have to say. They simply want to inform and have fun.

They tend to take life lightly and are naturally exuberant and positive. The more solid roles may feel "life wasn't meant to be easy" and that they are not facing up to their responsibilities, but the sage keeps skipping and joking along.

Sages can get along well with artisans, their complementary role, and with scholars. Both have a love of information gathering, the sage to tell it and the scholar to store it. Warriors may have some difficulty with sages because of their creativity with the news yet both have in common a rollicking sense of fun.

Sage: Relating to the Environment

Sages gravitate towards the professions of authors, actors, public speakers, journalism, and editing. Again unlike artisans their are few sages - they comprise about 11% of the population.

Sages like the media. Their greatest desire is make to sure that the information is communicated clearly and disseminated to all parts of the population.

They clamor the loudest for freedom of the press and journalistic access to international events. When reporting on these situations they bring their unique perspective to bear on the story, trying to find the human element, the surprise insight, or the hidden agendas.

To sum up, the sage's goal is to bring humour and fun to everybody else, and to teach them not to take life so seriously.

Famous Sages

Famous sages are Abraham Lincoln, Charlie Chaplin, Lawrence Olivier, Richard Burton, Shakespeare, Mark Twain, Cleopatra, Salvador Dali, Groucho Marx, Jesse James, Butch Cassidy, Bella Abzug, Ronald Reagan and Mikhail Gorbachev.

Positive Pole: Dissemination

Expressive, wise, entertaining, perceptive, dramatic, humorous, inquisitive, unruffable, informative, colorful; operate from their perceptions, knowledgeable, speak well, good in all media, teach through optimism and the light-hearted side of life, believe that you can achieve all you want in life and still have fun, they present fun and as a result grow up more slowly because they'd rather have fun.

Negative Pole: Verbosity

Oratorical, deceptive, attention-grabbing, loud, tasteless, overly dramatic, egocentric, boring, shove the information down your throat, teach you something whether or not you want to learn it, intrusive, gossipy, lying, slippery, irresponsible, wonderful sleazy characters.

The Action Roles: Warrior and King

+ Persuasion	+ Mastery
WARRIOR	KING
+ Coercion	- Tyranny

The action axis roles are warrior and king. These two types of people are gifted at getting things done. They are the most comfortable on the physical plane and enjoy the physical body and everything it can do.

WARRIOR   *(+ Persuasion, - Coercion)*

What does it mean to be a warrior and what functions do warriors fulfill in society? In a way they are like the soldier ants who offer protection for the nest or like the worker bees who accomplish so much for the hive. The warrior is the ordinal action role, focused and oriented to get the job done in a physical sense.

The following imitates the qualities of a warrior:

"What I'm best at is organizing. I can move into a disorganized mess and straighten it up.

Often I do most of the work myself because then I know it's done and done well.

I cut my teeth on a problems and challenges because I can generally devise a strategy to get around them. Challenges are what makes life worth living. If I don't have a goal I'm lost and depressed and feel I have no purpose.

Food, drink, good company and sex are how I really enjoy being in a physical body. I delight in sports that call for winning and excellence. Day-to-day I move from one goal to the next, methodically and focused. At work, I arrive and make up a list of things to do for the day. I spend the rest of the day simply working down the list."

Warrior: Relating to Self

Warriors approach life through their five senses. They are the most physical role and like to get into the center of things. They are highly focused, excellent strategists and tacticians. Warriors are goal setters and can become uncomfortable and ill-at-ease without goals.

Warriors are often so focused that they only see what is directly in front of them, and even then, only one thing at a time. Given that they are oriented towards action they prefer bodies that are strong and solid.

Warriors have a tendency to be solitary fighters and tackle a project all on their own. This type of workhorse approach often brings exhaustion, and it is commonly warriors that die from overwork. Warriors frequently have more lifetimes than any other role. They also tend to die earlier than any other role because of their active and adventurous approach to life. They have a proclivity to rush off into battle.

Another characteristic is that warriors like to earn what they have. Other roles can accept wealth or success as a gift but warriors delight in the striving. They enjoy success only when they know they truly earned it. Life is a contest to be won.

Enlightenment for warriors is knowing exactly what to do next and how to do it. They are most often than not the first to recognize what needs to be done in a particular situation. They can get frustrated with a group of people who are prey to other considerations. The warrior can get impatient as he sees action as the ultimate solution.

In the older cycles the warrior approach softens and the warrior can be a mellow, warm and gentle person. Warriors learn compassion late in the cycle. Even in the early part of the old stage the warrior tends to be ruthless with themselves rather than with others. Warriors self-deprecate often and can coerce themselves into certain high ideals and principles. This also relates to the ruthless honesty.

Because warriors are so single-focused they cannot handle more than one thing at a time. A warrior is apt to forget about family, friends, and hobbies while they are focused at work and vice versa.

Warrior: Relating to Others

Warriors love organization, planning and control. This makes them excellent businessmen, managers, and developers. They may stop at nothing to achieve their goal.

Warriors are the doers of society rather like the worker ants in an ant colony. Warriors have a sense of principle and desire to fight for what they believe is right. They tend to be combative and because they are an ordinal role they are most comfortable on a one to one basis.

In the early cycles warriors will gravitate towards conflict in a very physical fashion - pulling out their sword to settle their differences.

In the older cycles this combativeness becomes more subtle and can be seen on the courtroom floor or in corporate boardrooms.

> *That quintessential warrior, Clint Eastwood, converted the saying "Go ahead! Make my day." into a threat, epitomizing the negative pole of warrior (coercion).*

The archetype of the warrior is eulogized as the cowboy - a male archetype in the U.S.; Warrior qualities for males are deeply embedded and strongly upheld in this society.

Warriors make good parents because their families run like clockwork and children know exactly what to expect. The family's discipline tends to be just and quick. Children therefore are well behaved and know where they stand. Warriors make the best imprinters for children and young people and are usually in charge of the educational systems.

Warriors prefer to be direct and blunt and make poor liars. They distrust those who have a facility for presenting the truth in highly creative ways.

When they get bored, warriors hatch plots to entertain themselves. They may also create some confrontation for the same reason.

Despite their organizational prowess, warriors do not like to take ultimate responsibility. They like to have a king as the backstop.   The slogan of the warrior is, "To hell with meaning, give me results!" This one-eyed focused approach can be offensive to the sensibilities of the other roles.

Warrior: Relating to the Environment

Warriors are numerous in the world's population and make up about 20% of the population. The United States comprises mostly warriors and artisans (30% of each in the U.S.). One can see their influence in American society, such as the national propensity for litigation.

Their strong, solid bodies make it possible for them to be involved in highly active professions such as policemen, athletes, firemen, construction workers, national guardsmen, marines, sailors etc.   Nevertheless warriors may be found working as waiters, physicians, nurses or postmen. There is a tendency for warriors to be happiest in the more adventurous and active types of life that enhance what they do the best.

Warriors prefer to have male bodies because society gives men greater permission to be adventurous and active in the world. Female warriors can be frustrated by the limitations imposed by society. Presently, however, two thirds of warriors are women.

In the past, female warriors have gravitated toward being courtisans, or prostitutes. In many cultures these professions enjoyed a level of adventure and freedom and often courtisans were the only women allowed to learn to read and write.

Warriors are responsible for the creation and operation of large organized social bureaucracies such as the educational system, the military, and government.

The role of the warrior in the development of society revolves around the evolution of the military. As society changed from nomadic to stationary, the need for coordinated defense became necessary. The tribe's wealth and food stores were often kept in one hut and this had to be defended. This was the first need for a defense that went beyond merely the family. The principles of military organization that evolved from these early beginnings were also the foundations of modern bureaucracy.

Famous Warriors

General George Patton, Mao Tse Tung, Theodore Roosevelt, Attila the Hun, Eisenhower, Churchill, Rommel, Roosevelt, Gurdjieff, U.S. Grant, Grover Cleveland, Indira Gandhi, Golda Meir, Geraldine Ferraro, Martin Luther King, Henry Ford, Richard Wagner, Handel, Gertrude Stein, Ernest Hemmingway and John Wayne.

Positive Pole: Persuasion

Productive, structured, organized, aggressive, confronting, focused, Robin Hood, truthful, resourceful, determined, family-oriented, protecting, maternal (as opposed to paternal), defending, skilled, grounded, proud, principled, value the intellectual center, good at activities (moving centered skills) e.g. good with their hands, practical, reliable, loyal, love of challenges.

Good at setting up structures that care for the homeless, the weak, and the sick. Warriors organize schools, hospitals, fire departments, laws, so people feel protected and nurtured by society's structure; they are society builders, they add civilization so artisans can bring forth culture.

Good at teaching survival-oriented skills, e.g., teaching children how to make it to adulthood. Good at the physical plane and appreciating the physical - sex, smelling, touching, eating, etc.

Negative Pole: Coercion

Bullying, narrow-minded, intimidating, pushy, emotionally withheld, over-wrought, stressed, subjective, hot-tempered, overbearing, blunt, tactless, looking for struggle or conflict, argumentative, abrasive, hectoring, unforgiving, mistrustful, brutal, suspicious, devious, evasive.

Warriors are capable of strong-arming situations and if persuasion fails they can resort to force, pulling out the sword to get their way. This behavior is experienced as intimidation and frightening to the other roles who will normally withdraw under these circumstances. Sometimes because of their intense focus the warrior will not understand or be confused as to why everyone is going away from them. They simply do not see or understand that their coercive approach is offensive to others.

KING   *(+ Mastery, - Tyranny)*

Why are there so few kings and what is unique about them? How can you pick out a king or know if you are one? The first thing to remember is that the king is the exalted action role, given to doing in an expansive, wide-focused style. The king enjoys overseeing and directing the action. Because they are so broad-focused and impactful few are needed in the overall population. A little king goes a long way.

Here is how a king might think:

> *"When I think of life I think of how I can best do it - with the greatest dignity, mastery, style and productivity. Self-mastery is as important to me as mastery of situations and I like to use the other roles to help me achieve this. I am not afraid of delegation and like to use other people for what they are good at. I am visionary and can see how things can unfold. I see situations in the context of a larger picture, which I like to play with as I might play chess. While I like to delegate and use people to do things for me I always have in mind their well-being. I like to satisfy*

the masses and when I can't I feel I have not properly mastered the situation. I like to conquer, but only for the common good, i.e. let's all win!"

King: Relating to Others

Kings gravitate toward situations where they can delegate authority. You might hear a king say to subordinates: "This is the work I want done. Have it complete by the time I get back from my vacation." This is a part of their complete mastery and leadership.

Kings make excellent managers, politicians, and heads of corporations because these are all situations where they can direct activity.

They often have a naturally regal bearing and they inspire a sense of loyalty and devotion in other people. They have this gift for drawing people together for a cause. The loyalty they inspire is remarkable. They have the peculiar quality of achieving what they want through getting other people to offer it first. If a king is looking to buy a house, often someone will approach him with exactly what he wants. Not only is that convenient but the king retains the advantage because the other person is approaching him and not vice-versa.

Kings are leaders in investment fields (because of their mastery), rectors of parishes, and so forth. They can have a huge following and maintain personal relationships with each individual of the thousands that appreciate their talents.

Kings in particular can dominate the situation in an entire family. They prefer to be either the youngest or the eldest in a family. They feel an acute sense of responsibility for the outcome in many situations because they feel they are the final authority in the matter. This includes business situations, and families where they feel the need to launch all family members and look after their welfare. Old soul kings tend to demure and give in to this sense of responsibilty.

In the older cycles kings appear generous, magnanimous and highly compassionate towards others. In the younger cycles kings feel the drive toward fame and public recognition.

Kings get along well with most roles but they have a particular affinity for servers who frequently take care of them. Warriors usually group around kings and in turn the king responds to their loyalty. Artisans and kings enjoy one another because of their gift for expansive vision and scholars and kings make a good team. There can be difficulties between priests and kings or sages and kings because they all like the limelight.

King: Relating to the Environment

Kings account for 2% of the population. Although scattered widely throughout the planet, they gravitate towards more complex technological centers where they can exercise their abilities the most. Kings appear infrequently in India and China. In countries such as the United States, Japan, and Germany they are more prevalent. As the third world countries develop we can expect to see a higher number of kings born there or gravitating to those countries.

Kings, in desiring to master all situations will seek extremes of experience, sometimes knowing fame and fortune and at other times knowing the bottom rungs of society such as being a tramp, hobo, or societal reject. Note that kings are not always in positions of leadership and may be found in any socio-economic class and on every rung of society.

A classic occupation of an old king is to be the bartender where the bar is the social hub of a small community - or club president, neighborhood barber etc.

Famous Kings

Some examples of well-known kings include John Muir, John F. Kennedy, Alexander the Great, the man Jesus, Jack Kerouac,

William Randolph Hearst, Aristotle Onasis, J. Paul Getty, Franklin Roosevelt, Richard the Lion-Hearted, Mark Anthony, Raisa Gorbachev, the wife (and essence twin) of the Russian leader, Mikhail Gorbachev (sage) and Katherine Hepburn.

Positive Pole: Mastery

Excellence, imprint the concept of striving for excellence on those around them, gentle, natural leaders, magnanimus, charismatic, strategists, self-assured, stable, well-rounded, commanding, informed, visionary, good at delegating, good with money, quieter and more gentle than warriors, charismatic; get along with everyone, and inspire loyalty, commitment and devotion. Make good generals, presidents and heads of corporations.

Pull other people in so they get in touch with their karma, as well as getting in touch with the king.

Negative Pole: Tyranny

Demanding, controlling, intolerant, ruthless, overbearing, extravagant, unrelenting, arrogant in the extreme; usually get other people to do what they want.

The Assimilation Role: Scholar

+ Knowledge
SCHOLAR
- Theory

The assimilation axis is made up of one role only, the scholar. This axis is the neutral one and and makes it possible to mediate among all the others. Assimilation is concerned with absorption, making the dissimilar similar, comparing and incorporating. The scholar therefore studies, assimilates, and records.

SCHOLAR   (*+ Knowledge, - Theory*)

What do scholars contribute that is unique and different from the skills and talents of the six paired roles? How would you know if you were a scholar, or if you knew one? The most important thing to remember about scholars is their neutrality. They look neutral, they often feel neutral, and they respond neutrally to many situations that another role would not.

The scholar is at the hub of the wheel around which all of the other roles rotate. That is they occupy that neutral space that enables the other roles to communicate. When a scholar is present the other roles find greater ease in understanding one another and a greater ability to communicate with one another.

Here is how a scholar might think:

"Hmmmmm! This looks interesting. I'd really like to know more about this. I wonder if there's anything written about this or if anybody has compiled any information about this already. I'd sure like to get my hands on it. I wonder what would happen if I took some of this stuff and experimented with it. Sure would be exciting to find out. Even if I got some strange results that would be interesting too. What? You say you know someone in Tibet who has studied this and has a library on it. Pack my bags! There are no planes that go there? Well I'll have to start researching ways to get there. Let's study those maps and get some books about Tibet to prepare to go there. We'll take some notebooks and make a record of our journey."

Scholar: Relating to Self

The key word of the scholar is neutrality - scholars make excellent mediators for others. Especially in their older cycles they are much less opinionated than the other roles and have the gift of three hundred and sixty degree vision giving them objectivity and the ability to see all sides of a situation.

Scholars are oriented towards the accumulation of knowledge, not necessarily for the purpose of disseminating or communicating to others, but to keep it so it is available.

Scholars are usually best at recording, describing and analyzing what has gone on in a situation after it is over. They excel at hindsight.   They are synthesizers of information and make excellent historians. Scholars, being a neutral role, are frequently spectators or observers.

Scholars are exceptionally curious and driven to seek out anything which they feel they do not know about. They like to select a subject and study it *ad nauseam*... Scholars can devote an entire lifetime to the study of one object, attempting to understand every facet of the topic. Only a scholar could devote an entire lifetime to the study of a particular genus of flower or a particular type of insect. Because of this natural curiosity, scholars tend to go where angels fear to tread.   Sometimes scholars will, in later cycles, seek to study their own consciousness through experimenting with the use of psychedelic drugs and time spent in isolation tanks.

A scholar is a solid role as opposed to a fluid role like an artisan, server, or priest. As such, they appear grounded and appear quite physically oriented. They enjoy adventure and most physical experiences. Their sense of adventure though is different than that of the warrior. The scholar seeks adventure out of a curiosity to know more, whereas the warrior seeks new challenges and action. Scholars and warriors make good companions.

Enlightenment for a scholar is understanding as opposed to achieving any type of physical result. Because of their solidity scholars have more physical endurance than any other role. They are able to endure extremes of climate and adverse conditions.

Scholars accumulate information and store experiences kinesthetically in their bodies. This causes the scholar to have more physical problems (as aches and pain in muscle tissue and bone) than any other role; healing comes with the understanding that experience need not be stored in the body and that it may be consciously released.

Scholars like to experience a wide diversity during their lifetimes and accumulate information on intellectual, emotional, and physical levels. Commonly, scholars hold several different careers during their lifetime and, in addition, have a number of hobbies and interests. Because of their penchant for information, scholars like to have intellectual centering at least in part.

Scholar: Relating to Others

Scholars act as portable libraries for other roles who go to them for information. Other roles value scholars because they are able to keep a neutral view.

At the end of the cycle of lifetimes the scholar pours the sum total of his experiences and knowledge into the library of the universe, the Akashic Records. The next universe is derived from the experience of this universe that is stored there.

At times, scholars are unaware of the great store of information they have accumulated over the lifetimes and only when asked a specific question are they able to access what they know. Otherwise scholars can appear quiet and unassuming, and to the other roles they may appear emotionally held in. This is not to say scholars do not experience emotion. They may experience intense emotions and passion but reserve expression of these feelings.

Scholar: Relating to the Environment

Scholars make up about 13% of the population. Because they are oriented towards the accumulation of information they gravitate toward careers in philosophy, history and science. One could find scholars like any other role in any walk of life but they will be happiest in academia or in situations where they can have access to information.

The slogan of the scholar is summed up in George Santayana's famous dictum that "those who cannot remember the past are condemned to repeat it." Scholars feel it is their duty to keep track of that which has been learned so that society can move forward with new experiences and new information. In more primitive settings they gravitate naturally to the position of shaman or witch doctor.

Their scholarly nature makes them natural empirical scientists and so scholars are often experts with natural remedies, herbs, spices, naturopathy etc. They are the ones who would re-assemble parts of an aircraft after it crashed to investigate the cause. This kind of work calls for a fastidiousness that only a scholar could provide.

Famous Scholars

Examples of famous scholars include Heraclitus, Oppenheimer, Carlos Casteneda, Galileo, Earl Warren, Henry VIII, Saint Elizabeth of Hungary, Caesar Augustus, Pierre Curie, Immanuel Kant, Plato, Ouspensky, Howard Hughes, Rodney Collin, Picasso, Margaret Thatcher, Margaret Mead and Socrates.

Positive Pole: Knowledge

Understanding, knowledgeable, truthful, thorough, practical, integrating, neutral, mediating, grounded, solid, curious, observing, clarity, logical, adventurous, go anywhere once, brave yet reticent about it, keep people from repeating mistakes because they have remembered them; they are the clean-up crew for the other roles. They record what worked and what didn't after the artisans brought in chaos and the warriors structured it.

Negative Pole: Theory

Theoretical, abstract, confused, intellectualizing, reclusive, withdrawn, pontificating, overbearing, tedious, boring, slow, dull, dusty, fastidious, illogical because swayed by emotions, invisible, arrogant.

Scholars in the negative pole, rather than being knowledgeable about a situation, may think they know about it but are only developing theories. This theorizing masks actual ignorance of the situation but it gives the scholar a sense of control and a false appearance of understanding. In this fashion the scholar is able to fool other people and himself.

Find Your Role

Here are some statements that reflect a usual style of being. You may identify with all or many of them.

Try them on for size and see if they really fit who you are. Some of you, however, will know exactly which set fits immediately. Whatever the case, you can review the differences among roles through reading these statements.

1)   I love to take care of people and see to it that they are comfortable.
     I'd rather work behind the scenes making sure that everything is under control.
     Serving others directly is what inspires me the most in life.

2)   I often feel a strong urge to tell people what I see is best for them.
     I have a deep sense of mission about my life.
     Sometimes I am quite zealous in pursuing what I perceive to be the higher good.
     Most people don't appreciate their own spirituality.

3)   I love to create atmospheres, moods, and situations.
     Often I feel so creative I don't know what to do first.
     Life is my canvas and I want to express myself in a unique way.
     If I can't express my creativity by painting, sewing . . ., I can feel terribly blocked and frustrated.

4) Words and the way things are said are highly important to me.
   If it's not fun I usually don't want to do it.
   I like the attention of a group or crowd and entertaining them is a skill of mine.

5) I like to get things organized.
   I am a doer and most importantly I want results.
   It's the principle of the thing that counts.
   If I take on a dispute I generally win it.

6) If I do a task then I do it with excellence.
   I like to grasp the big picture and then see that it gets handled.
   I can be good at delegating what needs to be done to others.
   I don't stop until I really understand what I'm doing.

7) I am innately curious and like to study things.
   I feel neutral and I do not like extremes of emotion.
   I pursue knowledge avidly and record it all.

Code:
1) Server
2) Priest
3) Artisan
4) Sage
5) Warrior
6) King
7) Scholar

How to Use Your Role

The role is perhaps the most important overleaf of all to understand because it reflects your essence.

The role is your primary beingness. The role is not a pigeon-hole limiting your expression to one area. Rather it is a context to make what you do, feel, or express meaningful.

When you have figured out your role ask yourself whether you do the kind of things that your role likes to do, express, or feel. Are you frustrating your role by trying to please a parent or boss who wishes that you were different? Are you trying to be an athlete when you'd really rather paint or read? Are you trying to be meek and out of sight when you truly are good at delegating and leadership? Are you trying to be a craftsman when you'd rather be a nurse or serve people directly? Let us look now at the overleaves that comprise the personality and gain an understanding of this mask that we all wear.

Chapter Six

Introducing the Overleaves

What are overleaves and why are they called that unusual name? How do they operate and can you change them? Or do they remain the same? This chapter describes what overleaves are and shows you how to understand the upcoming chapters.

Imagine a human biology book that shows the different systems of the body on transparent sheets that overlay one another. On one sheet you can see the vascular system, on another, the muscular system, and on still another, the skeletal system. When you put them all together you see the complete system.

The overleaves, then, are personality characteristics that overlay the core or essence each lifetime. Together they create a complete picture of personality.

While the roles remain the same, lifetime through lifetime, the other personality characteristics or overleaves are chosen anew each lifetime. This enables the essence to set the scene in terms of personality traits. These personality characteristics facilitate the lessons that essence wants to learn for a given lifetime.

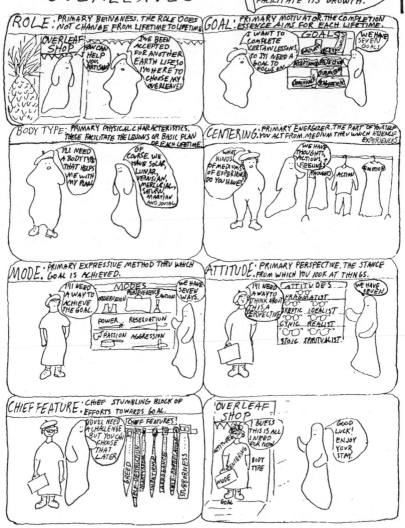

Essence has a 'basic plan' for each lifetime that it sets out to fulfill. The overleaves, bodytype and astrology are all selected to facilitate this plan. The whole purpose of a lifetime is oriented around the basic plan that essence formulates before incarnating.

An essence with the role of king in the young soul stage might choose a goal of dominance combined with power mode. To facilitate the young soul drive for power he might accentuate the impact of his personality by selecting a chief feature of greed and a natural inclination for action by being moving centered. An attitude of realist facilitates his aspirations. This is an immensely powerful combination and in fact these overleaves were chosen by the essence who became Alexander the Great.

What then is the value of knowing about one's own overleaves and those of others? It's often interesting to learn a new system for understanding personality, but in practical terms what is the point?

Here are some of the purposes of overleaves:

1.   The overleaves introduce variety, color, and richness into our lives. You always have choice about how to run your life and your essence chooses a different set each lifetime so as to learn more about itself and about life on earth.

2.   Without overleaves personality could not exist because by definition personality means being unique and different from others. Personality is the vehicle for our sense of separateness. Furthermore, karma is born from the thrust of our impulses and urges. The dance of self-knowing stems from this pattern of creation and repayment of intense experiences.

3.   Without overleaves we would be unable to cover the range of life experiences essence desires lifetime after lifetime. Leadership lifetimes require extroverted overleaves while contemplative lives

call for introverted characteristics. We seek the full gamut of all lifestyles throughout society, from king to peasant, and the overleaves set up our strengths and weaknesses relative to each other.

4.   Without overleaves we would be unable to challenge ourselves with difficult traits, grow with dynamic ones, or rest with easy ones.

Description of Overleaves

The overleaves overlay the essence and distort its purer energy. This distortion we call the personality and it is in imbalance in order to facilitate a lifetime of experience. The entire universe is in a constant process of shifting back and forth between balance and imbalance, much like a pendulum. Imbalance then is a natural state that leads to learning. Every lifetime is deliberately structured so that you learn.

You learn the most when encountering what you fear the most or love the most. The personality being what it is, we leap toward the ecstatic experiences and avoid the fearful ones. To redress this, essence sets up the fearful type of experiences with a degree of inevitability. So you get to have the experience either sooner (if you move toward it and confront it) or later (if you run like hell).

Nonetheless you will encounter your fears as well as pleasures. What happens around both is that as long as you continue to learn and gain intensity from being exposed to that situation, it will continue.

Eventually you become calloused to extremes. You encounter your loves, pleasures, fears and pains repeatedly until finally you no longer care. At that time you are neutral and complete.

The corollary of having many lifetimes is of course that you encounter death over and over again. You may be stabbed in a duel, have your ship sunk by a storm and drown in a freezing ocean; you are eaten by a crocodile or die slowly from leprosy. Ultimately you overcome your fear of death and learn to face it neutrally.

The overleaves make these experiences possible by providing a framework from which to act. They are like a set of tools which can be used effectively or ineffectively as the case may be.

Where essence can be seen as a form of beingness, the overleaves are a distorting filter upon the beingness. If you look at the Overleaf Chart, it forms an axis. Across the top is the "beingness" that essence is, and down the side are all the different types of filters that overlay beingness so that it can be expressed in an infinite number of different ways. Another word for overleaf would be "filter".

Each filter operates in terms of how it checks out reality (e.g. investigation versus suspicion for the skeptic) and how accepting (loving) it will be - e.g. persuasion versus coercion for the warrior. So the personality with all its overleaves is constantly making choices between illusion and truth, and love and fear.

Which is more important - truth or love? The lesson of this plane is whatever the function of the next higher plane is. The function of the astral plane is emotional, so physical plane lessons are preparatory to that. Love is the more important. In other words, truth is the path to love.

Briefly the overleaves are made up of the role [already discussed], the goal, the attitude, the chief feature, the mode, centering, and body types. There are seven of each of these characteristics contained within each set.

The personality comprises one each of the following. Refer to the Overleaf Chart at the back of the book for more detail.

The Seven Overleaves

Role   **Primary Beingness**
When essence is cast from the Tao it is cast in a role.
The role does not change from lifetime to lifetime.

Goal   **Primary Motivator**
The completion essence aims for each lifetime.

Attitude   **Primary Motivator**
The stance from which you look at things.

Chief Feature   **Primary Neutralizer**
This works to neutralize the goal thereby
maintaining barriers.

Mode   **Primary Expressive**
The method through which goal is reached.

Centers   **Primary Energizer**
The part of yourself you act from. The trap is the center
that facilitates the false personality best.

Bodytype   **Primary Physical**
                                  Characteristics
This facilitates the lessons or basic plan of each
lifetime.

Chapter Seven

Goals

The goal is the primary motivator in life and is the completion the essence aims for in each lifetime. Aside from the role, it is the most important overleaf.

The goal is what essence strives to achieve. Your essence will tend to create and bring situations into your life that bring you up against your goal. If you do not act from your goal then you may feel blocked and frustrated. When you act from the positive pole of your goal things flow smoothly.

People with the goal of dominance will find that when they lead a situation, (creating ideas, acting on them and organizing other people), that they are powerful, effective and self-actualized. When they act from say the goal of acceptance and do not lead, they may feel stuck and stagnant.

The opposite might apply to people with the goal of acceptance. If they try to lead, it may feel forced, pushy and uncomfortable. Their goal is to get in agreement with who they are and what their situation is, and to accept (love) others and themselves for who they are.

Goal - Primary Motivator
The Completion Essence Aims for Each Lifetime

Percentages Within the Earth's Population

Re-evaluation - 1%	Growth - 40%
Discrimination - 2%	Acceptance - 30%
Submission - 10%	Dominance - 10%
Stagnation - 7%	

The Seven Goals

Ordinal	Neutral	Exalted
Inspiration		
+ Simplicity		+ Evolution
RE-EVALUATION	———————	**GROWTH**
- Withdrawal		- Confusion
Expression		
+ Sophistication		+ Agape
DISCRIMINATION	———————	**ACCEPTANCE**
- Rejection		- Ingratiation
Action		
+ Devotion		+ Leadership
SUBMISSION	———————	**DOMINANCE**
- Exploited		- Dictatorship
	Assimilation	
	+ Free-flowing	
	STAGNATION	
	- Inertia	

Inspiration Goals: Re-evaluation and Growth

+ simplicity	+ evolution
RE-EVALUATION	GROWTH
- withdrawal	- confusion

RE-EVALUATION

Focus:

" I'm taking stock this lifetime."
" There is an underlying theme to my life that I'm spending years contemplating."
" My choices are more limited this lifetime."
(especially if I have a disability.)

Re-evaluation is a goal that is selected by only a small segment of the population at any one time - approximately one percent.

Re-evaluation relates to introspection and consolidation, a going over previous experiences of former lifetimes. It is sometimes a period of rest in anticipation of an extremely busy lifetime. (Years ago this goal was termed "retardation".)

People sometimes choose a physical disability that helps to promote this goal, for example blindness, mental retardation, or perhaps a major motor disability. This severely restricts movement and reduces the distractions so that the person is induced to contemplate.   Sometimes the lifetime is experienced in the custodial care of an agency, family, or individual who takes major responsibility for the individual's survival needs. Not everyone with a goal of re-evaluation suffers from a disability. However their lives will still be characterized by being focused on one or two main issues.

Often a temporary experience of re-evaluation can be brought on by a drug experience. Then people may slide into re-evaluation, becoming silent and withdrawn or perhaps look at the world around them with simplicity.

Because of the nature of the goal of re-evaluation there are no examples of famous individuals that illustrate it. If you know of a person suffering from Down's Syndrome or who is mongoloid, he or she will probably have this goal.

The principle behind Thoreau retreating to the simple life in cottage in a forest, as expressed in his book "Walden Two", expresses re-evaluation beautifully.

Positive Pole
Simplicity; naivety, inspection, review, state of awe or wonder, state of unaffected simplicity.

The positive pole of re-evaluation is simplicity. This suggests a lifetime with a minimum of intense experiences and karma. Life is experienced relatively simply and without complication.

Negative Pole
Withdrawal; internalized, stuck, bewildered, spaced out, regressed.

In the negative pole withdrawal is the attempt to hide and remove oneself from life entirely and this is usually experienced as unpleasant.

GROWTH

Focus:
"I want to learn and develop myself."
"It it's new and interesting, I'll give it a shot."
"Am I on the right spritual path? - Let's get on with it!"
"There are so many things to do in life that I don't know where to start."

The other inspiration goal is growth. To some extent it is the opposite of re-evaluation. Growth offers a lifetime of tremendous activity, a driving towards new experiences and constant development. Life in growth usually feels like several lifetimes all rolled into one. Growth is a popular goal and about 40% of the earth's population is experiencing it at once.

People in growth tend to select experience based on whether it will help them to grow or not. Growth is commonly chosen to facilitate a lifetime where a great deal of karma must be dealt with.

For a person in growth it is not important for the experience to be fun or not. What is more important is that the experience provides a path to development. Sometimes people in growth suffer because they choose challenges that either lead nowhere or prove painful.

If a person in growth feels that to run around the block twenty times will be a growth experience then the person will do that. Often people in growth discover to their chagrin that what they have been doing has really not led to growth at all. So, they will reorient themselves to a new situation which offers the prospect of growth.

Another characteristic of people in growth is that they love to talk about their experiences and what they mean. People in growth tend to be self-oriented and focus more on themselves than on others.

Since the goal complementary to growth is re-evaluation the person in growth slides there now and again to rest. Likewise someone in re-evaluation likes to grow sometimes to move forward. This sliding across to the opposite pole is true for all goals.

Some examples of well known individuals with the goal of growth are Galileo, Carlos Casteneda, Jimi Hendrix, Marshall McLuhan, Indira Gandhi, William Blake, Marie Antoinette, Eleanor Roosevelt and Gloria Steinem.

Positive Pole
Evolution; clarity, comprehension, progressive,   eager,   willing to take on challenges, essence directed.

The positive pole is evolution and this is the experience of overcoming all obstacles and developing oneself to maximum potential.

People with the goal of growth often say they spend a lot of time striving and the moments of brilliance and clarity are only occasional.

Negative Pole

Confusion; driven, complicated, absent-minded, ignorant of the needs of others, afraid of appearing ignorant or unmotivated.

The negative pole of growth is confusion. The notion of confusion is a self-deception. We are never really confused. We are merely between choices and do not want to acknowledge what those choices really are. We do not want to make a decision because we do not like the solutions we see. So confusion is a means of stalling.

Expression Goals: Discrimination and Acceptance

+ sophistication	+ agape
DISCRIMINATION	ACCEPTANCE
- rejection	- ingratiation

DISCRIMINATION

Focus:
"Is it good enough?"
"I am a sophisicated person."
"I draw the line here."

Discrimination is a goal that is found in only a few people, about 2% of the population. This goal is chosen as a challenge and usually accompanies a lifetime of intense karma. Discrimination is a difficult goal and is chosen only once in a number of lifetimes.

The aim of this goal is to approach life weeding out experiences that are inappropriate, selecting and savoring only the best.

The following are some examples of famous people with the goal of discrimination: Vincent Van Gogh, Rasputin, Marilyn Monroe and Jack Kerouac.

Positive Pole

Sophistication; refinement, perfectionist, worldly, discerning, well-developed critical faculties.

A person in the positive pole of sophistication might appear exceptionally picky about the kind of clothes they wear, who they choose as friends, or what kind of a job they wish to hold. For example a person in the positive pole of discrimination might be a wine critic or a literary reviewer wherin the person's skills at discrimination are called upon to select the wheat from the chaff.

Negative Pole

Rejection; prejudiced, judgmental, opinionated, aloof, snobbish, devoid of simplicity or naturalness, readily rejecting self and others.

A person in discrimination can slide to the negative pole of rejection and become prejudiced against other people and other experiences and reject them outright. This is not selecting the best but catagorically rejecting and makes for difficult relationships.

A person in this negative state can be prickly and difficult to be around and creates being rejected by others.

Feeling rejected reinforces the tendency to reject back or reject oneself in the process. This can become a vicious cycle and difficult to change. Sometimes an individual will seek help in psychotherapy only to reject therapist after therapist in a perpetual search for the best one.

A person living in the negative pole of rejection can appear like a tramp, a social outcast, a bag woman, someone you might find along the street. Often they will refuse assistance even when offered.

There is a tremendous difference between the way someone with this goal appears based on their choice to act out of the negative pole or the positive one.

A person in the negative pole of discrimination can slide to the positive pole through examination of the prejudices that he or she holds.

For example in a job interview situation the interviewer might be sexist and reject an applicant because of their sex rather than their qualifications. If the interviewer can see through the prejudice, he might realize he wants the best person for the job and select a person based on merit.

The goal of discrimination is often allied with an overleaf that assists in negativity - e.g. a cynic or skeptic attitude means they already doubt or disbelieve, and rejecting is a natural consequence.

Some additional points:

1. In the negative pole in relationships, people do a lot of rejecting. The basis is that although they may know intellectually that they are loved, they do not get the **feeling.**

To feel more loved they can focus on the love in the relationship. One way is through affirmations e.g. "I love you just as you are" - this takes away the discriminating element of " I would like to love you but you don't ..." The effect of this is to push people into the positive pole of acceptance, which is unconditional love.

One form of affirmation is to get in touch each day with some important feeling about your partner and express it to them. You are what you believe, so create wonderful beliefs.

2. A person who favors the negative pole (rejection) can hold a job that calls for a degree of discrimination. So as a book reviewer or theatre critic he or she can exercise their goal, including where

appropriate, a measure of rejection. This fulfillment of their goal in the work arena frees them up to some extent in say their private life and they will not be so rejecting in an ongoing relationship.

3. When you are rejected by someone acting out of the negative pole, rejection, you need not feel rejected. Rejection says more about the rejecter than the rejectee, and you don't have to buy into it.

4. In terms of the mating game, people usually pair off with someone with the opposite goal. So someone with a goal of acceptance likes being stretched to accept a spouse who is rejecting. The person doing the rejecting finds someone who accommodates their fastidious pickiness.

The alternative is that birds of a feather flock together and people in discrimination like pairing up and reinforcing each others' sense of refinement. Usually however, one will reject the other before too long.

The goal of discrimination can look prickly to people with other goals, but those who live there often like it. They feel good about being sophisticated and not being naive, gullible or unrefined.

ACCEPTANCE

Focus:

"That's fine."

"I'm easy to get along with."

"Sometimes I fear people don't like me."

"I like to do things that make people feel good."

"Sometimes I sacrifice being an honest person for being a nice person."

Acceptance is a popular goal which includes close to 30% of the population.

Where discrimination is a goal that is common with younger souls who seek to create karma, acceptance is oriented toward resolving karma which is appropriate for the mature and old soul stages.

People in acceptance accept whatever occurs in their lives and being accepted is a high priority for them. They are most agreeable.

They can have a difficult time saying, "no" and find themselves in situations that they have agreed to but then feel uncomfortable with. They may be uncomfortable in asserting themselves and putting forth their opinion for fear they will be rejected. People in acceptance are exceptionally vulnerable to any kind of rejection. They experience rejection as painful.

As it is the complement of discrimination, people in acceptance will sometimes slide over to discrimination and draw the line and say "No! This doesn't work for me."

People with the goal of acceptance may do some rejecting - that is, some will slide to rejection in certain situations that are stressful, or where they are fearful, such as with the opposite sex. Others may seldom reject anyone, no matter what. So having the goal of acceptance doesn't necessarily mean you are always in nodding agreement with everyone.

Some examples of well known individuals with a goal of acceptance are John Muir, John F. Kennedy, Socrates, Carl Jung, Aristotle and Bella Abzug.

Old souls who find themselves back on the planet after they have experienced every conceivable variation of overleaves often choose the combination of idealist attitude, passion mode and the goal of acceptance. This ensures a challenge in striving for balance and they tend to collect intense and colorful experiences.

Positive Pole

Agape,   friendly,   outgoing,   warm,   understanding,   altruistic. humanitarian.

The positive pole of acceptance is agape which is translated as unconditional love or acceptance. This leads one to be loving and tolerant of oneself [despite limitations] as well as totally accepting of others for who they are. This does not necessarily mean tolerance for what they do.

Acceptance is generally chosen as the goal for the old soul in the final lifetime because agape is the final or ultimate goal of all lifetimes.

The starting point of unconditional love is learning to be mildly tolerant of those whom you find uncompromisingly reprehensible.

Negative Pole

Ingratiation; insincere, afraid of not being liked.

The negative pole, ingratiation, is the desire to please others so much that you lose yourself in the process. Ingratiation frequently leads to feelings of resentment and eventual rejection by all parties involved.

The person doing the ingratiating begins to tire with the constant strain of being "nice" and performing to be acceptable. He eventually becomes resentful that he does not feel appreciated for who he is. This sometimes leads to passive aggressive behavior - i.e. indirect anger.

The ingratiator may politely agree to do something for another that he really does not want to do. Inwardly, he rebels and fails to show up, disappointing the other. The other person feels let down and is motivated to reject the ingratiator. The negative pole thus leads to that which the person fears the most, rejection. This is the way negative poles tend to work.

Action Goals: Submission and Dominance

+ devotion   + leadership
SUBMISSION   DOMINANCE
- subservience   - dictatorship

SUBMISSION

Focus:
"I bury myself in work or a cause."
"If I can't devote myself to someone or something, I feel hollow and empty."

About 10% of the population is in submission at any one time.

Submission is the experience of placing oneself in the service of a cause or a situation or a person. Often the goal of submission will cause someone to seek a life in a monastic order or convent, or to follow the teachings or dictates of a guru. Everyday examples would be someone who is devoted to their job, their family or a deserving cause. People with this goal put others needs before their own.

Here are some famous people who exemplify the goal of submission: Pearl Buck, Andrew Wyeth, Mother Theresa, Joan of Arc and Mr. Rogers.

Like re-evaluation, the goal of submission does not often lead to a life of fame and fortune. The examples here tend to be exceptions.

Positive Pole
Devotion, caring, helpful, sensitive, selfless, dedicated, loyal.

Individuals with the goal of submission in the positive pole will bring themselves satisfaction through devotion. This is a tremendously valuable goal - for example bringing up a large family, dedication in marriage, or devotion to a particular career pursuit. People with the goal of submission can dedicate themselves to the study of science or the arts in a devoted way.

Here again people like to pair off with the opposite goal. So submission likes the way dominance charges into a situation and grabs the bull by the horns. Submission stands fairly and squarely behind, providing the backup of equipment, encouragement and refreshments. It is a common ingredient in business where both people are brilliantly capable at their different tasks. Dominance launches an audacious takeover bid for a company ten times their size and wins. Burdened by mountains of debt, and a hostile staff of the new company, submission brilliantly beavers away restructuring the accounts and the debt, persuading the people they are now better off etc. Within a year or two the amalgamation is a Wall Street success story. Neither of the two, however, could do it without the other. One is the bulldozer, the other the fine tooth comb.

Negative Pole
Subservience; helpless, dependent, martyred, victimized.

The negative pole of submission is subservience and it can be experienced most unpleasantly. For example one might be victimized or feel at the effect of the world. There is almost a feeling of being enslaved or in bondage.

The individual in this negative pole of subservience can get out of it by sliding to the positive pole of dominance or leadership. He can step up and take charge of his live and shift from being exploited to finding out what he really wants to be devoted to.

DOMINANCE

Focus:

> "We can really win here."
> "I'll lead the way."
> "I can show you what to do."

Dominance is the complement of submission. Taking charge is the main theme of this goal. Like submission, about 10% of the population who have dominance as their goal.

People with the goal of dominance tend to rise to the top of any given situation that they are in. They reach positions of leadership in their families, or their careers, or sometimes in social situations. It is important to be aware that people in dominance cannot help but desire to control. This can be experienced by other people as bossiness.

Dominance is an action overleaf. People with that goal will find that their lives work best only when they themselves step forward and lead. Generally the person in dominance knows best.

The style of dominance will be greatly influenced by the other overleaves. Some people control through silence, while others dominate through sheer verbosity. Some control by virtue of generosity and wisdom, while others dominate by threatening suicide and martyring themselves.

When dealing with people with the goal of dominance it is important to let them be boss of their area. So a family with three individuals in dominance would divide up areas and responsibilites that each would have, and operate with clear demarcation.

There are numerous examples of famous people with the goal of dominance because it lends itself to the kind of leadership that brings public attention. Here are but a few: Karl Marx, Ho Chi Minh, Julius Caesar, Gertrude Stein, Barbara Stanwyk, Mao Tse Tung, Mozart, Alexander the Great, General George Patton, and our favorite artiste, Lady Godiva.

Positive Pole

Leadership; authoritative, determined, outgoing, capable, win-win attitude, governing.

In the positive pole they are a model for others. They demonstrate capability and lead through their natural ability. They like to operate from a position of "Let's you and me both win - we can do this one well together."

Negative Pole

   Dictatorial,   demanding,   pushy,   overwhelming,   insensitive, selfish, "I win - you lose" attitude, controlling, dominating.

   Through the negative pole of dictatorship they try to force others to do what they want. They tend to be pushy, insensitive, and approach life from a winner-takes-all attitude.   Persons in the negative pole of dominance which is dictatorship can reach the positive pole by first sliding across to the positive pole of submission, devotion. This calls for a measure of surrender. Through devotion they can submit to the demands of the situation and then lead appropriately.

Assimilation Goal: Stagnation

+ freeflowing
STAGNATION
- inertia

STAGNATION

Focus:
   "Never do today what you can put off until tomorrow."
   "No need to be concerned - everything will work out fine."
   "What! Me worry?"

   The seventh and last goal is stagnation, the neutral goal which has no pair. Stagnation is the goal of approximately 7% of the population and is often considered a lifetime of rest.

   The aim of stagnation is as it sounds, to let life flow easily and effortlessly in order to take a rest. Some people spend most of their lives fighting this and it may take a long time before they learn to go with the stagnation.

   People who have chosen lives with the goal of stagnation have often had a number of intense lives previously. They seek to enjoy their present lifetime and experience the beauty of the world, and recuperate.

One of the characteristics of stagnation is that life is experienced without much drama. People's lives tend to unfold without intense effort on their part. Things tend to come to them easily and they do not have to work as hard as other people. Often they are born into wealth and have a natural flair or skill that enables them to walk into a well-paid job. This, of course, feels unfair and feels irritating to those with more demanding goals. They feel that stagnation is either cheating or that those in it are lazy and without ambition.

Again, because of the nature of the goal of stagnation there are few examples of famous people who illustrate it. Buddha epitomized this goal and showed that really the universe will provide if only you trust it.

Positive Pole
Freeflowing, unstressed, easygoing, fun-loving.

A person in stagnation in the positive pole will move from one thing to another in life without effort. The idea is to let things happen as they will and everything turns out well.

Allowing events to unfold in their own way without seeking to shape them is the purpose of stagnation. Those with this goal approach life with a major difference in outlook and speed from those of other goals. The easygoing outlook has an ease and tranquility unknown to those driven by growth, for example.

Negative Pole
Inert, lazy, uncommitted, ignorant.

The negative pole of stagnation is inertia and acts as a blockage causing situations to not work or flow at all. People in the negative pole often struggle more than they need to. The task is to let life be and merely step out of the way as people do in martial arts.

Goals in General

Relating Goals with Modes

All the goals are eventually experienced by all the roles but each role has likes and dislikes. For example, servers find that the role of submission facilitates their role, whereas warriors may find submission irritating and difficult. Kings find dominance easy whereas they might find re-evaluation difficult. Since scholars enjoy an on-going stream of fresh experiences, they tend to enjoy the goal of growth. All the roles experience the goal of acceptance about equally.

The goals manifest differently depending on the role. For example, a young warrior in discrimination appears quite different from an old server in discrimination. Whereas the young warrior in discrimination would probably create much karma, the old server in discrimination would be more likely to resolve karma. The warrior brings action to the goal of discrimination whereas the server brings inspiration to the role, and so on.

Find Your Goal

By now you know the process. Inspect the alternates below and see if you can identify the one that motivates you most.

1) If things aren't going my way, I fear I'm losing.
   Life looks competitive to me.
   I always want to win, no matter what.

2) More than anything else, I want to be dedicated to someone or something.
   I'm most comfortable when I feel devoted.
   I put others ahead of myself regularly.

3) More than anything I want people to like me.
   I hate being rejected.
   If someone went around saying unkind things about me I would be deeply wounded and find it difficult to confront him or her.

4) I don't enjoy things unless they are exactly right.
   I am picky about who my friends are, what I wear, and what I do.
   I am critical and I find others highly critical of me.

5) I like to be constantly learning, experiencing things, and changing.
   Just when I get everything just right I seem to move and start something new.
   Often I get overwhelmed, confused, and have to sort things out.

6) My life seems to revolve around the same issue over and over.
   Everthing in my experience is affected by my physical condition.
   I am severely limited as to my mobility or ability to get around.

7) I don't feel ambitious or driven to accomplish anything major in this life.
   I seem to ride from one thing to the next without the problems that others seem to have.
   Often it seems that life is uneventful but pleasant.

Code
1) Dominance
2) Submission
3) Acceptance
4) Discrimination
5) Growth
6) Re-evaluation
7) Stagnation

How to Work With Goals

The goal is most often selected for the duration of a lifetime yet occasionally it is exchanged for another one within the lifetime. On rare occasions, a person may decide to move from growth to acceptance or from discrimination to acceptance. Usually this occurs only in the older soul cycles and is accompanied by a traumatic life event.

The most effective way you can approach your goal is to move into its positive pole as often as possible. The negative poles are useful on occasion to throw you into karma yet they usually are uncomfortable to remain in. As has been mentioned before, if you find yourself in the negative pole you can shift out of it by sliding to the positive pole of the opposite goal in the axis. If you are in the negative pole of stagnation, the positive pole of any other goal will do.

In order to know more about how to work with your goal you will have to know about modes - the means of achieving your goal.

Chapter Eight

Modes

The mode is the method or action one takes to achieve one's goal. This does not necessarily mean the goal in the context of these discussions but anything that a person seeks. The mode is the method or "how" of one's general approach and is one of the strongest or most influential of overleaves after the goal. The goal is what you want, the mode is how you get there. Your attitude is how you decide on those things.

Percentages Within the Earth's Population	
Caution - 20%	Power - 10%
Repression - 2%	Passion - 10%
Perseverance - 4%	Aggression - 4%
Observation - 50%	

Mode - Primary Expressive
Method through which Goal is Reached

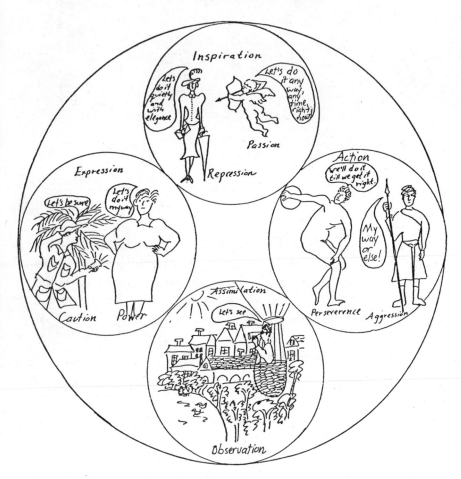

The Seven Modes

Ordinal	Neutral	Exalted
Inspiration		
+ restraint		+ self actualization
REPRESSION	————————————	PASSION
- inhibition		- identification
Expression		
+ deliberation		+ authority
CAUTION	————————————	POWER
- phobia		- oppression
Action		
+ persistance		+dynamism
PERSEVERANCE	————————————	AGGRESSION
- immutability		- belligerance
	Assimilation	
	+ clarity	
	OBSERVATION	
	- surveillance	

Inspiration Modes: Caution and Power

+ deliberation	+ authority
CAUTION	POWER
- phobia	- oppression

CAUTION

Focus: "Be careful!"
"Think before you act."

Caution mode is the fear of doing something wrong. It is self-blocking by nature, tending to hold a person back.

Popular with a younger soul population, it facilitates the purpose of young and baby souls because they are newer on the planet. Caution helps them approach life more carefully, balancing their natural inclination to tangle with the world and create intensity.

For example, a person in caution mode is less likely to tangle with a bank robber making his or her getaway. The fear of doing something he may later regret (in this instance, getting hurt) is always uppermost in his mind.

If older souls select caution mode, it is usually   to facilitate certain outstanding karma. For example, growing up with abusive parents would be easier if you were cautious about avoiding possible provocation.

About 20% of the population choose caution as their mode. A person in caution mode is careful about consequences, self-deprecating and conservative. The person may avoid responsibility (for example, refuse a promotion) because of their fear that they are "not up to it."

Caution is an ordinal mode and tends to be an intense experience for the person involved. It is an introverted type of mode, directing the attention inward (by being concerned with what may go wrong) rather than an outgoing mode that impacts others. In other words, it is more self-karmic than karmic.

Clearly this way of being will be difficult for people in outgoing situations.

Caution mode for an army general would be a mixed blessing. In a war situation he might let risky but potentially winning opportunities slip past because he is risk-averse. When he finally does send his troops into battle it is because he has deliberated (positive pole) and assessed that this is the occasion when they are most likely to win.

Caution mode by its nature does not lead many people to become famous or widely known. Those that become renowned have generally managed to act from the midpoint of caution and power modes, finding the balance position and sliding to power mode when appropriate.

Positive Pole
Deliberate; checking, proceeding carefully, taking time, avoiding risks or dangers.

In the positive pole, people in caution mode do a great deal of deliberation because they fear what they do might go wrong. To others they may seem slow and dragging their feet because they want to be certain that the right choice is made.

This person would say "Let's check for any dangers before we proceed", or "Let's not be too hasty."

Negative Pole
Phobia; irrationally fearful, superstitious, stuck, unable to decide, endless deliberation of possibilities.

The negative pole of caution mode, phobia, is best descibed as an irrational fear. This can be a phobia about being in a closed-in space or about traveling in cars or elevators, or extend to animals, birds, or food. The fear can be a wide-ranging, pervasive and intense experience. People who have phobias are acutely aware of them and often this causes them to do what otherwise seem to be funny things as they try to alleviate a phobic situation.

This person may be heard saying, "Let's take the train, I don't like to fly. I am uncomfortable about the number of recent plane crashes."

A second form of phobia is being frozen in inaction. That is they say "Whatever I do will probably go wrong so I'll do nothing." The fear of going wrong overwhelms them and they feel blocked at every turn.

POWER

Focus:
"I know the best answer."
"You know you should do it my way."

Power mode is an outward-going sense of confidence and authority. The complement or flip-side of caution, power mode impacts others directly. People in power mode feel they know what they are talking about. Other people easily notice those with power mode because of their style and approach. They account for 10% of the total population.

Whereas caution mode is a matter of being held back or underconfident, power mode is an expression of confidence and authority and is enabling. They are opposites.

> *For example at a medical staff meeting doctors, head nurses and supervisors may stop and heed the advice of an orderly who is in the power mode. The power mode person however, quickly rises to the top and is given a position of authority.*

Power mode is a natural leadership position and is common among national figures. However many women who have elected to remain at home to raise children may be in power mode, and their sense of leadership is expressed through family dynamics or community involvement.

> *Historically women have had more difficulty with power mode because of cultural and societal restrictions. Other females and males may resent the power mode female and accuse her of not knowing her place.   This dynamic may be similar among members of an oppressed minority who choose the power mode.   Under these circumstances power mode may facilitate public recognition, or even assist a karmic struggle for power with others.*

Certain roles handle power mode better than others. For example kings and warriors handle power mode well, whereas artisans feel less familiar with this *modus operandi*. Power and creativity require a great deal of experience to synthesize well.

Power mode is often confused with the goal of dominance or the role of king or warrior. Power mode is a way of approaching things whereas king is a way of being; dominance applies to the situation only whereas power is pervasive. Insight and practice may be required to distinguish between them.

Examples of famous people in power mode are easy because it leads so often to leadership and the public eye. These individuals exemplify this mode: Earl Warren, Malcolm X, Mao Tse Tung, Socrates, Rasputin, Machiavelli and Hieronymous Bosch.

Power mode is often chosen by people who become influential spiritual teachers as it helps them to be a convincing authority, and in the negative pole they may be overwhelmingly controlling.

Positive Pole
Authority; confident, commanding, presence.

In the positive pole, authority, the power mode person is confident, able to take responsibility, and highly influential with other people. The person stands out energetically in a crowd and he usually gets what he wants.

This person might say, "I know the answers to your questions so let me handle the situation."

Negative Pole
Oppression; threatening, pushy, bullying.

The negative pole, oppression, is difficult to define. The person in power mode rarely recognizes or feels that he is harrassing or oppressing others. However the negative feedback he gets from others may tip him off because they experience the oppression intensely. Those who are experiencing oppression often feel that they must comply with the other's will no matter what. Sometimes this is the case when the power mode person is not even present.

Others have described this invisible heavy sense of oppression as if there was a big black cloud in the room that was poised to swallow you up. Power mode, you *feel*.

In the negative pole the person in power mode conveys that if you don't fit in with their plans you should quake in fear and trembling.

Expression Modes: Reserved and Passion

+ restraint	+ self actualization
RESERVED	PASSION
- inhibition	- identification

RESERVED

Focus:
"I am holding in my feelings."
"What I express is precisely what I wish to express."

Reserved has the quality of being held in, contained or focussed in expression.

Reserved mode is found in about 2% of the population. This is an ordinal mode and therefore tends to be more self-karmic and introverted.

The experience of restraint is often seen in figure skaters, martial arts, ballet, and other disciplines wherein the motion of the body is contained and focused. Some reknowned artists are in the reserved mode; the discipline helps them in their art and creativity.

People in the reserved mode can be seen as withholding. The truth is that they often do not know what they are feeling. These people may undergo a dramatic personality transformation when they are under the influence of alcohol, drugs or wild friends.

The normally inhibited person who, with a measure of intoxication, wears a lampshade on their head at the New Year's party, is a classic example of reserved mode unleashed for the evening.

Reserved is usually easier for a warrior than for the more expressive roles, artisan or sage. The warrior can do well to hold in his feelings during a protracted march through the desert. Artisans and sages may feel constrained by repression in ways they are not used to.

Here are some well-known figures with a mode of reserved Marlon Brando, Ernest Hemingway, Ludwig Wittgenstein and Candice Bergen.

Positive Pole
Restraint; graceful, disciplined, refined.

The person in the positive pole of reserved, restraint, brings a refinement to their work. They will not tolerate anything crass or vulgar. They are able to hold in spontaneous action to such a degree that they can master difficult and complex patterns of movement as in ballet, gymnastics, and detailed artwork. They can be exceptionally tactful and make good diplomats and mediators.

This individual may be heard saying, "I need candlelight, good music, and fine wine, and then I'll be in the mood." There is a sense of drawing out specific feelings.

Negative Pole
Inhibition; blocked, cut off from emotion, withdrawn, reserved, witheld.

The negative pole of reserved, inhibition, causes a person to feel blocked or unable to express at all. The person will appear overly reserved, unable to speak, sing, or play music in front of other people.

You might hear this person saying, "I can't do it, there's too many people, I just can't find my voice."

PASSION

Focus:
"Let's do it now! Anyway! Anyhow!"
"Yah! Yah! Yahoo!!!"
"I'm leaping in, and to hell with the consequences!"
"Let's publish and be damned!"

Passion is the complement of reserved, and rather than being a blocking mode it is an enabling mode. Because it acts on other people it is more karmic than self-karmic. It is characterized by great intensity of feeling, or movement and is present in about 10% of the population.

Passion mode is often coupled with emotional centering [discussed later] and indeed lends an inspirational touch to all activities.

If a person in passion mode is trying to decide what to do, the clue is to choose what holds the most passion for them. If the course of action does not excite and challenge them then they are unlikely to want to bother with it. When making the choice they should ask themselves "What do I feel most passionate about?"

Passion mode is a favorite among mature souls because this stage is characterized by heavy identification. Priests and artisans love passion mode because it lifts them to ever higher levels of inspiration and creativity. On the other hand passion for these roles is difficult to handle because it can have an ungrounding effect rather than a stabilizing one.

Passion is a mode which often leads to widespread public recognition. The following famous people are examples: Joan of Arc, William Shakespeare, Bach, Muktananda, Ludwig Beethoven, Thomas Merton, Walt Whitman, Mozart, Vincent Van Gogh, James Joyce, Goethe and Lady Godiva.

Positive Pole

Self-actualization, heightened awareness, involved, intensely alive.

Self-actualization is the experience of heightened awareness. For example the experience of listening to music or seeing something of beauty is intensified. They feel more alive and involved in their experiences. The positive pole of passion mode suggests self-assertion and a means for people to get what they want. Passion is the royal road to the achievement of their goal.

You might overhear this person saying, "Life is so wonderful I can hardly stand it, everything is just so beautiful!" (or the opposite of this).

Negative Pole

Identification, overly involved, invested, boundary-less; not "I have the problem" but "I am the problem."

The negative pole of passion, identification, is a matter of becoming like or at one with the experience at hand. For example, a person may be passionately identified with his automobile. If the automobile is dented or harmed in some way the person may feel that he has been dented or harmed.

Just as one can identify with an object, so one can identify with a person or a relationship. In listening to a friend's woes, the passion mode person can introduce the same suffering in himself and not know the difference. People in passion are capable of suffering acutely and unneccessarily at times. This suffering does nothing to alleviate the other person's problems.

This person might be heard saying, "Oh my gosh, did you hear my poor friends have been slugging it out in a divorce court? They are such lovely people and now there is so much bitterness and anger. I am totally distraught." It is fine to feel grief or upset, but identification is the process of taking it on as happening to yourself.

Action Modes: Perseverance and Aggression

+ persistence
PERSEVERANCE
- immutability

+ dynamism
AGGRESSION
- belligerence

PERSEVERANCE
Focus:
"No matter what comes up I'm going to finish this".

Perseverance is the quality of sticking to something resolutely.

An action mode, it is found in about 4% of the population. Being ordinal it is once again self-karmic in that it describes how people experience themselves rather than being thrust out to experience others.

Thomas Edison tried some ten thousand experiments before he successfully created the electric lightbulb. Perseverance is a common ingredient in success.

Perseverance can readily be mistaken for stubbornness. This is because it tends to make a person seem solid and unswerving. However stubbornness comes from a fear of loss of integrity, while perseverance is a modus operandi and not rooted in fear.

A person in perseverance is able to totally focus on the problem at hand but can be blind to peripheral matters or the big picture. Perseverance can make a person look like a warrior even though that is not their role. A warrior in perseverance will look even more focused and driving.

Perseverance is a favorite of scholars as it helps them stay at endlessly detailed and fastidious tasks, such as being an historian.

The mode of perseverance is often chosen with the goal of submission. This facilitates the ability to stay with and devote oneself to a cause or a person e.g. caring for a retarded child.

As an ordinal mode perseverance does not often lead one to a life of fame and fortune.

The Guiness Book of World Records has a number of references to persons with a mode of perseverance. Some famous people include: Thomas Edison and Sir Ernest Shackleton.

Positive Pole
Persistence;   *disciplined,   staying   power,   stick-to-itiveness,*
enduring.

The person in the positive pole of perseverance is disciplined, able to endure hardship, and able to pursue a goal without deviation. This kind of approach allows a person to complete a painstaking task such as completing a doctoral dissertation or crossing a desert on foot - not entirely dissimilar pursuits!

This person may be heard to say, "When the going gets tough, the tough get going", or "I'll see this project through to the end!"

Negative Pole
Immutability; fixed, unchanging, stuck, repetitive.

The main quality here is being unwilling to change. People stick with what worked in the past without seeing that the situation has changed and calls for being handled in a new and different way. They keep doing it the old way and won't change.

Often people in the negative pole of perseverance repeat stories over and over again to the irritation of their audience. They have simply forgotten that they have told the story before to the same people.

Perseverance makes a person so focused on a problem that he becomes blind to the bigger picture.

This person might say, "I'll keep doing it (the old way) even if it kills me!"

AGGRESSION

Focus:
"I'm here everybody!"
"If it's not done this way there will be trouble."

People in aggression are gamblers, risk takers and adventurers with a love of danger. They assert themselves constantly and approach others directly both verbally and physically; they tend to be outspoken and are impossible not to notice when they enter a room.

They can frighten other people or intimidate them, causing them to move away. This can leave people in aggression mode confused and lonely, wondering what they did wrong. After all, they were just being themselves.

Aggression mode is found in about 4% of the population. An exalted mode, it is more extroverted, and acts on other people thus facilitating the creation of karma.

Aggression mode by definition is one of the more difficult to master and handle appropriately.

Some examples of well-known people with aggression mode are: Adolf Hitler, Idi Amin, Mohammed Ali (many boxers), Mr. T. (television personality), and as a model of appropriate usage, Shirley Temple Black. Also Khadafy and Kruschev; a caricature of aggression mode is Donald Duck.

Postive Pole
Dynamism; adventurous, risk-taking, assertive.

Aggression can be powerful in great actresses or actors who approach their role aggressively. A dynamic person is a constant ball of action from early morning to late at night.   They are involved in a multitude of activities and out-strip the pace of those around them.

The dynamism can lead to athletic prowess such as that held by Mohammed Ali and other great boxers.

The dynamic person might say something like, "Hello everybody, who's in charge here? I want to talk to her right now!" Or "I've got people to meet, places to go, things to do; either keep up or get left behind!"

Negative Pole

Belligerance; assaultive, destructive, attacking.

Belligerance, the negative pole, is seen in individuals who run afoul of the law. This includes people who feel that they are defending their interests by attacking. People find it difficult to be around a person in the negative pole of aggression mode because they can feel like they are being attacked either verbally or physically.

Aggression mode characterizes the leadership of certain countries ruled by terror - for example, Idi Amin, the dictator of Uganda until he was deposed in 1979.

The belligerant person might be heard to say, "I'm going to do this and don't try to stop me." or "Do it my way or else." The way to handle people in agression mode is to convince them that you are on their side and that you agree with them.

Assimilation Mode: Observation

+ Clarity
OBSERVATION
- surveillance

OBSERVATION

Focus:

"Let's see."
"I like to learn by watching how it is done."
"I love to people-watch."

Observation is a popular mode appearing in about 50% of the population. Because it is a neutral mode one can slide to any of the other modes at will.

People in observation approach their goals and all of life by watching and noticing what is going on around them. This penchant for observing explains the enthusiasm of spectator sports, parades, or watching television. In Europe and other countries cafe sitting is a national pastime as is promenading in the evening.

Observation is a proven method for learning and often accompanies the goal of growth. Scholars in particular enjoy observation mode because it helps them to assimilate knowledge. A warrior in observation would watch an action oriented activity such as football, whereas a sage might prefer to enjoy an expression oriented event like the theatre. Each person uses observation according to their role. These are some examples of well-known people with a mode of observation: Carlos Castaneda, Gertrude Stein, Aristotle, Allen Ginsberg, Francis Bacon, (note all have written based on their observations of the world) and Julia Child.

Positive Pole
Clarity, aware, alert, insightful.

A person in the positive pole of observation, clarity, sees things clearly and as they are. This is the kind of person whose observations come as a breath of fresh air and are most insightful.
The proverb "look before you leap" is pure observation mode.

Negative Pole
Surveillance, spying.

In the negative pole, a person becomes scrutinizing and watchful for possible danger. The person may gather information so as to control others. The intelligence services of various countries exemplify the observation mode in the negative pole with endless spying and counterspying. The McCarthy (obsessively anti-communist) era in the U.S. is an example of the negative pole in operation.

Another example of the negative pole is surveillance in the service of jealousy.

Modes in General

Relating Modes with Roles

Although all roles choose all modes at one time or another, there are certain combinations which are favorites and others which are more difficult.

As a rule of thumb, the exalted roles king, priest, and sage will experience more difficulty with the ordinal modes caution, repression, and perseverance. Likewise, the ordinal roles artisan, server, and warrior may experience some difficulty with the exalted modes power, passion, and aggression. These combinations are usually chosen to facilitate karma and not to simply rest or enjoy life.

Exalted roles usually enjoy and are familiar with exalted modes and ordinal roles are comfortable with ordinal modes.

As mentioned, scholars being the neutral role feel well-matched with the neutral mode observation.

Relating Modes with Goals

The following illustrates most common combinations or typical patterns of modes with goals:

GOALS	MODES	
	Passion or Power	Caution or Observation
Growth	more karmic	less karmic
	more emotional	more intellectual
Acceptance	more spiritual	w/caution self karmic
	more emotional	w/observation, teacher
Stagnation	more psychic	rest

Find Your Mode

Again, these are designed to help you find the one closest to you.

1)   I like to carefully gather all the information before deciding.
      The more important the decision, the more I like to deliberate.
      There is potential for any situation to come unglued, so it's best to play it safe.

2)   I usually know what to do and am not afraid to lead others.
      People often look to me for the answers.
      People often notice me and see me as having presence.
      I like people to take notice of me and listen to my input into a situation. Usually I'm right and it is done my way.

3)   When I set out to do something, nothing can stop me.
      I am incredibly disciplined and can see something through to the end.
      I am often reluctant to move on to something new and different.

4)   I approach others first.
      People are often intimidated by me.
      I am a risk taker, adventurous, and don't mind taking a gamble.

5)   I love elegance.
      Others often see me as classy or refined.
      At times I find it hard to speak up.

6)   Others experience me as a vivid and emotionally intense
        person.
        I tend to plunge into things without any concern for myself.
        Often I get so involved in things I lose myself.

7)   I learn by watching other people do it first.
        I like to draw conclusions from what I see.
        I love to watch people, events, and things.

Code
1) Caution
2) Power
3) Perseverance
4) Aggression
5) Reserved
6) Passion
7) Observation

How To Work With Modes

The mode is rarely changed because you chose it specifically for
this lifetime in order to get what you want done.

You can operate out of the positive pole most of the time unless
you want to use the negative pole for a purpose. For example, when
being hunted by a tiger it may be extremely useful to be in the
negative pole of observation, surveillance - it might save your life.
(However, not all students of this system have this problem!)

If you find that you are acting from the negative pole and
choose not to stay there, you can slide to the positive pole of the
complementary mode.

For example if you have moved to identification, negative pole
of passion, you could choose to exercise some restraint, positive pole
of repression. This will help you arrive at self actualization,

positive pole of passion. So, instead of identifying too closely with your friends' divorce you restrain yourself and can experience your own happiness.

+ restraint	- self actualization
RESERVED	PASSION
- inhibition	- identification

The mode then is the method of doing or action, the means by which we reach our goal. The attitude is our perspective and the chief feature is the emotional challenge to be learned along the way. Let us now take a look at attitudes, and how we make decisions.

Chapter Nine

Attitudes

What is the best attitude a person can have? What is the worst? Is it better to be a skeptic or an idealist, a spiritualist or a pragmatist?

The truth of the matter is that no attitude is better than any other, and none is worse than any other. At an essence level each one of us chooses to look at life from a certain angle. Each one of the seven attitudes has its own advantages, and its own usefulness.

The attitude is the primary perspective: the stance from which we look at things, how we go about deciding what to do. It governs the way we form concepts about what is going on and where we fit in. The seven possible attitudes are: stoic, spiritualist, skeptic, idealist, cynic, realist, and pragmatist.

The attitude interacts with the goal and the mode in a particular way. Through our attitude (how we see the world), we form a concept of our goal (where we want to get to). Then we go about getting there through our mode of action (how we operate).

Attitude - Primary Perspective
The Stance from which You Look at Things

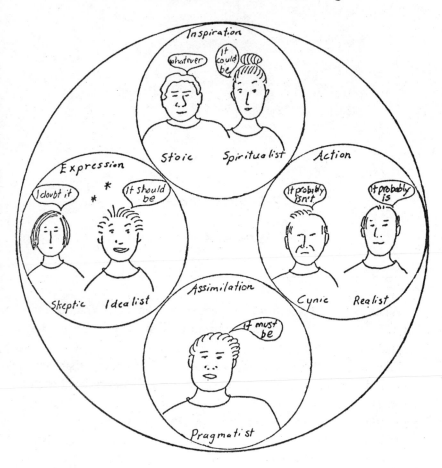

Attitudes

Ordinal	Neutral	Exalted
Inspiration		
+ tranquility		+ verification
STOIC ——————————— SPIRITUALIST		
- resignation		- beliefs
Expression		
+ investigation		+ coalescence
SKEPTIC ——————————— IDEALIST		
- suspicion		- naivety
Action		
+ contradiction		+ objective
CYNIC ——————————— REALIST		
- denigration		- subjective
	Assimilation	
	+ practical	
	PRAGMATIST	
	- dogmatic	

For example, suppose that someone had an attitude of idealist, a goal of dominance, a mode of aggression, and a chief feature of greed (next chapter). You can see that this kind of person would boldly and aggressively attempt to dominate others through the adoption of an idealistic vision of how things ought to be. The greed would make the person dissatisfied until everyone had been dominated according to this or her vision. Our favorite villain, Adolf Hitler, had these overleaves.

Percentages within the Earth's Population	
Stoic - 5%	Spiritualist - 5%
Skeptic - 5%	Idealist - 30%
Cynic - 5%	Realist - 30%
Pragmatist - 20%	

This system says that you can change your attitude. Once your attitude changes, you can change your life direction and how you get there.

Note that the degree of a person's consciousness is reflected in their attitude to life in general. The phrase "to be philosophical" about, say, a minor disaster is to view the broader picture from a high position.

The Meaning of Attitudes

What is the value of having seven different attitudes? Why have seven unique perspectives instead of one absolute viewpoint on the way things are? Here are some points:

1. The attitude is the intellectual view, flavored with emotion - pessimism or optimism - and directed inward or outward. Sometimes essence sets up a failure situation and from failing you learn more about your attitude. For example, a woman with an idealist attitude may choose to marry and divorce alcoholics repeatedly, expecting each time to be able to rehabilitate the man. Eventually, she will learn how to use the idealist attitude more appropriately.

Attitude reflects the concepts that you hold. From those concepts you get feelings, and you then act. Attitude is what changes the most throughout your lifetime, from childhood (inn

changes the most throughout your lifetime, from childhood
(innocence) through to old age (wisdom). The purpose of life is to
reveal yourself to yourself, a process that changes how you see
things.
2. Attitude is a vehicle for individual differences. Ten people
with the attitude of idealist, for example, will manifest idealism
in their own unique ways (depending on their other overleaves,
role, soul perceptivity etc.). There are infinite gradations and
permutations of idealism, realism, and so on.
3. If we all saw the world in the same way and were in nodding
agreement it would be excruciatingly dull and boring. Having
multiple points of view ensures that we will each, in our own way,
investigate the world from our own particular angle. Faced with
the same situation each of us makes a different appraisal and a
different decision.

Mottos

Ordinal	Neutral	Exalted
Inspiration		
STOIC ——————————— SPIRITUALIST		
"whatever"		"could be"
Expression		
SKEPTIC ——————————— IDEALIST		
"might be"		"should be"
Action		
CYNIC ——————————— REALIST		
"probably isn't"		"probably is"
	Assimilation	
	PRAGMATIST	
	"must be"	

What is the point of knowing about attitudes? Without this knowledge, it is all too easy to feel different and even inadequate because you see things differently from other people.

The feeling of loneliness can make you feel defensive about your way of seeing--"I'm an outsider, but that's because I see the truth and others don't." Without understanding the importance of different attitudes you can sell yourself out on your unique lens on the world and convince yourself that you see things "just like everybody else" to feel part of the group.

Everyone in fact does this "selling out" to a greater or lesser degree as children in the course of growing up. We forgo a measure of our individuality so that society may have a common denominator to enable it to function. For example, we all agree to use money as a medium of exchange.

Understanding the attitudes enables you to be clearer on your individuality and others.

...Or it can make you want to convert others to see things the way you do--much like Professor Higgins, "Why can't a woman be more like a man?"--because you are convinced that the way things look to you are the way things really are.

Once you know that there are actually seven possible attitudes rather than only one, you   get to understand WHY someone else sees something else differently. (All the people who you thought were mad...)

Once you know your own attitude, you can become more comfortable with your own way of seeing things; you can accept yourself more easily and see the benefit of the vantage point you have chosen. In addition, you can discover how to use your attitude purposefully, to move yourself toward your goal rather than away from it.

Once you are aware of which attitude you are operating from at a given moment, you can actually change it in the light of your purpose. Some attitudes are self-blocking, so by shifting attitudes you free yourself up.

We all touch into all seven of the attitudes. Some we visit a lot, some a little, some never or hardly ever, and one we live in. The one where we live, our basic perspective on life, despite other perspectives we might visit, is our own attitude, the one that is our habitual viewpoint.

The attitude is pervasive in that it affects our perception of every aspect of our lives. It determines how we see ourselves as well as other people and all our experiences.

Of all the overleaves the attitude is the easiest to change. You can practice stopping and asking yourself what attitude you are using at the moment and how matters would look with a different attitude.

For example, a skeptic may block himself from starting a project. He may doubt it can be done, that it is worthwhile and so forth. When he sees that he is operating from a skeptic's viewpoint. He can say "Aha!" and slide to the opposite of the pair, the idealist. The idealist says "It should work." It is an enabling attitude and may inspire him to action. This is simple but effective.

Each attitude, except for the neutral attitude, is linked with its opposite or complement.

If your attitude is stoic you will slide at times to the opposite pole of spiritualist. If you are a spiritualist you will likewise slide to stoic temporarily. This is true of all the other paired attitudes. Only pragmatism is neutral rather than paired.

The pragmatist slides to any of the other attitudes, although there will be one or two favorite attitudes. The ability to slide to the appropriate attitude is one of the most pragmatic aspects of a pragmatist.

Inspiration Attitudes: Stoic and Spiritualist

+ tranquility	+ verification
STOIC	SPIRITUALIST
- resignation	- faith

STOIC

Focus:

"I'm holding my expression in."

The stoical attitude can be summed up as "whatever happens is, and that's okay." Stoics generally reserve their expression, and their faces take on a masklike quality. What is the stoic feeling? It is often hard to tell, on the basis of outward appearance, since stoics don't express or demonstrate their emotions easily. They reserve their feelings to themselves. This can come in handy in a game of poker, in police work, or during military operations, but can be a disadvantage in a romantic relationship.

Because stoics don't show their feelings, they often are accused of being unfeeling. But this is not true. They have feelings just like anyone else, and sometimes feel emotion very intensely.

The military has a tradition of stoicism because taking time out to express one's emotions is inappropriate in the midst of a battle. As the commonest emotion is fear in this context, stoicism enables the emotional center to be closed down in favor of moving center. Feelings can become pent up and then explode - either inwardly or outwardly.

Stoics won't interfere or state their position to the contrary. They often put up with more than they really want to because they don't try to influence things by speaking up. This can happen to the stoic in the work setting when told by a hard driving boss that a difficult project must be accomplished in too short a time. The stoical attitude then becomes an issue in a person's life.

Stoicism is chosen infrequently, by only 5% of the population, because in some ways it is more difficult than other attitudes. Being a stoic places a definite limitation on a person's ability to convey their feelings.

Sometimes this creates a unique quality of expression such as that of Marlon Brando whose stoicism enhances the tension of the roles he plays.

Certain roles find the attitude of stoic easier than others. Warriors do not mind a stoical attitude because it goes along with many of the activities they choose to do, for example, being a soldier or an athlete. On the other hand, the more expressive roles of sage and artisan would find it more difficult to be a stoic, as stoicism goes against what they do best: expression.

Famous people with the attitude of stoicism: Marlon Brando, Joan Baez and Julia Child.

Postive Pole

Tranquility, capable, able to handle anything, emanates calm, peace and harmony; nothing can go wrong because they are so stable.

The positive pole enables the stoic to become serene and tranquil and develop inner peace and awareness. Stoics in the positive pole are capable of handling just about anything. Their stability gives others the feeling that as long as they are around, nothing can go wrong. People who practice meditation often exhibit these qualities. Many stoics are attracted to Zen Buddhism and in fact the picture of stoicism in the positive pole is the Buddha in meditation.

Negative Pole

Resignation; resigned to their fate and not showing it; slogging along, despairing, exhausted.

The negative pole of stoicism is resignation. In this position stoics give in or submit themselves to whatever circumstances are at hand, be it an unhappy relationship, political oppression, or a natural disaster like flooding. Stoics persevere and slog along where they might more profitably confront the situation, or turn away from it.

Giving up is quite different from enduring what must be endured. One way to tell the difference is that endurance can feel appropriate, while resignation simply feels bad. Nor can stoics easily draw compassion for their problems, since they don't show their distress and are resigned to their fate.

SPIRITUALIST

Focus:
"There are sixteen different ways to approach this one."
"Most people don't realize a fraction of their potential."
"Often I think of God."

The other inspiration attitude is spiritualist. Spiritualists tend to see all the possibilities of how things can be. They can see the big picture and have a wider perspective than most of the other attitudes. A spiritualist can see what a person could accomplish if he realized all his talents. The spiritualist attitude is far-reaching and is more able to look into the future than most other attitudes. They make up about 5% of the population.

The spiritualist attitude has to do with what we associate with spirituality - God, theology, and matters of religion. Spiritualists often gravitate towards religions or a religious way of life because these traditionally are oriented toward a grander view of life that includes the unseen. However not all people with the spiritualist attitude are intensely religious. The spiritualist is a person who has vision in any arena, so this attitude can be directed toward business and politics. The spiritualist attitude is not usually an issue in life. It is especially compatible with certain roles such as priest and server and no role finds it disagreeable.

Famous people with the spiritualist attitude: Joan of Arc, Aristotle, Muktananda, Thomas Merton, Ludwig Beethoven, William Blake and nearly all the well-known evangelists.

Positive Pole

Verification; visionary, sees possibilities others can't see, expansive, pursuits of a philisophical nature.

The positive pole of spiritualist is verification, which requires him to check out and verify with his own experience what his beliefs are. In the positive pole, the spiritualist dedicates himself to higher pursuits with the attitude that these are of higher priority than mundane matters.

Negative Pole

Beliefs; takes things on faith, can look like a priest in the negative pole, doesn't investigate appropriately, doesn't live in reality, diffuse.

In the negative pole spiritualists have blind faith. They tend to be naive and believe anything they hear. This gullibility can cause them anguish.

Expression Attitudes: Skeptic and Idealist

+ investigation	+ coalescence
SKEPTIC	IDEALIST
- suspicion	- naivity

SKEPTIC

Focus:
"I won't believe it until you prove it to me."
"If it is important, I check and double check, and then check again."

The skeptic by definition is a doubter. He will tend to approach a topic or a situation or even a product disbelievingly and want to check it out before believing or buying it.

One of the characteristics of skeptics is that they can be eternally doubting. If they find something that might be really good they question it endlessly. The higher its potential importance, the more relentless their questioning. If eventually they accept a concept or situation they put their whole weight behind it and become tireless advocates of it. They may swing from one extreme to another.

Skepticism involves much consideration, conceptualizing and questioning, and so is one of the more intellectual attitudes. Skepticism accounts for approximately 5% of the population.

Positive Pole

Investigation, tries to see all sides of a situation, nonjudgemental, checking that all the facts are in, striving for knowledge.

In the positive pole, investigation, skeptics perform a great service because they keep belief systems or anything that they happen to be examining, truthful. They are excellent at checking out any possible errors or discrepancies. In some ways they act as clean-up people. They may inject discipline into study groups or act as an exacting scientist or investigator.

The skeptic Socrates said, "The unexamined life is not worth living." He lived out of the positive pole of investigation.

Negative Pole

Suspicion, picking apart, doubting everything, lack of trust.

In the negative pole, suspicion, the skeptic may become overly doubtful and suspicious of everyone and everything. In fact skeptics in the negative pole are so doubtful, suspicious, and exacting that they become difficult to be around and are inclined to drive others away.

IDEALIST

Focus:

"I see a better way."

"It ought to be done right."

The other expression attitude is idealist. The idealist says how things should be and his conversation can be studded with shoulds and oughts. This is a popular attitude and about 30% of the world population has it.

The idealist looks at ideas and situations in light of how they ought to be to progress. Idealists are always enthusiastic about making progress and pushing forward and they are in fact responsible for major breakthroughs in many fields of work. They have a tendency to put people on pedestals and are frequently disappointed when their idol turns out to be all too human with real limitations.

Idealists can be hard on themselves by putting extremely high standards out for themselves and when they do not reach them they feel frustrated and suffer from low self-esteem. When they succeed, they act as pioneers modeling how one ought to live meeting maximum potentials.

"Ask not what your country can do for you, but what you can do for your country," is a classic statement of an idealist, John F. Kennedy.

In other words, the idealist can be very hard on himself and other people. He may think that others should think the way he does, and gets confused when this is not the case. He often has a tough time of it because he is always desiring that things be different from (better than) what is. Whatever is at the moment is not right because it can always be improved. This leads to eternal dissatisfaction, yet on the other hand, is challenging and stimulating.

Sometimes people on this axis are idealistic about people and skeptical about situations.

The following are famous idealists: Earl Warren, Galileo, Goethe, Adolf Hitler, John F. Kennedy, Mao Tse Tung, Jimi Hendrix and Ernest Hemingway.

Positive Pole

Coalescence; combines the best of all possibilities, pushes for improvement, brings all parts together; practical.

The idealist can perform a great service when in the positive pole by pulling together all the necessary ingredients to make a situation work in the best possible manner. Idealists pull things forward to a new and improved state by virtue of their vision and far-reaching ideas. They are able to visualize and then produce new improved products, buildings, organizational structures , and better societies.

Negative Pole

Naivety; unrealistic, abstract, ungrounded, perfectionistic

In the negative pole the idealist becomes identified with the pictures of how things should be and is shattered when these don't come to fruition. The idealist can become rather abstract, as with someone who has utopian ideas of how things ought to be and is unhappy with the way things are.

This might be an architect who conceives of how a building could look but cannot implement the project because it is quite impractical. This can be frustrating and disappointing because the architect can truly see the tremendous value of his project. He can move to the positive pole of idealist and reduce the grand concept to what will actually work.

As with the role of artisan, idealism has inherent creativity. The idealist creates how things *should* look. The negative pole of naivety has an element of self-deception - the naive person doesn't know he is naive. The trap is "you don't know what you don't know."

An idealist who is being naive can be most difficult for others to be around. The idealist is inclined to take an unrealistically simple viewpoint.

Idealists in the negative pole can be demanding and hard on people around them. They can often be seen as perfectionists. Of all the attitudes they are the hardest on themselves.

Ideals are necessary for progress. Clearly the effective idealist is the one who progresses the most. So the attitude of idealist is the one with the potential for the most growth. The degree of inner stress that occurs within the breast of the committed idealist reflects their determination. So idealism is both the most respected and the most difficult attitude.

Take the idealist architect who has modified his ideals so that a building may be constructed. He then has a choice of being unhappy with the result because it is not perfect, or happy because, although not perfect it is the expression of the best possible building under the circumstances. This exemplifies the positive and negative poles - the choice of being happy or unhappy, even though the subject of one's attention is neutral.

Action Attitudes: Cynic and Realist

+ contradiction	+ objective
CYNIC	REALIST
- denigration	- subjective

CYNIC

Focus:
"If things can go wrong they will."

The cynic tends to be on the watch for what is negative. They are quick to identify what will not work, forseeing possible problems. This preoccupation with what is negative is a serious obstacle for the cynic and those around them. Because of the difficulty involved with this attitude, cynicism is held by only 5% of the population.

Cynics approach relationships, projects, and experiences from the point of view that they will not work out in the long run. This can be a self-fulfilling prophecy. For cynics, it may be difficult to accomplish tasks and achieve goals as they tend to stop themselves.

People who are idealists and spiritualists have difficulty with cynics because they are diametric opposites. Idealists and spiritualists see the multitude of possibilities, and the cynic sees the prospect of multiple disasters.

This is primarily a self-defending attitude. People who have difficult karma to handle in a life time, such as physically and mentally abusive parents, choose cynic to avoid the worst of an unpleasant situation. This attitude has the practical application of helping them survive.

> *For example, throughout history warriors constantly engage in battle and all too frequently meet death. A warrior with the cynic overleaf, however, might look a little longer at the prospect of getting killed and defer rushing into battle so as to live a little longer. Cynics have a knack of avoiding difficult or unpleasant situations that others might rush into with well-intentioned enthusiasm.*

The way other attitudes can handle a cynic is to contradict him. This brings the cynic to the reality of another point of view. Some of the people who handle cynicism well are comedians such as Woody Allen. They can be natural humorists, teasing people with their opposite viewpoint.

This attitude can be changed when a person no longer needs it to assist in their survival. So people in their twenties and thirties commonly work on leaving this essentially negative outlook, trading it for the positive of the pair, the realist. The key to changing the cynical attitude lies in how closely he is able to monitor his attitude and ask himself, "Am I looking for the negative or the positive?"

Positive Pole

Contradiction; seeing the other side, constructive criticism, questioning commonly held beliefs.

The positive pole of cynicism is contradiction, the ability to see the other side of the situation or the opposing view. This attitude can be useful when considering the consequences of carrying out an idea. Because there's bound to be something wrong with any scenario, the cynic will find out what can go wrong and avoid it. He will pick something apart, and eliminate the weaknesses before they manifest.

Negative Pole

Denigration, defame, bad-mouth, put down, quash, reject.

The cynic in the negative pole feels that the whole world and life in general is rotten, and denigrates everyone and everything. The cynic tends to disbelieve everything and put everything down. In the negative pole it's a tough one!

REALIST

Focus:

"This is probably what will happen."

"I can see all sides to a situation."

The complementary action attitude is the realist. The realist tends to see all sides of situations, and because this is a popular point of view, about 30% of the population has it.

Realists see how a situation is; they see what is so about experiences, relationships, and events. Realists tend to see what is with simplicity rather than complexity. They see all sides of a situation or problem. Realists make good consultants because they can see into a situation that a person with another attitude may be confused about. They tend to have good judgment and rarely overextend themselves in business or in relationships.

> *The realist says, "it probably is," whereas the cynic says, "It probably isn't."*

Because the realist is so good at seeing all sides to a problem, he sometimes has difficulty making a decision or committing to a single course of action. A realist who is buying a car can drive himself and others crazy because he can see both the good qualities and limitations of each model and make that he simply cannot make a decision.

Robert Oppenheimer, General George Patton, and the philosopher Alfred Whitehead were all realists; also Bella Abzug.

The children's book Winnie the Pooh is a parable about attitudes. Winnie himself is a realist ("Maybe it will and maybe it won't, let's see.") and his colleague, Eeyore the donkey, is a cynic ("It always rains on my birthday").

Positive Pole
Objective; present, sees all sides, sees what is.

The positive pole of realist is objectivity. This is the experience of living in the moment and seeing what is really going on. The realist in the positive pole is not trying to change anything, he simply flows with it. He does fine because he is not expecting any surprises. Of all the seven attitudes, this is the attitude that is striven for in courts of law where an objective judge attempts to sort out fact from fiction.

Negative Pole
Subjective; supposition, biased, based on inappropriate data.

The realist in the negative pole believes he is seeing what is, but is instead seeing a more   positive or negative picture and therefore he is not operating from objectivity. If feeling negative he may slide to cynic.

The negative pole of realist is subjectivity or supposition, supposing all the different things that could happen. This can lead to indecisiveness and a great deal of researching without any firm conclusion. That is, the realist sees all the realistic possibilities and gets lost in the maze of alternatives. As the realist is an action attitude this stuck subjectivity does not feel good.

Under the influence of the negative pole the realist becomes unduly influenced by emotions and loses sight of the objective facts.

This is classic in the stock market where a person refuses to sell out their holding when the price falls as they don't want to take a loss. The price continues to fall to the point where their losses are so large they are forced to sell. Some readers may have experienced how financial pressures cause subjectivity to give way to objectivity.

Assimilation Attitude: Pragmatist

+ practical
PRAGMATIST
- dogmatic

PRAGMATIST

Focus:
"Do it my way because it's most efficient..."

The pragmatist says, "It must be." He has eliminated the inefficient and impractical alternatives. Pragmatists make good efficiency experts because they reduce things down to the simplest functions or forms. The pragmatist is a practical person and tends to do things efficiently and simply. Like most neutral overleaves it is popular and has been assumed by 20% of the population.

Pragmatists sometimes have difficulty because they overlook what is pleasurable or a more fun way of doing things. The efficient way is not always the most enjoyable.

> *For example, the pragmatist may feel compelled to take a short cut through an ugly part of town rather than take the longer, more beautiful route through the country. This metaphor applies to workaholics ignoring their children and so on. Their criterion of productivity and usefulness ignores feelings, relationships, beauty, fun and so on. They can end up emotionally beached, with no feelings and no relationships.*

As the neutral attitude, pragmatists may slide to any of the other attitudes. Scholars tend to like the attitude of pragmatism because it facilitates learning and studying in an efficient way. An artisan, however, may find pragmatism unfamiliar and difficult because he must wrestle with how to be creative and practical at the same time.

Marshall McLuhan and Ho Chi Minh were both pragmatists.

Positive Pole
Practical; efficient, simple, functional, sensible rule-maker.

The pragmatist in the positive pole exhibits good judgment in handling everyday matters and affairs. He is mindful of the advantages and disadvantages of action or procedure and tends to see things in terms of their usefulness.

He is like a realist in that he takes what is, and seeks to use it practically. He seeks to save time, effort and money. He has a tendency to make up rules and regulations so as to make things run most efficiently in the existing structure. Also he is willing to slide to other attitudes if it is useful.

Negative Pole
Dogmatic, opinionated, narrow-minded, rigid, creates red tape, preachy, anal retentive.

In the negative pole the pragmatist allows the rules and regulations to overrun him. He becomes dogmatic and preaching, believing that his way is the only way and any other way is wrong, because it is probably less efficient. He ignores other people's feelings as they slow him down, and he can be ruthless like the negative pole of warrior (coercion).

When the pragmatist becomes dogmatic he can become narrow-minded; things must be done his way because he knows best. He tends to lay down the law - ("Do it my way, you fool" is pragmatist combined with the attitude of arrogance).

Dogmatism is sometimes manifest in certain religions such as having to say prayers at a certain time of the day and having to perform rituals in a certain way. This eliminates spontaneity and flexibility, blocking development and keeping things the way they are.

Attitudes in General

Relating Attitudes with Soul Ages

Infant, baby, and young souls favor specific attitudes to assist them in their lessons. Stoicism helps them with stability in these early stages while spiritualism helps them to be forward looking. Pragmatism helps them to get things done. Mature and old souls prefer the more intense attitudes: cynic, realist, skeptic, and idealist. They are looking for greater emotional intensity and more detailed and focused challenges in their experiences - such as working on a specific relationship.

Relating Attitudes with Roles

In the long run, all roles experience every attitude a number of times in order to have the full experience of life. Nevertheless, there are favorites among the roles. In general exalted roles (sage, priest and king) are more comfortable with exalted attitudes (idealist, spiritualist and realist) which tend to put them out into the public eye more. Ordinal roles (artisan, server and warrior) are more comfortable with ordinal attitudes (skeptic, stoic and cynic) because these attitudes are more inward looking. Scholars being the neutral role are happiest with pragmatist but can handle any attitude more easily than most roles.

On the other hand the solid roles that are inherently more intellectual (scholars, kings and warriors) often prefer an emotional attitude like idealist for balance.

Relating Attitudes with Goals

People with goals of growth and acceptance go for any attitude, but cynic and realist are favorites for growth. Those with the goal of re-evaluation prefer idealist or realist because this attitude facilitates that experience.

For those with the goal of discrimination, cynicism works well to give these persons the experience of the negative pole of this overleaf. Think of the cynical person who rejects most people and expects rejection by them.

An attitude of skeptic helps the person in discrimination to experience the positive pole more: e.g., the highly discriminating wine critic who is skeptical of most wine before deciding which is best.

People who have selected the goal of dominance prefer the attitudes of realist or cynic which give them an action orientation. Submission goes well with stoic or spiritualist attitudes which gives them an inspired perspective for this goal.

The goal of stagnation is most facilitated by the attitudes of stoic, spiritualist, and pragmatist. These again provide the inspirational or assimilative perspective needed to flow with experiences.

Find Your Attitude

First read all the statements and try them on for size. All of us use all the attitudes from time to time. However look for the one that you habitually use, or how other people would describe you. You may even ask someone who knows you well to pick you out from the list. If you really have trouble identifying with any one attitude then you are probably a pragmatist, who slides to all or several of them frequently.

The attitude is your primary perspective and is how you view your goal as well as everything else in your life.

1) I usually doubt what I hear until I check it out for myself.
   I am mostly suspicious of new products until I have tried them out.
   I frequently investigate something thoroughly before accepting it.

2) I can usually see what should or ought to be done in a situation.
   I am rarely satisfied with the way things are.
   I have high expectations of myself and others and am frequently disappointed when these are not met.

3) It is important to see the potential in people, things, or events.
   I often take things on faith without checking them out much.
   The possibility of things, what could be, intrigues me most.

4) Others often say I am hard to read; they wonder what I am thinking.
   Often I look at things calmly while others are losing their heads.
   I usually resign myself to whatever is happening. No use trying to change it.

5) I like to focus on what can go wrong in a situation. What may go right will look after itself.
    Often people and situations aren't what they're made out to be.
    I expect the worst and then if it turns out okay, I am glad.

6) I usually can see all sides to a situation.
    Often I have a hard time making a decision because I can see the pros and cons of everything.
    I can be more matter of fact than most people.

7) I like to do things the most efficient way.
    I am good at seeing what will work in a situation.
    Frequently, I am frustrated by what looks to me to be a clumsy approach to something.

Code
1) Skeptic
2) Idealist
3) Spiritualist
4) Stoic
5) Cynic
6) Realist
7) Pragmatist

How to Work With Attitudes

Of all the overleaves, the attitude is the easiest to change. If you're considering what to do about a problem, it is relatively easy to ask yourself, "What attitude am I using right now?" If you find you are using an   attitude that works against getting what you want, you can then take a different viewpoint.

Suppose a hardened skeptic, John, has always secretly wanted to learn to play the piano. If he is acting from his skepticism, he may be too blocked to even begin. He may doubt that it can be done ("I'm probably too old to learn"), or that it is worthwhile ("I certainly won't be any Beethoven no matter how hard I practice"). However, if John can recognize that he is looking at the subject from the viewpoint of a skeptic, then he can deliberately slide to the opposite attitude on the axis, idealism. Then John can start to think, "It ought to work" and set himself in motion to rent a piano to practice on. Of course he may continue to be skeptical about it all, but at least he does not have to block himself.

Escaping from the Negative Pole

When people fall into the negative pole of their attitude they can resolve it by moving into the positive pole of the opposite attitude. For example, an idealist who has been operating out of the negative pole of naivety can move to the positive pole of the skeptic attitude, investigation. From there he or she can gather information to bring things together and move to coalescence, the positive pole of idealist.

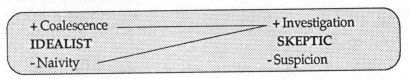

```
+ Coalescence ————————————  + Investigation
  IDEALIST                     SKEPTIC
- Naivity                     - Suspicion
```

Negative Pole of Attitude Introduces Chief Feature

When you slide into the negative pole of your attitude you automatically go to your chief negative feature.

To understand this more we will look at chief negative features and explore the riches that they have to offer.

Chapter Ten

Chief Features

What is the worst chief feature a person can have? Is stubbornness more of a hindrance than impatience? Is self-deprecation easier than martyrdom? Does everyone have a chief feature and how do we develop them? What can we do about them? Let us now examine these questions and see how the chief feature influences us and relates to the other overleaves.

The chief feature is the primary stumbling block we have set up so that we can learn about the characteristics and consequences of that particular fear. It neutralizes efforts towards the goal.

The chief feature is the chief neutralizer or the chief negative obstacle. It is the one overleaf that is possible to erase completely so that it no longer exists in your personality. In fact, erasing the chief feature is one goal of this system of knowledge.

Remember, that the goal is what motivates us, it is something to achieve. The attitude gives us a habitual perspective, a way of looking at the goal. The mode is the modus operandi, the method by which we strive for the goal. And lest, we breeze through this scenario too easily (after all a cheetah gets no challenge from

Chief Feature
Primary Stumbling Block to Your Goal

Ordinal	Neutral	Exalted
Inspiration		
+ humility		+ Pride
SELF-DEPRECATION	————————	ARROGANCE
- abasement		- vanity
Expression		
+sacrifice		+appetite
SELF-DESTRUCTION	————————	GREED
- suicidal		- voracity
Action		
+ selflessness		+daring
MARTYRDOM	————————	IMPATIENCE
- victimization		- intolerance
	Assimilation	
	+ determination	
	STUBBORNNESS	
	- obstinancy	

Percentages within the Earth's Population	
Self- deprecation - 10%	Arrogance - 15%
Self-destruction - 10%	Greed - 15%
Martyrdom - 15%	Impatience - 15%
Stubbornness - 20%	

racing with a tortoise) we also have a chief feature–a stumbling block to ensure that we learn what we need to learn while in pursuit of our goal.

Together, the chief feature, the attitude, and the mode form a triad that is the means by which a person achieves their goal.

The chief feature is the emotional leg of the triad together with attitude and mode. The attitude is the intellectual center, the mode is the moving center and the chief feature relates to emotional center. Centers are discussed in detail in a later chapter.

Meaning of the Chief Feature

Since the chief feature is an obstacle, a stumbling block and a handicap, the real question is, "Why do we need a chief feature? Why set up the whole scheme so carefully, a goal to reach, an attitude, and mode to help you reach it, and then throw in a monkey wrench so you can't get to it?"

Here are some reasons:

● If we had no handicaps, if we remembered and used our full capacities, we would breeze through everything and win without even having to interact with others or ourselves. It would be like playing Scrabble with a twenty pound dictionary on your lap and an infinite supply of wooden letters at your disposal. In short, there would be no game.

● Being aware of one's overleaves and handicaps like the chief feature is a challenge to our natural forgetfulness. Holding an awareness of the larger picture of who we are and our absolute origins calls for a high level of beingness.

● The chief feature, unlike the other overleaves, can be erased. It forms a large part of the false personality. Eliminating it allows the true personality to shine through. Achieving this feat can transform your life and bring you closer to your goal.

● When you know your chief feature, you know specifically where you tend to trip up. For example, "It's not that I am a no good pile of garbage; it's that my chief feature is self deprecation, and I put myself down unnecessarily." Or, "it's not that I'm slow witted, it's that my chief feature is impatience and I don't allow myself (or even other people) enough time to learn."

● When you go easy on yourself for tripping over your stumbling block, you become more self-accepting. "Oh, I was just being stubborn again, okay." Or, "oh, I'm thinking I'm martyred again, okay." In tolerating your own stumbling blocks, you can also tolerate, or at least understand, those of others.

The Nature of the Chief Feature

The chief feature varies from individual to individual in intensity and degree. For one person it may be very mild, for another it could be intense. Despite its strength the chief feature is only visited momentarily. It can be erased through observing it and then choosing if that is the way you want to be.

As we have seen, the chief feature commonly springs from the negative pole of our attitude. If I am a pragmatist and I become dogmatic, I can easily become arrogant as well or perhaps stubborn depending on my specific chief feature.

Not everyone chooses to have a chief feature. It is more common for the older souls to be without one, although most people choose one for purposes of growth or karma.

Where all the other overleaves are chosen at the beginning of each lifetime, the chief feature is selected by each person during the formative years. Adolescence is a time of experimenting with all the chief features - greed, arrogance, martyrdom, self-destruction - all are played with and sampled. This is why adolescents can be so trying to be around. They experiment with all the chief features - martyrdom, self-destruction, impatience, stubborness etc. This is exacerbated by their hormonal changes that throw them out of balance. Most people settle on one main chief feature in early adulthood or even middle life, although a few choose it as young as five years old, depending on their upbringing.

The chief feature is a flexible overleaf and people can change to the complementary one several times in a lifetime.

> *For example, one may easily slide to martyrdom from impatience. When you experience impatience in heavy traffic you are feeling victimized by the apparent lack of time and that which is preventing you from moving forward, cars, road repair, or whatever. Feeling a   victim of the situation is the hallmark of the martyr.*

The chief feature blocks the achievement of the goal and can slow down the speed of growth.

Like all the overleaves, the chief features break up into ordinal and exalted. The ordinal chief features (self-destruction, self-deprecation and martyrdom) tend to hold a person back; they are self-blocking.

The exalted chief features (greed, arrogance and impatience) encourage a person to be outgoing and to put themselves forward in the world.

Another way of looking at the two types of chief features is that they divide into self-karmic (inward and personal experiences) and karmic (outward and interacting with the world).

Stubbornness is neutral and the person can experience both the blocking and also the enabling aspects of the chief feature. With this chief feature the person tends to slide to other chief features and use them heavily.

Chief Features and Their Underlying Fears	
	SELF-DEPRECATION **ARROGANCE**
The fear of...	...being inadequate ...being judged
	SELF-DESTRUCTION **GREED**
The fear of...	...life is not worth having ...not having enough
	MARTYRDOM **IMPATIENCE**
The fear of...	...being a victim ...missing out
	STUBBORNNESS
The fear of...	...change

Inspiration Chief Features:
Self Deprecation and Arrogance

+ humility	+ pride
SELF DEPRECATION	**ARROGANCE**
- abasement	- vanity

SELF DEPRECATION

Focus:
"I am unworthy."
"When I'm right no one remembers, when I'm wrong no one forgets."
"I get in my own way when it comes to being successfull."

In self deprecation a person assumes that his or her self worth is quite low. This is the proverbial inferiority complex in which self esteem suffers greatly through self-putdown.

A person with self-deprecation often apologizes before or after they say something as in: "I don't really know anything but..." or, "I guess I don't know what I am talking about." They will kick themselves verbally like "Gosh, am I stupid," or "Gee, that was really dumb of me, I can't do anything right." Other people try to build the person up but give up after awhile and feel annoyed instead. This results in a self-fulfilling prophecy that one is not liked because he is inferior. Self-deprecation can be erased through an accurate understanding of personal self-worth and self-esteem building. ·

The actor and director Woody Allen has achieved fame and fortune through his portrayals of self-deprecation.

Positive Pole

Humility;   proper   perspective,   understanding   of   position relative to others.

The positive pole of self-deprecation is humility. In this context that refers to being modest about fantastic achievements.

An example might be Mother Theresa's self-effacing remarks after she was awarded the Nobel Peace Prize.

Negative Pole

Abasement, putting oneself down.

The negative pole of self-deprecation   is abasement, i.e. outright self-devaluing;   the person feels that he is probably worthless and so he figures it is not worth taking care of himself, either physically or emotionally. Typically, the person in the negative pole will look unkempt and downtrodden i.e., unwashed, uncombed, slumped, and dejected.

ARROGANCE

Focus:

"I'm so good at what I do that I make others look foolish."
"I'm afraid others will see my weak spots and won't like me for them."

Arrogance is the feeling of shyness or low self esteem that is covered by a veneer of high self-worth or an air of superiority. "I don't know my self-worth and I am afraid it might be low. So, I'll try to convince myself and others that it is very high instead."

People in arrogance have a great deal of attention centered on themselves. Sometimes they find the attention of others painful and this results in shyness. It is as if they are holding up a shield. If you were to get past it and strike a vulnerable spot where they feel exposed and defenseless, they would be mortified.

Arrogance is the fear that others will pass judgement and find them wanting. Often those with arrogance secretly pass heavy judgement on themselves first, and then pass judgment more openly upon others. About 15% of the population have the chief feature of arrogance as their stumbling block.

Arrogance and self-deprecation are sourced in low self-esteem. Interestingly, mature and old souls often choose these two chief features to facilitate them in their lessons around self-worth and self-acceptance. Whereas, younger souls more often choose chief features that are more outward going and less inward looking.

Arrogance can be erased by building one's self-esteem, and realizing one's self worth.

Here are some examples of famous people who have displayed arrogance: Mozart, James Joyce, Gertrude Stein, Joan of Arc, Aristotle, Mohammed Ali ("I'm the greatest"), Liberace and Gurdjieff (vanity).

Positive Pole
Pride, perspective on accomplishments.
The positive pole of arrogance is pride - a good feeling about who one is and about the value of one's works. One may experience pride in one's family or nationality i.e., proud to be a Frenchman or an Arab; or, pride in having completed a major task such as a doctoral dissertation or book. Such pride is appropriate for the situation and is not truly a feeling of superiority over others.

Negative Pole

Vanity, superiority, aloofness, lording over.

The negative pole is vanity, a kind of over-importance bestowed upon oneself. Here, the person believes that he is better than other people. There can be a sense of embarrassment that everyone is noticing him and judging him so he puts on airs. In the negative pole he cares about this intensely and goes to great lengths to keep up the show, sometimes with ostentatious displays of wealth or power. People love to watch television programs that depict a character who epitomizes vanity often in the guise of the arch villain.

Expression Chief Features:
Self-destruction and Greed

+ sacrifice	+ appetite
SELF-DESTRUCTION	GREED
- suicidal	- voracity

SELF-DESTRUCTION

Focus:

"I can't help myself drinking (drugs etc.)."
"I want more and more ... (excessive greed)."
"I don't want to be here anymore."

The chief feature of self-destruction is the act or motivation to harm oneself either physically or emotionally out of the belief that life is not worth living. This expressive chief feature is found mostly in emotionally centered people, trapped in the moving part. (See the chapter on Centering.) About 10% of the population have the chief feature of self-destruction. We often see it most blatantly in alcoholics, drug abusers, wild dare-devils, and actively suicidal individuals.

Some individuals attempt self-destruction in some quick, possibly violent act. Others prolong it over a number of years or a whole lifetime as they slowly destroy themselves. Sometimes self-destruction is a maneuver to jolt oneself out of a stuck place.

The chief feature of self-destruction is often associated with a fear of losing control. So people may take high risks to prove they can control an extreme situation, e.g. a dare-devil motorcycle rider who leaps with his machine over longer and longer lines of cars. Or ,in battle, it is well documented that those who survive a number of battles where people around them are killed-off like flies gain a sense of invulnerablilty, that they cannot be killed. They deliberately take greater and greater risks until they, too, eventually die.

The nature of the overleaf is that it is a one-way street - people keep on doing something dangerous more and more until it kills them.

It manifests in compulsive gamblers who lose some money and then believe that by risking more they can win it back. They lose more, and then really want to recoup it, so they borrow some to try again. Eventually, they become washed-up and bankrupt. The theme is that they can't let go and surrender to their losses.

Here are some well known figures who had a chief feature of self destruction: Vincent Van Gogh, Jimi Hendrix and Marilyn Monroe.

Positive Pole
Sacrifice; surrender, give up something valued for the sake of something greater.

In the positive pole a person may sacrifice his life or his freedom for a purpose higher than himself. For example, a soldier might throw himself upon a hand grenade to prevent six others from getting killed. Or a mother might dash into a burning building to save her child and either be killed herself or badly injured. This chief feature may be chosen by someone who desires the motivation to pay back an outstanding karma.

Negative Pole

Suicidal,   self-sabotage,   masochistic,   sadistic   or   ruthless internalized parent (superego).

In the negative pole people attempt self destruction either as a quick possibly violent act, or prolonged over a number of years or a whole lifetime as they slowly destroy themselves. Out of self-hatred they might overeat, drink too much, take drugs, or engage in dangerous activities. These actions are based on the fear that their life has no value to them and is not worth living.

With the next chief feature, greed, we see how "too much of a good thing" results varying degrees of self-destruction. Drinking too much at a party and regretting it the next morning is an example most people can relate to. Overdosing on drugs or stimulants ranging from nicotine and   caffeine to more potent substances   reflects excessive greed sliding to self-destruction.

GREED

Focus:

"My needs are always greater than what I have and I truly want to meet them."
"There is never enough of what I want."
"I want more and more and more..."

Greed is the experience of wanting, or desiring, out of a fear that there will not be enough to go around. This is a type of poverty consciousness that no matter how much one has, more is desired. There is a feeling of losing out. The chief feature of greed is often found in emotionally centered persons trapped in the intellectual part (see section on centers). About 15% of the population has the chief feature of greed.

Greed is often manifested in the body as an insatiable craving for food, drink, sex, or drugs. Thus, the person with this chief feature may overeat even when they are not really hungry. Usually they feel remorse after gorging themselves and purge themselves of the food only to gorge again. This condition is known as bulimia. The reverse of this condition , anorexia, is also a derivative of greed.

Greed   may not manifest physically, but, emotionally as a craving for more and more experiences, relationships, love, goods and profits. This relentless craving often has the effect of driving others away. People in greed can be utterly ruthless in striving for their ends. They can be driven and possessed by their craving.

William Kellogg, the "King of Cornflakes," who founded the Kellogg Foundation (assets $1.2 billion), lived for 91 years, nearly all of them miserable. His doctor said: "In my long practice of psychiatry I do not know of a more lonely, isolated individual."

Ben Weingart, of the Weingart Foundation (assets $275 million), lived for 92 years. He divided his spare time between two women, seeing one on Wednesdays, Fridays and Sundays and the other on Tuesdays, Thursdays and Saturdays. On Mondays, he rested. Before he died he said he would, if only it were possible, like to order a larger shroud and take his money with him.

Greed can be eliminated by confronting the fear of lack and looking at the root fear. There is always a specific fixation with greed and a feeling of not enough. Identifying the "not enough" helps come to terms with the obssession.

The expressive and more dramatic roles of artisan and sage often favor the chief features of self-destruction and greed. Howard Hughes is a good example of a person with a chief feature of greed (wealth), as well as those described above.

Positive Pole

Appetite, allowing abundance, seeking fulfillment.

The positive pole of greed is appetite, a desire for all that life has to offer. This is the experience of allowing yourself to have everything you want in great quantity - almost no quantity is great enough.

Younger souls become enthusiastic about glory, fame and power; mature souls want lots of love, relationships and affection; and old souls develop a tremendous appetite for spiritual knowledge and experience.

A person in self destruction may happen upon something or someone in their life that is really worth living for, and they may slide to greed. The romantic notion of falling in love, where one suddenly feels a new zest and aliveness is an example of gaining an appetite for life, the positive pole of greed. And the reverse, losing a loved one, has occasionally caused the expression of grief in self-destruction.

Negative Pole

voracity, eternal dissatisfaction, bottomless pit.

The negative pole is voracity - an all-consuming enthusiasm that cannot be filled. This extends to life itself, where the person goes overboard in pursuing a maximum of experiences or intensity in one experience. The feeling is like being a bottomless pit with eternal dissatisfaction.

Often greed causes the person to slide to self destruction and to do something that hurts himself or to nearly do it. This can jar him out of feeling so greedy.

Because self-destruction and greed are a pair, an individual having the chief feature of greed may slide to self-destruction through the negative pole, voracity. As mentioned earlier, the greedy person, in consuming too much liquor may overdose and become very ill.

Action Chief Features: Martyrdom and Impatience

+ selflessness   + audacity
MARTYRDOM   IMPATIENCE
- victimized   - intolerance

MARTYRDOM

Focus:
"If it wasn't for xxx, I would be happy."
"I can't do this because..."
"Why do I always get the bad end of the deal?"
"After all I've done for you..."

In martyrdom, a person puts himself through needless suffering. He feels a victim of the situation, that it is beyond his control and he feels he can do little about it. About 15% of the population have this chief feature.

Martyrdom is the fear that one is not free but trapped by circumstances or by another person. There are noisy martyrs and silent martyrs. The noisy ones complain loudly and incessantly. The silent ones act like their suffering is too great to describe, and besides they are such lowly worms that no one would want to support them by listening to them. Martyrs are victims and nobody loves a victim.

This person has a difficult time acknowledging pleasure or fun because it would interfere with their suffering. Martyrdom has the effect of enraging others to the point of retaliation. They alienate others and create a self-fulfilling prophecy of mistreatment:

> For example, "You never call me anymore" with a reproachful tone. Or "No, it's okay, you go have a good time, I'll just stay home alone like I always do on Saturday nights and wash the floors, although my arthritis is so bad I can hardly hold the mop to clean your room."

Most of us slide to martyrdom periodically. For example, if I am ready to drive somewhere and I discover that my car battery has been stolen, I might feel a victim of the situation. This is fairly typical when sudden and unfortunate situations occur.

People in martyrdom sometimes flirt with death. They go near the edge, e.g. a suicide attempt, and sometimes they go too far and kill themselves. This can create difficulties for therapists because the client in martyrdom sometimes takes the attitude of "I'll show you - I'll kill myself," and every now and again they do.

Famous persons with a chief feature of martyrdom: William Blake, Ludwig Beethoven (deafness in later years so he couldn't hear his compositions), Karl Marx, John F. Kennedy and William Shakespeare. No points for guessing Joan of Arc.

Positive Pole
Selflessness; putting oneself out.

The positive pole of martyrdom is selflessness. This is giving to others instead of thinking of oneself. The positive pole was the ideal of the early Christians who gained a place in history through their persecution by the Romans.

In political circles the power of martyrdom to draw sympathy to a cause is well known. The murder of Mr. Aquino in the Phillipines in 1983 led to his wife, Corazon Aquino, being elected President in 1986. The impetus for change happened largely because of the intense feeling generated by the martyrdom of her husband which drew peoples' attention to Marcos' unsatisfactory style of dictatorship.

Negative Pole
Victimization; immolation, humiliation.

This occurs when martyrdom is taken into the realm of "poor me, I'm giving and giving and never getting what I need." Of course ,the person has put himself in that position and he can realize that he is in charge and can do something about it. To do so, he would have to express his resentments directly and forgo the pleasure of sympathy and self-pity.

As said earlier, this can be the most unlikable of all the chief features and elicit disgust from others because it is the position of lowest self-esteem.

People who remain in the negative pole for long periods of time frequently develop a martyred posture that looks like they carry the world on their shoulders. The negative pole of martyrdom can also be used to experience embarrassment. If a person has the chief feature of impatience and slides to martyrdom, they can become intolerant and dismissive of themselves. They might think, "Oh my God, I've done a really dumb thing that everybody's noticed. Now I'm in utter humiliation."

IMPATIENCE

Focus:
"I don't have time to wait for..."
"If those S.O.B.s don't hurry up..."

Impatience is a feeling of frustration or tension that comes from the fear of missing out. Often this is seen as "Hurry up or you'll miss out!" i.e. the fear that there is not enough time.

On the subject of time, a note here for advanced students. Of course, all time is simultaneous, and so you are never late. The time of your arrival is always appropriate, otherwise, simultaneous time would be a lie. It is impossible to arrive at an inappropriate time. You can observe the truth of this for yourself.

The frustration of impatience can lead to martyrdom, its complementary chief feature. About 15% of the population choose impatience as a chief feature.

Although a popular trait in our society, impatience is negative. When you are busy rushing you miss the fullness of the moment. You never arrive and enjoy your life because there is always planning and arranging to be done.

Impatience can lead to a desperate attempt to get something done in such a hurry that either something is broken or further delay is created. For example, a person caught in traffic may become so impatient that they speed on a different route only to get a speeding ticket or get hopelessly snarled in much worse traffic. Or, in an attempt to make a quick correction on a piece of work, the person damages it beyond repair and must start over which would be enough to put anyone into martyrdom.

Positive Pole

Audacity; spontaneity, daring.

The positive pole of impatience, audacity, suggests a bold, daring and spontaneous act that relieves the situation and enables one to move decisively forward. In order to reach the desired end more quickly, the person takes a risk.   For example, one can encounter endless red tape in foreign countries and a bold move, like words with the right official, might get one across the border instantly while everyone else waits impatiently.

Negative Pole

Intolerant, judgmental, frustrated.

The negative pole is intolerance. A person operating from here will reject people or situations that are unsatisfactory from his point of view.   Intolerance is a result of heavy frustration, the inability to achieve things in the time frame that he would like. A person might be caught in traffic and feel frustrated that he will not arrive on time. In the negative pole he may give full vent to his frustrations abusing other drivers, his car and himself.

Assimilation Chief Feature: Stubbornness

+ determination
STUBBORNNESS
- obstinancy

STUBBORNNESS

Focus:
> "I'll do anything but change."
> "I'm sticking to my guns."
> "You can't make me."

People with this feature have the characteristic of taking a stand in the face of real or imagined opposition. Stubbornness is the fear of change, not wanting to let go of one's position.

About 20% of the population choose this chief feature, making it the most popular one. Stubbornness is also a favorite chief feature for older souls, a phenomenon that is discussed in an upcoming section.

Stubbornness affords the opportunity to slide to all the chief features at will, making it both a flexible and convenient obstacle.

The remedy for this chief feature is the practice of letting go appropriately in the face of resistance. For example, in arms negotiations stubbornness only increases the likelihood of open hostilities, whereas letting go of the fear of change might open the door for progress and peace.

Famous people with the chief feature of stubbornness: Margaret Mead, Andrew Wyeth, Rasputin, Pearl Buck, Carlos Casteneda, Ho Chi Minh, Galileo and General George Patton.

Positive Pole
Determined, resolute, possessing strong intention, fixed in purpose.

The positive pole appears useful to individuals forging ahead in spiritual growth or any other endeavour. Determination is about willpower, the firm intention to slog through and persevere no matter what the obstacles. People in the positive pole do not get daunted easily.

The positive pole of determination is like applying the gas and really moving forward. This person says *"Yes,* I will do it."

Determination is often an ingredient of success in our society. It relates to putting a lot of energy out to achieve your goal. As energy seeks to complete a circuit, it generally comes back as success, money or what have you.

Negative Pole
Obstinate; pig-headed, closed-down.

The negative pole of stubbornness, obstinacy, is like applying the brakes and grinding everything to a halt. The person says "*No*, I won't do it."

The negative pole can make a person blind to certain information, to certain parts of the total picture. They become unyielding and hold on fast even when it is detrimental to do so. This sometimes is merely fear of change.

Chief Features in General

Relating Chief Features with Soul Ages

Baby and mature souls prefer martyrdom and impatience because these chief features facilitate well the lessons of these two stages. Both get into feeling the victim and martyrdom leads them toward interaction with others.   Impatience accompanies their frequent feelings of being out of control.

Infant and young souls often go for greed because they both want to accumulate vast quantities of experience or material goods. For the infant soul, it is a question of amassing for survival and for young souls it is more a question of winning.

Old souls show a preference for self-deprecation and arrogance. These chief features concern questions of self-worth that are central for old souls. They have been around long enough to realize that in the great scheme of things they actually know very little. They are likely to say "Who am I to speak? I know nothing."

Relating Chief Features with Attitudes and Goals

The following are some examples of chief features and how they work with attitudes and goals.

1. Let us take for example, an individual whose goal is acceptance and who's attitude is cynic. If he is standing in a long line he may slide to the negative pole of cynic and denigrate the situation: "It's hopeless and I'll be here forever." This makes him feel a victim of the situation, the negative pole of martyrdom. Or, perhaps intolerant, the negative pole of impatience. Now, it is very difficult for him to achieve his goal of acceptance. If the cynic can reach the positive pole of realist he can become objective and reconsider how to reach his goal of acceptance.

If, however, he already finds himself caught in his chief feature - say impatience - can move to the positive pole--- audacity and do some positive direct act that remedies the situation and helps him reach his goal of acceptance as well.

For example, he might decide to leave and come back later when there is no line, thus accepting the situation at hand.

1. Consider a person with the goal of growth, a pragmatist attitude, and the chief feature of arrogance. If he is teaching his son to play the piano he may get frustrated and slide to the negative pole of pragmatism, dogma. He then may arrogantly insist that the child does it his way or else. The child may quit which under those circumstances may not feel good to either of them. On the other hand, if the father can slide to efficiency, the positive pole of pragmatism, he may cut the lesson short for the day and take his son outside to play instead. Arrogance does not arise and he can grow from the experience.

In each of these examples the individual's mode would determine how all of what they do is accomplished: cautiously, passionately, aggressively and so on.

Relating Chief Features with Centering

The chief features relate to different centering. The table shows common associations of centering and trap with the different chief features. See also chapter on Centering.

Chief Feature	Center	Part (trap)
Martyrdom	moving	intellectual
Impatience	moving	emotional
Greed	emotional	intellectual
Self-destruction	emotional	moving
Arrogance	intellectual	emotional
Self-deprecation	intellectual	moving
Stubbornness	no preferred centering	

Find Your Chief Feature

You will find a bit of yourself in all of these because you have done them all from time to time. Your chief feature is the one that characterizes you the most. Since you are frequently blind to your own chief feature it may be best to ask someone else how they see you. Others can always see your chief feature. When they all say "Boy, are you stubborn," or, "You are totally impatient" and you deny it vehemently, that is probably your chief feature.

1) At times life is just not worth living and suicide seems like the only answer.
   I often feel that it does not matter what happens to me or what I do to my body. Who cares?
   I sometimes deliberately do things that I know will be harmful to myself but I just can't stop myself.

2) At times I am terribly afraid I will miss out on things and I desperately want them.

Often, I can't seem to control my appetite for money, food, drink, sex, or some other experience.

I just never feel like I get enough.

3) Others never appreciate me for what I do.

I often feel trapped by what I have to be or do and I fear I'll never come out from under it.

It's other people's fault that my life is so hard and if they would just be nicer to me it would be better.

4) I hate to wait for anything.

I become intolerant easily when others move too slow for my taste.

I frequently fear that there is just not enough time to accomplish everything.

5) I often feel that I'm really not much good at anything.

I feel I do not measure up to other people in many situations.

I am extremely hard on myself and beat myself up relentlessly.

6) When they first meet me, others frequently think I'm a snob.

Sometimes I feel very shy and shun attention. Then I feel left-out.

Often, I feel like I have much more to offer if others would just shut-up for a minute and listen to "me".

7) When I set my mind to something, that's it, nobody can move me.

Sometimes, even when I know I'm wrong about something, I won't give in.

Nobody can tell me what to do. I make up my own mind.

Code

1) Self-destruction
2) Greed
3) Martyrdom
4) Impatience
5) Self-deprecation
6) Arrogance
7) Stubbornness

Now that the role, goal, mode, attitude and chief feature have been covered, we are ready to go on to centering. Centering is how you interact with the world in terms of thinking, feeling and doing.

Chapter Eleven

Centering and Higher Centers

This chapter covers the seven centers, their three parts, and the traps within them. Centers are a more complex set of overleaves than the others because of the interaction of the three parts within each center.

First, a brief description will be given of all the seven centers and then each center will be discussed in detail. Then, the parts of centers will be described, as well as, the traps that keep us stuck. Finally, we will discuss methods of becoming free of the trap so as to become balanced in our use of the centers.

The seven centers roughly correspond to the seven major chakras located along the spinal column. Chakra is a Sanskrit word meaning wheel or vortex and refers to the seven subtle centers of consciousness located along the length of the spinal column.

The Importance of Centering

You do not experience anything outside of your centers. They are the medium through which essence experiences the world.

Center	Chakra	Location	Related Role
Instinctive	1st	Base of spine	King
Higher Moving	2nd	Above sex organs	Artisan
Moving	3rd	Solar plexus	Warrior
Emotional	4th	Heart	Server
Intellectual	5th	Throat	Sage
Higher Intell.	6th	Third eye	Scholar
Higher Emot.	7th	Crown	Priest

The experiences gained in each life depend on how we use our centers in the context of the overleaves that we have chosen for that life. Our personality has a favorite way of using our centers and overleaves. That way determines the particular map of experience that essence gains from that lifetime. Nonetheless, we have access to all the centers and all the overleaves all the time.

Difficulty understanding the function of centers can be a product of our own centering. Intellectual center will have difficulty understanding emotional center, and vice-versa. We are prejudiced according to the center we operate from. Gaining a perspective on the other centers increases self-knowledge.

What is Centering?

Centering has to do with how you go about operating in your daily life. Centering is what you do immediately, without premeditation. It is the primary automatic response.

It is how you react to a situation and how that reaction is expressed.

Although their are seven centers, people actively operate out of one of the main three - moving, emotional, and intellectual centers. We experience through whichever center we use most of the time. So we predominantly move, feel or think according to our preference. We use other centers secondarily to back them up.

The fourth, instinctive center, operates mostly unconsciously and the three higher centers are experienced only occasionally.

The Seven Centers in a Nutshell

Center	Description
Intellectual	Words, concepts, thinking
Emotional	Feeling states - joy, sadness, anger
Moving	Moving the body - walking, dancing, fidgeting
Instinctive	Keeps you alive, body functions, heart beat, breathing, cellular growth etc.
Higher Intellectual	Truth
Higher Emotional	Love
Higher Moving	Beauty, sense of wonder, sex connectedness

As mentioned, each person has seven functioning centers. Certain of the centers may however be closed-down or relatively unused. Others may be used or even over-used. For example, a person may have a rich emotional life, be quick to move, but be blocked around grasping concepts intellectually, and so on. All centers work but to different degrees.

The primary centering is determined by the center that one uses first in any situation. That is, if people respond to situations mainly with feelings then they are emotionally centered. If they usually think first then they are intellectually centered, and if they act first then they are moving centered.

Suppose there is a car accident outside a cafe:

● The person inside who hears the crash and analyzes what happened and who hit whom is intellectually centered.

● The person who immediately feels terrible because people may be hurt is emotionally centered.

● The person who jumps up to go and have a look is moving centered.

The Seven Centers

● Primary Energizer
● The part of yourself you will act from
● The trap is the center that facilitates
   your personality best

Ordinal	Neutral	Exalted
Expression		
+ insight		+ truth
INTELLECTUAL ———————		HIGHER INTELLECTUAL
- reasoning		- telepathy
Inspiration		
+ perception		+ love
EMOTIONAL ———————		HIGHER EMOTIONAL
- sentimentality		- intuition
Action		
+ productive		+ integration
MOVING ———————		HIGHER MOVING
- frenetic		- desire
	Assimilation	
	+ Aware	
	INSTINCTIVE - All centers available	
	- Mechanical	

Parts of Centers

Each of the centers has three parts: the moving part, the emotional part and the intellectual part. These are not to be confused with the centers by that name. For example, each of the centers, moving, emotional, and intellectual have a moving part, an emotional part, and an intellectual part. Each part governs a different aspect of experience.

The distribution of centers and parts of centers worldwide is perfectly balanced. Within the U.S. it is skewed and the following diagram shows how.

Percentages within the United States' Population

	Emotional Center 40% of pop.	Intellectual Center 50% of pop.	Moving Center 10% of pop.
Emotional Part	N/A	1/2	1/4
Intellectual Part	3/4	N/A	3/4
Moving Part	1/4	1/2	N/A
	1.00	1.00	1.00

The Trap

When a person chooses one part to operate out of (perhaps out of habit) in response to most situations, this is called the trap. For example, if a person is primarily centered intellectually but frequently worries about what he thinks, he is responding out of the emotional part of intellectual center and may in fact be trapped there.

It is important to distinguish between parts and traps. Each center has its parts. A person may find himself trapped in a part. That is not to say that a part is problematic. It is to say that a person's habitual response out of that part may be inappropriate. In other words, the trap occurs when you are not in the part you ought to be in.

The Meaning of Centers

Centers convey the experience of personality to essence. They are like bridges, tunnels, or energy vortices between essence and personality. You might think of them as communication lines between the central command and the outpost. These lines carry information back and forth giving direction and guidance to the outpost or personality and giving feedback to the central command or essence. The personality determines what to do with the information although essence tends to influence the long-term developmental direction and certain specific events (i.e. karma).

Before you are born, essence decides what your centering preferences will be and your overleaves. Personality chooses the part of the center and the pole of the overleaves (positive or negative).

Essence says "This lifetime I will be emotionally centered." The personality says "Okay - I am emotionally centered this lifetime and I choose the moving part - I am going to act impulsively on my emotions. This centering and part means that the intellectual side of me is under-developed. I will sometimes be trapped in the moving part, and be doing and doing and lose the original purpose." This is a personality experience.

So a large part of personality is determined by choice of the positive or negative pole and the part of a center. You can look at where you go most of the time and then decide if you would then like to do differently. There is quite a bit of choice involved.

Relating Centering to Soul Ages

Soul ages rather than roles influence the use of centers. These are the centers that assist the different soul ages.

Infant & Baby	Use instinctive center a lot.
Young	Like moving center for conquering the world; more action, doing and success.
Mature	Emotional because you are the same as me. Being a mature soul is mostly about relationships.
Old	Use intellectual center to get the perspective that there's you, me and the entire picture.

Being an old soul is more about directing attention, especially toward cycling-off. You never cycle-off without realizing you're doing it.

The Centers in Use

As mentioned, the centers determine how the other overleaves are used.

For example, one person with power mode may be a strong intellectual presence such as Socrates, while another person with power mode might be moving centered like Mao Tse Tung who changed an entire society. An intellectually centered spiritualist like Thomas Merton writes books while an emotionally centered spiritualist like Beethoven writes music. An emotionally centered person with a goal of growth, an idealist with observation mode, might look like Allen Ginsberg, observing with feeling, and growing through writing poetry.

You can see then how the centers govern all our experience. The experiences gained in each life depend on how we use our centers in the context of our overleaves. That way determines the particular map of experience gained from lifetime to lifetime.

INTELLECTUAL CENTER

+ Insight
INTELLECTUAL
- Reason

This center comprises a lot of different things but can be simplified to thought, concepts, and language. The intellectual center uses words and vocabulary as its basic tool and is therefore somewhat slower than the emotional center.

The intellectual center is where you hold the concept or form the reason about why you're doing what your doing. This is called "directed attention" or intention because you have a thought or intention behind what is happening in other centers. (See later - Parts of Centers.) So when you place your intention upon what you are doing, you do it not until you're tired of it (as in other centers) but until it's done.

This center also places our perceptions in a linear time sequence, identifying events as being in the past, present, or future.

People generally have a two year intellectual cycle in their lives. This means you only get the concept and clarity of what you did two years afterward.

When the intellectual center is overdeveloped or out of balance with the other centers the person may be seen as an "egghead" - all ideas and no action or emotion.

Intellectually centered people have an advantage in Western culture because society is structured around rewarding them. Reading, writing, and speaking are all functions of the intellectual center and based on the retention of a wide vocabulary. Intellectually centered people naturally gravitate to philosophy, journalism, law, research, and literature and the like.

Thomas Aquinas, Earl Warren, Carlos Castaneda, James Joyce, and Socrates are all intellectually centered individuals.

Positive Pole
  Insight
  The positive pole of intellectual center is insight or thought. Thought is best described as an original idea that appears out of nowhere. Pure thought is not linear but spontaneous like an Aha! or a realization and does not require labored effort.

Negative Pole
  Reason
  The negative pole of the intellectual center is reasoning. When we string together a number of ideas and attempt to chain them together with logic, that is reasoning. Reasoning is the poor man's approach to working things out. It is slow and tedious compared with the power and speed of the emotional and instinctive centers.

EMOTIONAL CENTER

+ sensibility
EMOTIONAL
- sentimentality

This center governs the area of basic feelings - the experience of liking or disliking, e.g. a painting, a landscape, another person. In emotional center you see your feelings with distinctness.

The response from emotional center is "I like it" or "I don't like it." This emotional response is much more rapid than thought. It takes only an instant to respond with joy, anger, amusement or sadness. The emotional center includes the physiological response of the body's glands to experiences of either an internal or external nature.

Emotional center deals with perception and feeling. People

confuse feelings with sensations and thoughts quite a bit - more than they realize. In simple terms, emotion is feeling. But pain, for example, is the instinctive center. Also, intellectually centered people are, by definition, out of touch with their feelings. They tend not to have feelings but merely *think* they have feelings. - "I think I feel..."

On the other hand, objectivity is a quality of the intellectual center. Loss of objectivity happens when emotion distorts the intellectual center. It is summed up in the saying - "The heart has its reasons the mind knows not of."

> *Institutions such as the stock market depend on swings of emotion to generate market action - without that the market would be dull, flat and boring. The stock market indices are literally graphs of swings in optimism and pessimism. Likewise, surges in economic growth occur when people are optimistic - no other reason. (Called the Pigou effect after the English economist, Mr. Pigou, who described this.)*

When the emotional center is balanced, we see the person as emotionally open and responsive.

Emotionally centered people often gravitate to the arts, fashion design, theatre, and music. They may be perceptive and accurate in their hunches about situations or people. When asked to explain how they came to their conclusion they often can't, so they manufacture reasons to satisfy their intellectually centered friends. They can be highly sensitive and easily hurt.

Feelings are like muscles. You may feel what you feel simply because that muscle is exercising itself. People often look for a reason - e.g. "I feel depressed because..." and in fact there is no reason. They are simply having a feeling. Note also that when people feel good they seldom look for a reason but simply enjoy feeling good.

Jack Kerouac, Jimi Hendrix, Marilyn Monroe, Ernest Hemingway, Beethoven, and Albert Einstein were all emotionally

Positive Pole
   Sensibility; feelings.
   The positive pole of emotional center has to do with the ability to sense and feel directly. The person operating out of this pole is highly perceptive and able to assess a situation rapidly.

Negative Pole
   Sentimentality.
   The person operating out of the negative pole of the emotional center is highly subjective and gets caught in excessive and irrelevant feelings about a situation. For example, the sentimental person may fail to throw out some possession that is obvious garbage because they are attached to some memory associated with it.

MOVING CENTER

+ productive
MOVING
- frenetic

   Moving center retains everything you've ever learned ever since you came into your body. You learned how to walk and talk, move your eyes, run, throw and so on. Doing all of what you have learned is moving center.
   Moving centered people are constant balls of activity. They tend to be restless and move about the room changing positions frequently. Often they are attracted to such occupations as professional athletics, aviation, police work, traveling sales, or anything that will keep them on the go.
   When the moving center is developed to the exclusion of the emotional and intellectual centers we see someone who acts like a veritable machine - no thought and no feeling. This person may not think or have any feelings about his actions. When the moving

center is balanced, the person is physically fit and excels at getting things done, often of a physical nature.

Mao Tse Tung, Gertrude Stein, Malcolm X, Don Juan Matus, and Gen. George Patton were all moving centered. Notice the level of activity exhibited in their lives.

Positive Pole
Productive; enduring.

The positive pole is productive movement or movement with a purpose. These are movements of an enduring quality and include the voluntary nervous system, walking, talking, hugging, dancing, playing, and working. Productive movement also refers to any intentional motions that produce something which endures like a sculpture, a building, or a tool. This person carries through their motions to their natural conclusion.

Negative Pole
Unproductive, wasted, fidgety, restless, frenetic.

The negative pole of moving center is unproductive movement. This includes all motion which has no purpose such as pacing nervously or tapping one's fingers anxiously and so on. Energy is dissipated without any tangible results.

Shifting from one thing to the next without completing any one task is the kind of useless activity characterizing the negative pole.

Someone wandering around aimlessly in shock after a disaster or racing around frantically or hysterically would be another example.

INSTINCTIVE CENTER

+ aware
INSTINCTIVE
-automatic

The discussion of instinctive center is a longer one because it is complex. It is the neutral center for all the other centers everything that happens has some bearing on the instinctive center.

The instinctive center governs all those processes in the body that keep us alive, also known as the involuntary nervous system. This is the work of the heart, the lungs, the glands etc. The instinctive center is needed for survival and includes all fight or flight functions. When we leap out of the way of a speeding car or instinctively brake to avoid hitting a child on the road we are operating out of instinctive center. The instinctive center operates spontaneously without the interference of thought or emotion.

The instinctive center has access to information about both current environmental conditions and past life memories. Therefore, sometimes this center will go into operation to avoid a seeming threat which is not appropriate to the current situation such as a phobic reaction to crossing a bridge. The bridge may be perfectly safe but if the person has a traumatic past life memory of being attacked on a bridge and being killed, they could instinctively respond with fear or even panic.

Likewise, the instinctive center operates from symbolic information which may have gone through several translations or associations.

Therapy case studies have shown that, for example, if a child falls down and hurts herself just as a black dog barked, the pain becomes associated with black dogs. The pain may become further associated with anything soft and black such as a scarf, or blouse, or sweater. As an adult, the person may react with irrational fear or discomfort when presented with a black scarf. She may even begin to feel the old pain in her elbow where she fell down, but may not consciously remember the event. This train of association is a common phenomenon in the therapeutic situation.

The instinctive center is a powerful survival mechanism and does not function according to linear time as understood by the intellectual center. To the instinctive center all time is now.

The instinctive center has a special function as a gateway to higher center experience.

The instinctive center as a whole has often been portrayed by many spiritual traditions as something base and gross, something to rise above. However, as mentioned, the instinctive center is the doorway to the higher centers, a fact well known to practioners of shamanism, Sufi dancing, deep meditation, or spiritual ritual. How can the instinctual center be both something to be transcended and yet something to enter into in spiritual practice? Let us begin with a mundane example. One way to experience the instinctive center consciously is to notice the state you are in while either defecating, urinating or washing under the shower.

People often report experiences such as insight or understanding while attending to toilet activities. It is not uncommon to hear someone say "I do my most creative thinking on the toilet." Some great inventions have been conceived there as well as ideas for books spawned. Why is this so? You will notice by observing yourself, others, or even animals during this activity that one enters into a mild trance state. The body totally relaxes and intellectual center and emotional center cease their activities briefly (unless of course you are not relaxed). Instinctive center takes over, the chatter ceases and higher center experiences become available.

In the same way, with a near-death experience people frequently report great insight and spiritual awakening. Here too, the body has become completely instinctive in order to survive and the gateway to peak experience has opened.

Likewise, certain consciousness-altering drugs stimulate the instinctive center which causes the person to either react in great fear or in other cases enables the person to reach higher centers and the associated peak experiences.

Trance dancing, fasting, deep meditation, drumming, deep breathing techniques, etc., are all ways of opening the instinctive center as the pathway to higher centers.

Loud rock music is a good example of a method by which adolescents and others open the instinctive center to accomplish an unconscious review and assimilation of their recent life processes.

A person can use the instinctive center to change the direction of their life or to let go of an old pattern and take on a new one. This often takes the form of becoming ill. The person experiences the instinctive center for a few days or weeks and in fact conducts an extensive unconscious review. When this happens it is common that when they recover, they may   make some immensely difficult decision that they had been deeply blocked about.

Being incapacitated in bed stops most moving centered activity, feeling unwell inhibits intellectual activity and limits much emotionally centered activity.   So, the other centers are closed down and the person is driven into instinctive center where the review takes place.

This involuntary use of the instinctive center is often accomplished by the essence that wishes the body to stop its activities and pursue a different course in their life. Sometimes a person who is in battle or a high tension career may fall ill, preventing them from continuing. So, illness can act as a pivotal experience, causing people to change careers, shift out of a marriage or live a little longer by getting out of the battlefield situation.

The alternative to getting ill is to choose to be in touch with one's instinctive center and to be aware of one's deeper processes. One way is through meditation.

An infant a few days old is a good example of being immersed entirely in instinctive center. As he becomes older, the other centers come into play and the instinctive center becomes buried. Later in life the experience of being an infant can be relived by opening the instinctive center in any of the ways described. This can be a powerful therapeutic tool.

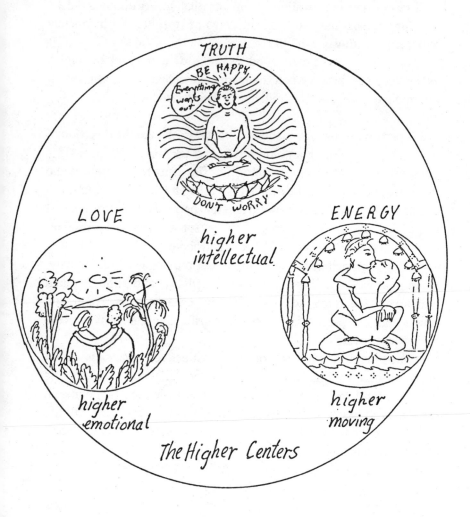

Helen Keller is one of the few examples of famous people who have lived much of their lives in instinctive center. Other examples would include people in deep comas, profoundly retarded individuals, and those with extensive brain damage.

Positive Pole
Aware; atomic, natural, childlike, basic, simple.
The positive pole is basic awareness of being. However, it extends also to a retarded person, someone in a trance state, or a person in deep meditation. This person would appear childlike and would operate at an extremely simple level. The person handles living functions naturally but with awareness.

Negative Pole
Automatic; mechanical, anatomic.
The negative pole is automatic or mechanical behavior that takes place without awareness such as is the case in extreme autism. Sleepwalking is another example of mechanical behavior taking place without awareness.
It refers to anyone who is acting automatically and is in a state of "waking sleep".

The Higher Centers

The higher centers enable people to see connections and understand the bigger picture in life. The lower centers are more separate and are used to divide and categorize. They may be used to separate out the individual sensations of an experience. The higher centers are of essence, the lower centers of personality.
The higher centers exist to remind us that in reality we are not separate, but are all part of a greater whole. This self-remembering is the experience of unity and rememberance that the physical plane is an illusion. Loneliness and forgetfulness do not exist on the other planes.

The higher centers are available to everyone, although not everyone will value the experience. The older the soul, the more they are experienced and enjoyed. Younger souls by contrast need to forget themselves to create karma and create the lessons of separateness.

> *Imagine you are a budding author, beavering away one page at a time, attempting to keep all the storylines in your head and evolve a diabolical plot. One evening you are taking a shower when the picture of the entire plot for the rest of the book floods into your mind. You rush to your desk still dripping wet and start quickly running off all the details. You get so concerned about losing the flow that you work for three days without stopping for sleep. By the time you are done you have broken the back of the project and only fill-in work remains. This is an exaggerated higher center experience.*

Although that is typical of an intense higher intellectual center experience, all the higher centers tend to have a quality of merging about them. You can't always be clear which higher center an experience relates to, because you can perceive or feel such a sense of unity that divisions and labels don't make sense.

Higher centers are high energy places to experience, and for that reason, people generally don't spend long periods of time there. The centers can be seen as like a thermometer - you use energy to rise out of the lower centers and into the higher ones. The impact and value of being there is high as you transcend the mundanity of everyday life.

The Poles of the Higher Centers

The negative poles of higher centers are not the same as those of the lower centers, because they have a different meaning. In the lower centers, negative poles are related to the functions of false personality and consequently they do not feel good to either party.

Elements of Higher Centers

	Intellect	Emotion	Moving
Positive	Truth	Love	
Neutral			Understanding
Negative	Illusion	Fear	

In the higher centers, the negative poles represent a narrower band of conscious awareness of an enlightening experience. Negative poles of higher centers usually feel good, unlike lower centers' negative poles.

Each one of the centers, higher and lower, has positive and negative poles that form a triad that is an energy circuit. For example, intellectual center has the positive pole (insight), the negative pole (reasoning) and a position which is neutral where the center simply fulfills its function neutrally. The center itself is a triad and you are in choice as to where on the triad you operate from.

Looking at the larger picture of all the centers, the entire seven centers form a septant. That is a larger form of energy circuit.

In the positive poles of the higher centers, there is no sense of separation. All of life is seen as interrelated and an integrated whole.

In the negative poles there is still a sense of separation, an awareness of you and I. Whereas, the positive poles of the higher centers are experienced with intense awareness, the negative poles are usually experienced unconsciously. One may not be aware of a telepathic communication or an intuition, for example. Increasing your awareness of those subtle energy flows is a rewarding practice.

HIGHER EMOTIONAL CENTER

+ love
HIGHER EMOTIONAL
- intuition

Positive Pole

   Love

   The way to enter the positive pole of higher emotional center is to love one's neighbor as oneself - because he is yourself. This sense of emotional connectedness creates a clear wordless state for those experiencing it. This is a state of pure love that meditators strive for in their spiritual path.

   Some spiritual teachings are primarily focused on this higher emotional experience of love. The teachings of Jesus Christ are an example. When asked to give the ultimate lessons he responded that they are to love oneself, one's neighbor, and God.

Negative Pole

   Intuition

   The negative pole of the higher emotional center is intuition, a high level ability to perceive the state of another person from a place of empathy. As such, this represents a narrow band of loving, that is, not being completely and fully loving in all directions. This is the act of being able to put your feelings in the place of someone else, e.g., "I know just why you're grieving and upset - I know how it feels." This of course does not mean taking the feelings on, or identifying with the person; it is being perceptive about oneself and also about others. Nor is it necessarily loving in general. The focus narrows onto a particular individual one feels empathetic with.

   This ability to see patterns, dynamics, and deeper feelings in oneself or others includes psychic   abilities.   In the higher emotional state, the psychic literally bypasses the usual emotional and intellectual processes and is able to pick up and understand immediately the past, present, or future probability of events or conditions.

Psychics sense what is going on in a person's life path from the negative pole of the higher emotional center. This is not as accurate as perceiving from the state of total love and being, the positive pole of higher emotional center, yet it is definitely service of a high order.   The Hindus have called the negative pole the state of siddhis, powers and supernormal abilities that develop on the path to enlightenment. They warn the student that this is only a step on the way to the positive pole and not to mistake it for the real thing.

HIGHER INTELLECTUAL CENTER

+ truth
HIGHER INTELLECTUAL
- telepathy

The higher intellectual center experiences the Truth of all that is.   Reality experienced through the higher intellectual center is permanent and immortal.

Word descriptions do not do justice to higher center activities because the experience transcends language. Language tends to break down experience into compartments that the higher centers fuse and unite. Higher intellectual center experience has to do with a realization of truth beyond what can be described.

Spiritual teachers are often   confronted with the task of relaying this experience to their students. They have usually resorted to directly challenging the student's habitual and conditioned view of reality through the use of paradox and koan so that the student can glimpse the higher intellectual truth. This truth about reality has to do with the essential oneness and inseparableness of all that is. Of course this truth is often fought by false personality because, being programmed for independent survival, it does not want to acknowledge its own finiteness.

Positive Pole
Truth

The positive pole of intellectual center is Truth. This is not about this or that truth but truth about all that is. This was the center out of which the spiritual master Lao Tsu taught.

There are of course degrees of truth - personal, world and universal, and furthermore they can change with time. Truth for one person is not always the same as truth for another. In higher intellectual center you tend to perceive wider rather than narrower truths.

Negative Pole
Telepathy

The negative pole of higher intellectual center is telepathy, a narrow band of high order truth. Telepathy has to do with knowing what is true for another person, the intellectual insight of who they are and where they are coming from. This is an intellectual rather than emotional experience and can be a valuable tool for spiritual growth.

HIGHER MOVING CENTER

+ integration
HIGHER MOVING
- desire

The higher moving center is concerned with beauty and pure energy. Higher moving center represents energy in its pure form, just as higher emotional represents love and higher intellectual represents truth. Together they form the triad Truth, Love, and Energy, the basic building blocks of the universe.

This center was originally called sexual center, and then changed to be consistent with higher emotional and higher intellectual centers.

Calling it sexual center resulted in people thinking of individuals experiencing sex, and the focus shifted to sexual matters. Sexual intercourse and its many variations is actually mostly moving centered experience. Higher moving center has to do with every sense of connectedness - sex in the higher sense. That is, one being connected and intimate with everyone, and everything in the universe.

Literally, the term sexual center is true. Life on all the planes of existence is about sex, and the combining of individuals.

The higher moving center governs energy. This relates to a more subtle or core energy than what you use to walk and talk and move your body around as in the lower moving center. The higher moving center has to do with the manipulation of energy beyond the normal functions of walking and running, into a higher and more sophisticated form.

The higher moving center comprises three main areas:

1. Sexuality - sexual energy can be used strictly for sexuality or it can be employed in creative pursuits. Creative energy originates from the higher moving center.
2. Money, career, or the manifestation of what you want as goods in your life.
3. Physical health - how you take care of your body and whether it is sick or healthy.

We can look at this another way, which has three parts:

The first is your physical relationships - corresponding to sexuality. This includes how you relate to people in general, how you feel about them: it is an interactive energy flow.

The second is your outer experience of energy and what you do with it in the world - what you do to manipulate the physical environment out there.

Third, there is your inner experience of energy, or how the energy flows through you. This relates to your health and your general level of vitality - where your general level of energy is and whether or not it might be blocked.

The higher moving center is a feeling of intense energy. In groups it is contagious and manifests as a feeling of camaraderie, well-being and excitedness. Individually the energy may be experienced as a feeling of being in love, or a feeling of intense connectedness with other people.

The higher moving center is the seventh and final center of the seven. It represents the integration of all the centers and the integration of all the lessons that have been learned relating to each of those centers. It is about integrating all the centers into our physical bodies - all that has been learned on the emotional, intellectual and spiritual levels.

The higher moving center is a Buddhaic plane experience. The energy is already present in the universe and this center determines how you bring it into your body and let it flow through, directing it in terms of intentional behavior.

Positive Pole
Integration, beauty, energy.

As said earlier, the universe comprises truth, love and energy. This means you understand what is true in your life, see that everything you value centers on loving and feeling loved, and the application of both these principles is integration.

In other words, it is getting it all together.

Beauty includes the perfection of energy. When you see something as beautiful, such as a sunset perhaps, you are perceiving through your senses that the form of energy appears perfect to you. All the component parts of energy add up to a perfect total or whole. Thus, beauty is our response to a sensation of energy. The appreciation of art and beauty in nature is a higher moving centered experience. The teachings of the Buddha are related to the positive pole of this center.

Negative Pole
   Desire; erotic.

The negative pole of the higher moving center is desire or a craving to have what you feel you do not possess. This is indicative of a perceived separation from the person or thing that you want. This is an experience of imperfection with a desire to perfect or balance the energy.

Desire is sometimes seen as a cause of suffering as in Buddhism, which recommends the elimination of desire or craving. However, it is desire that motivates us to combine and unite with others, to reach ever more satisfying states of consciousness. Without desire, for example, a meditator would have no cause to seek further.

Desire, then, is a narrow band of the total state of beauty or energy that is the positive pole of the higher moving center. Rather it is attachment that causes suffering and this is a lower center function, i.e. of the false personality.

The Higher Centers	
Higher Intellectual	"I know"
Higher Emotional	"I love"
Higher Moving	"I am one with"

Centering Related to Soul Ages and Roles

As mentioned before, although all centers are potentially available, people do not live in higher centers. In general, people live out of the intellectual center, the emotional center, or the moving center.

A few individuals focus on the instinctive center for a lifetime for purposes of karmic lessons or experience and experimentation.

Infant and baby souls use the instinctive center heavily. Young souls enjoy the moving center, mature souls like the emotional center and old souls rely on the intellectual center a good deal.

Infant and baby souls rarely experience the higher centers. Mature and old souls like the higher center experiences and may focus there up to one third of the time.

The choice of a particular center often relates to the choice of overleaves. Certain centers are favored by particular roles - for example, scholars prefer intellectual center.

Priests and artisans are most comfortable with the emotional center. Warriors and kings like the moving center.

All centers are chosen and developed by all roles over many lifetimes. The ultimate goal is to learn to balance all the centers, especially the lower centers, so that intellectual, emotional and moving centers are used equally.

Many spiritual disciplines teach methods and techniques to balance the centers. These usually consist of movements that have both an intellectual and emotional component. This was the aim of the dances developed by Gurdjieff.

Certain cultures foster different centers. Italy is a favorite place for emotionally centered souls, whereas the USA is technologically sophisticated and we find mostly intellectually centered people. Similarly, for Germany and Japan. Early Greece developed the Olympics and this may be seen as a celebration of the moving center. The USA makes room for moving centered people by rewarding them with scholarships to universities based on their sporting and not intellectual prowess.

The Parts of Centers

Recall that each center is composed of three parts, the moving part, the emotional part, and the intellectual part. Thus, there are seven centers with three parts apiece or twenty-one possible parts to use. The parts of the higher centers, however, are not discussed because of their esoteric nature.

Intellectual Center	Emotional Center	Moving Center	Instinctive Center
Intellectual Part	Intellectual Part	Intellectual Part	Intellectual Part
Emotional Part	Emotional Part	Emotional Part	Emotional Part
Moving Part	Moving Part	Moving Part	Moving Part

The quality of the part of each center is as follows:

1. **The Moving Part** of each center has to do with placing one's attention externally, toward outside objects. This may look like a certain fascination with something or someone. The moving part is like mechanical attention. That is, like watching television or walking down the street; anything that can be done in a rather mechanical fashion.
("fascination attention").

2. **The Emotional Part** of any center includes "divided attention" - attention toward an outside object, and an awareness of oneself at the same time. In the emotional part of any center the attention is held by the object.

3. **The Intellectual Part** of any center includes three parts of a triad: Awareness of oneself, awareness of the object one is looking at or talking to, and also awareness of something greater that includes both.   In the intellectual part of any center, the attention is directed - it is more intentional. With this triad an energy circuit is established - the term is "self-remembering".

Our personality chooses which part of the center to be in. The essence chooses the center.

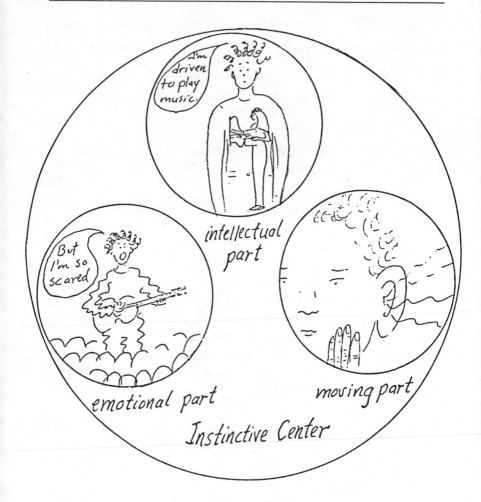

Instinctive Center

Intellectual Part - past life memories stored in various parts of the body. Essence programs personality from here to do karmas.

Emotional Part - physical emotions - likes and dislikes.

Moving Part- reflexes, the five senses.

THE PARTS OF INSTINCTIVE CENTER

The **Moving Part** of the instinctive center includes the five senses: reflexes, laughter, yawning, hearing, sight, touch, taste and smell.

These are all automatic inner functions. Yawning for example is a device which transfers energy from one center to another. This is the instinctive center operating automatically and distributing energy as needed.

The **Emotional Part** of instinctive center has to do with physical emotions; that which is experienced as pleasant or unpleasant, to like or dislike, to be attracted to or repulsed.

Persons experiencing profound disorientation such as schizophrenic persons may find themselves caught in this part of the instinctive center.

This part also governs the experience of fear. In the extreme this may make a person appear paranoid.

The **Intellectual Part** of instinctive center has to do with the hidden cognitive part of the survival machinery. This is the primitive logic that protects the organism, e.g., fight-or-flight situations. This part of the center governs weight, temperature etc. Included in this are all mechanisms which defend the body against bacteria, fight tooth decay and so on.

Also, memories of past lives are stored here. These subconsciously influence behavior. These memories may be stored in various parts of the body, in the cells. When these memories become conscious, these are experienced in a different center. Hypnosis often pulls the intellectual part of the instinctive center to the surface and transfers this information to the intellectual center where it can be recalled anytime.

Essence uses this part of the instinctive center to program the personality to respond in certain ways so that various lessons may be learned, agreements kept and so forth. For example, the urge to take a day off work and go to the beach where you meet your worst enemy who throws a brick at you, breaking your arm, is a karma that was instigated through the intellectual part of the instinctive center.

The Parts of the Instinctive Center	
Intellectual	"I am driven to." (Complete karma, have children etc)
Emotional	"I am in fear and trembling." (Survival issues)
Moving	"Uhhhh!! " (Automatic body functions)

THE PARTS OF MOVING CENTER

The Moving Part of moving center (or kinesthetic center as it is also known) has to do with learned functions such as walking, speaking, eating, writing etc. It also governs functions of memory and habitual responses. These are functions which require no particular feeling or thought.

The Emotional Part of moving center governs emotional aspects of movement. That is, movement with emotion, such as dance, sexual play, sports, gestures, postures, the language of the body - all the expressive forms of movement.

The Intellectual Part of the moving center has to do with intelligent movement such as martial arts. These are movements requiring substantial attention. They include acting, creating inventions, mathematics (i.e. fast calculations). A person trapped in this part will tend to rely very heavily on thoughts about moving. Leonardo Da Vinci was a good example - he was brilliant at knowing how to do, rather than actually doing.

Moving Center

Intellectual Part - movement with a purpose requiring substantial action, the martial arts, creating inventions, calculations.

Emotional Part - movement with emotions, dance, sexual play, sports, gestures.

Moving Part - learned function that require no particular feeling or thought - walking, speaking, eating, writing.

THE PARTS OF EMOTIONAL CENTER

The Moving Part of emotional center has to do with acting on emotions, and spontaneous activities such as hugging someone, or clapping them on the back. Tantrums and fidgeting would also fall into this category. This is basically about acting on what you feel.
This part governs mob psychology such as rioting, or the mass emotions we may encounter at major sporting events.

In addition it governs imprinted emotions such as nurturance, sentiments and so on.

The moving part of emotional center also governs spontaneous memories. A person who is trapped in the moving part of emotional center may be rather impulsive in his acts. They also may be capable of moving on their feelings, putting into action what they have felt and becoming very creative. Artisans often like operating out of this part as it fosters their natural creativity.

Walt Whitman, Andrew Wyeth, and Ernest Hemingway all operated from this part.

The Emotional Part of emotional center has to do with pure emotion. There is no cause or thought behind it - such feelings as joy, grief, nostalgia - spontaneous feeling. No action is necessary. There is no place to go with the feeling, no reason to analyze the feeling. It is a condition of pure sobbing, pure laughing - pure emotion.

The Intellectual Part of emotional center has to do with the perception of what is true, and the reasons behind emotions, seeing the relationships, knowing the plot. This intellectual part governs perceptive discrimination. This is an excellent place to function from because it is speedy and accurate - more so than any other centering. In other words, being emotionally centered you can have perceptions that are more accurate than intellectual analysis and much faster, and having had the emotional perception you then work out why from the intellectual part.

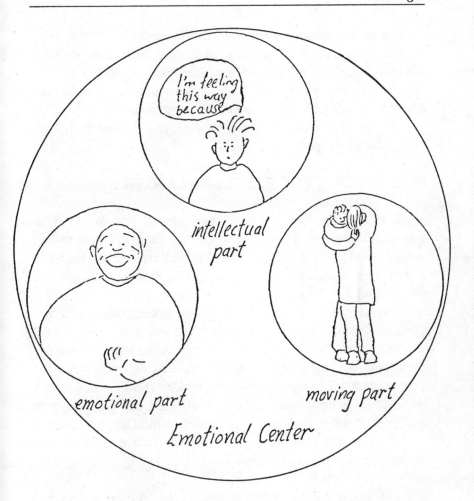

Emotional Center

Intellectual Part - I'm feeling this way because...

Emotional Part - pure sobbing, pure joy or laughter.

Moving Part - acting on what you feel.

If a person becomes trapped in this intellectual part they may over-intellectualize their feelings, give very little time to their emotions, and spend most of their time thinking about them.

The way out of this dilemma is to move directly on to the next emotion. (This requires the operation of moving center.)

Marilyn Monroe, William Shakespeare, and Vincent Van Gogh operated from this part.

THE PARTS OF INTELLECTUAL CENTER

The **Moving Part** of intellectual center has to do with intellectual memory. This part also governs communication and all actions based on thought. War, premeditated murder, embarking on a particular career are all actions based on thought - i.e. first the thought and then the action.

This is the part from which goals emerge, making a list, checking items off the list after achieving them etc.

The person trapped in this part may move rapidly from one thought to the next without finishing the first thought. This could lead to an attack of frenzied thinking which is not productive. It is difficult for scholars with this trap as they can get caught in endless deliberation without ever going into physical action.

These people really go for the Logos and want to use it - i.e. thought translated into usefulness.

The **Emotional Part** of intellectual center governs desires and interests, decisions, anxieties, depressions, optimisms, pessimisms. These are thoughts that result in emotional responses. Anxiety or depression can become a response to an original thought.

The thought may be for example - "I don't have enough money for a new coat." A rush of emotion may follow this thought, then depression or anxiety.

Many types of psychotherapy set out to deal with people who are trapped in the emotional part of intellectual center.

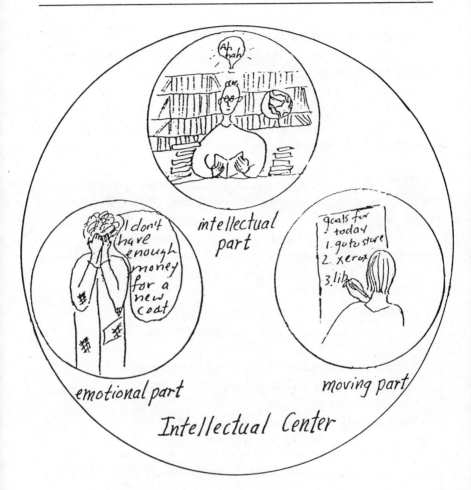

Intellectual Center

Intellectual Part - pure logic.

Emotional Part - thought that results in emotion.

Moving Part - first the thought then the action.

Worries, anxieties and depressions are not true emotions. They are based on thought. So they cannot be relieved by any form of release or satisfaction.

One can only experience true emotion and the release of that emotion in the emotional center. The intellectual part of intellectual center must be called upon to change the original thought, idea or belief to a new one.

The Intellectual Part of intellectual center governs pure thought, an original idea or a new belief. This part governs philosophy, logic, conscious awareness, sentience, the knowledge that we are alive and exist, and the evolution of new concepts.

INTELLECTUAL CENTER	
Intellectual Part	Thinking about thinking e.g. pure logic (Pure thought)
Emotional Part	"I can't stop brooding/worrying." (Think then feel)
Moving Part	"Let's be logical." (Think then move)

EMOTIONAL CENTER	
Intellectual Part	"I'm feeling this way because..." (Feel then think)
Emotional Part	Feeling an emotion e.g. laughing, crying. (Pure feeling)
Moving Part	"I'm feeling compelled to..." (Feel then act)

MOVING CENTER	
Intellectual Part	"Why did I do that?" (i.e. shoot first, ask questions later.) (Move then think)
Emotional Part	"I'm afraid I'll move before perceiving." (i.e. they leap then feel) (Move then feel)
Moving Part	Moving the body e.g. run, skip, jump. (pure movement)

Find Your Centering

Pick the center which most characterizes your daily behavior.

1) I like to analyze situations and figure out what happened.
I love philosophy and kicking around ideas.
Usually I think about things before doing anything.

2) I tend to cry easily.
I change moods rapidly and am drawn to music, dance, and art.
I am quite perceptive and able to feel out what is needed.

3) I am drawn to activities of all kinds.
I find it hard to sit still.
I'd rather do something than talk about it.

Code
1. Intellectual
2. Emotional
3. Moving

Find Your Trap

Remember that you will identify with all of the following statements to some extent because we all do them all from time to time. Pick out the group of three statements that is most typical of your daily approach.

1) I tend to be a worrier.
   I'm often anxious about what will happen.
   Sometimes things come to mind and then I get depressed about them.

2) I am often driven to wash dishes or do something active while I am thinking about something.
   I tend to take one idea to the next and the next until I get somewhere.

3) Often I know the plot way before the end of a mystery book or movie.
   I am extraordinarily perceptive in most situations.
   Sometimes I get so caught in thinking about my feelings I stop actually feeling them.

4) I tend to be spontaneous with my feelings, letting them dictate my actions.
   I have a tendency to be impulsive and sometimes I regret having bought something on impulse.
   I often put my creative ideas into action right away.

5) I love to dance and express myself exuberantly.
   My postures, expressions, and gestures communicate most about what I have to say or am feeling.
   I have a flair for the dramatic.

6) I like disciplines like martial arts, marching, and finely executed maneuvers requiring mathematical precision.
I enjoy plotting out the movements for dances, machine parts, or computer programs and graphics. I am inventive.
In sports I like to figure out ahead of time where the plays will be made.

Code
1. Emotional part of intellectual center
2. Moving part of intellectual center
3. Intellectual part of emotional center   ←
4. Moving part of emotional center
5. Emotional part of moving center
6. Intellectual part of moving center

How to Work with Centers

Once you grasp how the centers work, it is useful to stop and observe several times a day which center you are operating out of - called "photographing".

As a result, you can choose to operate differently if you want to. The habitual way isn't always the most appropriate. In general you can change centers in any given situation through an act of will or intention. However, if a center is heavily blocked it must be cleared and freed before this becomes possible. Clearing can be accomplished through a number of methods including hypnosis, psychotherapy, meditation, concentration, visualization, body-work, acupuncture, and healing.

For example, if a person's emotional center has become shut down due to painful childhood trauma such as the death of his mother, feelings will be cut off for the most part. This tends to occur because the pain of the experience is overwhelming and resisted by the child because of survival instincts. The memory of the painful experience must be released and experienced via one of the methods mentioned.

In American society men are often trained to block out pain, e.g. so as to play sports, and this leads to them learning to cut off firstly physical sensations, and secondly emotions.

Efforts are made in most cultures to make sure the emotional center is not blocked when a crisis occurs. For example, historically, wailing women were sometimes employed at funerals to make sure the feelings of grief were released. In modern days frightening or sentimental movies perform a similar function of releasing pent up emotions.

Nevertheless, some cultures like current western society tend to block emotional expression especially in men. The result is that most men are 80% emotionally shut down and those that aren't often doubt their masculinity. Emotional opening requires first a willingness to be open, second permission to be open, and third some attention and energy put into releasing. Group therapy and men's groups have become popular methods of dealing with this.

Western society promotes intellectual development and restricts those who are intellectually blocked. Blockage may be karmic and the result of brain injury or genetic defect. However, many kinds of intellectual blockage result from simple conditioning and programming that one is not smart. This type of blockage can be removed through reprogramming and validation of one's cognitive abilities. The key to this lies in instinctive center healing, where the fears and beliefs were originally recorded.

The moving centers are perhaps the least understood and so more time will be devoted here to discussing how to use them.

Moving center and higher moving center issues are harder to handle than those of the other centers.

Consider the intellectual centers. In our society you can usually get as much education as you want, and as much knowledge as you wish, to do what you want to do. You generally get it handled. You acquire sufficient skills to make your life work, either to a lesser or greater degree.

Similarly, for the emotional centers. Even people who are emotionally blocked are willing to realize this and are able to work on opening up emotionally to some extent. A person can make advances on this according to where they are and how they feel. Everyone still feels emotions, even those who are emotionally blocked. No one feels no emotion. They will sometimes at least feel happy or sad, confident or fearful.

But considering the moving centers, how many people have their sex lives, their monetary havingness, their careers, and their health the way they want it?

So, moving centered issues tend to be the issues people have the greatest amount of difficulty with. They are more complex and more demanding than the other centers. People often see their bodies as merely vehicles that cart them around, the business of making money to live off as an undesirable burden, and sex, they'll have it when they can get it.

However, you can focus on these issues, and place your intention on getting them the way that you want them. This includes addressing your habit patterns, the hallmark of the moving center. They are inefficient and take a while to change.

Look at what it is you want in these areas and look at your habit patterns. Look at starting habit patterns that will bring you towards your goal. Being habits, by repetition they will bring you towards what you want. Moving centered issues turn over very slowly.

You can have a thought very quickly, you can have an emotion in a flash, but you can't change a physical habit that fast. Ask someone who has tried to stop smoking, for example. It takes longer to get the habit of lighting up out of your system than it does to purge the craving for nicotine.

In setting out to establish new habits, new patterns, and fresh levels of handling these issues, be tolerant and accepting of the time it will take you and the difficulty of the task. Don't look for results within a few days or even weeks.

We actually train our higher and lower moving centers to handle energy. The energy manifests as issues, or as physical problems, and we learn how to handle them. In experiencing this energy it is important to let it flow through the body. If it is blocked it may manifest as aches and pains, sickness, colds etc. For example, if we wish to raise our level of prosperity, we will feel a surge of energy especially as our goals begin to manifest. If this surge is resisted in the body, physical distress occurs in the forms just mentioned. The resistance of course comes from a variety of habitual beliefs and patterns that want things to stay the same, e.g., "If I become prosperous, I'll lose all my friends."

Let the issues that arise have their full sway and take the opportunity to explore what it is that you are really doing. Examine each belief and habit pattern and then release it.

The point is that this process takes as long as it takes, from three weeks to six months. It may take your moving center that long to get the point that change is wanted and needed. Ridding oneself of unwanted habits can take time but can be done.

Chapter Twelve

Bodytypes

Bodytype has to do with such factors as the height and weight of the entire body; bone structure including length and size of bones, teeth, and nails; the coloration and texture of hair and skin; the strength or weakness of the organs and their size relative to one another; the responsiveness of the nervous system; the shape, size and strength of muscles, and every facet of the physical body. The configuration of the body has much to do with the development of the body personality and its foibles.

In other words, bodytypes have two components:

Physical - The attributes that have positives and negatives, e.g. Saturn bodytype has the positive of high physical indurance and the negative of frequent chiropractic problems.

Emotional - There are personality traits associated with each bodytype, e.g., Mars bodytypes have the positive of tending to support the underdog, and the negative of being impulsive.

On the Overleaf Chart the physical and emotional traits are intermeshed, and the most important attribute - either physical or emotional - has been chosen. So the positive and negative poles are not solely emotional or solely physical.

Bodytypes are directly related to planets. A person's physical makeup is, in large part, determined by the positioning of planets at the time of conception. The fetus draws from the gene pool of each parent and selects those qualities that are appropriate for the purpose of the lifetime.

The position of planets acts as a kind of architectural blueprint for the body in general. This is why we see that children of the same family, although they may clearly resemble one another, vary greatly in terms of coloration, size, and shape. Usually people are a combination of up to three planetary types - one principal type and two minor types. Occasionally, a person may be a combination of two planetary influences and rarely do we see a pure type influenced by one planet only.

Bodytype is a difficult topic because it is the least clear-cut of all the information offered in this volume. As people are a mixture of types, recognizing the permutations and combinations is difficult. The information is useful where people recognize one influence and can then gain insights around it.

Why do we have a combination of bodytypes? Simply speaking the combinations provide us with variety on the physical plane. However, as we shall see, they also facilitate and retard the influences of the other overleaves we have chosen.

Sometimes essence uses bodytype as a vehicle for eccentricity. So, being extremely tall, with people walking into your kneecaps, would be an interesting challenge to the goal of acceptance. The opposite might be seen in Napoleon, who took on the challenge of being intensely dominant when very short.

So bodytypes can be used to promote certain karmic experiences and add spice, intrigue and humor to one's existence.

Conventional good looks bring a different set of circumstances to bear than a bizarre or grotesque physical appearance might. An unhealthy body or one with a limited genetic makeup would fit the bill if, because of a karmic debt, a person needed to be cared for by another.

You can readily see on a daily basis how physical attractiveness makes it possible for many persons to become involved with one another when a karmic debt is in need of payment - or creation... without the attraction element they might never seek the romantic entanglements.

Bodytypes relate also to astrology itself. It is likely that a person's bodytype or one of the three major parts is manifest astrologically in that the relevant planet will be located in the First House (physical body). It could be there as a more subtle influence, e.g., showing up in the house of family. Perhaps the person spends time as a child in the family the influence manifests and the body takes on that aspect; more often the bodytype is transmitted genetically through the parents.

These are seven main planets that influence bodytype:

Axis	Ordinal	Neutral	Exalted
Inspiration	Lunar		Saturn
Expression	Mercury		Jupiter
Action	Venus		Mars
Assimilation		Solar	

The Seven Major Bodytypes

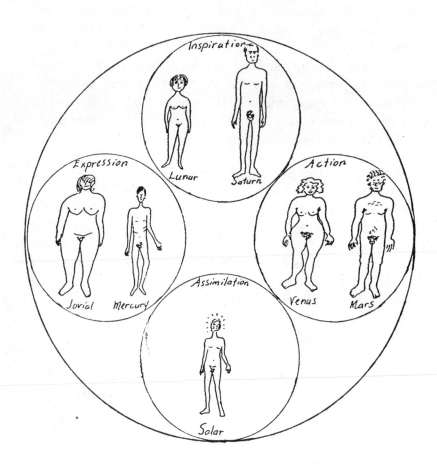

Two other planets influence bodytype and they are Uranus and Neptune. They are the furthest planets and their influence can reach a maximum of only 30%. The planet Pluto is a rare influence.

Stereotypes

Bodytype	Stereotype
SOLAR	THE CHILD
MARS	THE ATHLETE
VENUS	THE GODDESS
SATURN	THE LEADER
LUNAR	THE GENIUS
MERCURY	THE PERFECTIONIST
JUPITER	THE EMPEROR
URANUS	THE ECCENTRIC
NEPTUNE	THE STAR
PLUTO	THE MASTERMIND

Bodytypes affect infant, baby and young souls much more than mature and old souls. Infant and baby souls will tend to select bodytypes according to role much more than other soul levels. For example, a baby soul warrior would make a massive and strong body a top priority; whereas, for an old soul warrior this would be a minor consideration.

Certain roles prefer specific bodytypes. For example, warriors and kings like the Mars bodytype for physical strength and perhaps Saturn for endurance. Kings are partial to Jupiter because of its grandeur. Priests like Saturn because of its height and Solar because of its radiant qualities and ability to attract attention. Servers go for Lunar, artisans enjoy Mercury for its quickness and sages favor attention getters like Jupiter, Saturn, and Venus.

Scholars, being neutral go for any body type but prefer Mercury for its rapid processing. The bodytypes facilitate certain overleaves and retard others. For example, a Venusian body type would promote emotional centering. Saturn would facilitate a goal of dominance but not particularly a goal of submission. Mars goes well with aggression mode but not particularly with caution.

The ordinal planetary types are all feminine ones, whereas the exalted planetary types are characterized by masculine energy. The sun or solar type is neutral and does not occur often. The ordinal planets are more passive and influence a person to be more internal, the exalted planetary bodytypes are more outgoing and push a person to be active out in the world.

Planetary types flow according to the model of an Enneagram. That is, each lifetime you select a principal bodytype. There is a direction of flow, with the main emphasis resting with the central bodytype of the three - so your bodytype may be seen as a triad. That is, you are leaving one planetary type, fairly immersed in the next and already starting into the third. This provides for constant variation and change so all bodytypes are experienced by all roles over time.

Diagram 1

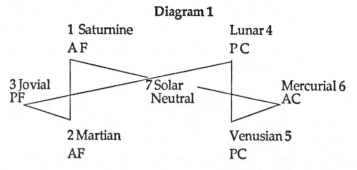

1 Saturnine   Lunar 4
  A F   P C

3 Jovial   7 Solar   Mercurial 6
  P F   Neutral   AC

2 Martian   Venusian 5
  AF   PC

*Note the numbers are only to show the direction of flow.
A = active   F = focused (masc.)   P = passive   C = creative (fem.)

There is of course no better or worse bodytype, just a flow from one to another according to a definite pattern.

Diagram 2

Lunar   Saturnine

Jovial ◯ Venusian   Martian ◯ Mercurial

PASSIVE   ACTIVE

Diagram 1 shows the direction of flow of bodytypes from lifetime to lifetime. It is an unending flow. The solar type is neutral and is pulled in only occasionally. For example, the Saturn bodytype will gradually begin to appear more and more like a Mars type. In their next lifetime they will perhaps select Mars as being their principal bodytype.

Then during that lifetime they may gradually change physically toward becoming a Jupiter type, and so on and so forth.

As mentioned earlier, pure bodytypes are rare and occur when someone selects only one planetary influence.

They are often used for effect in cartoons, mythology and caricatures, e.g. Snow White (Solar), Santa Claus (Jovial), Charlie Brown (Lunar).

It is interesting to observe that the society's ideal bodytype also moves around the enneagram. The ideal model of the 1920s was tall and thin; this has gradually shifted to the trim, fit and athletic Saturn-Mars bodytype that is common in today's advertisements. The old art works of the previous century frequently focus on voluptuous women, the Venusian ideal at that time.

Each of the major planetary types are associated with certain familiar symbols, myths and visions of time.

Diagram 3 - Associations

Day	Planet	Deity	Characteristic
Sunday	Sun	Apollo	beauty
Monday	Moon	Diana	fertility
Tuesday	Mars	Aries	volatile, war
Wednesday	Mercury	Hermes	messenger
Thursday	Jupiter	Zeus, Thor	father
Friday	Venus	Aphrodite	love
Saturday	Saturn	-	weather

Diagram 4 - Glands and Chakras

Planet	Gland	Chakra	Characteristics
Sun	Thymus	4th	Immune system, body growth
Moon	Pancreas	3rd	Lymphatic system, digestion
Venus	Para-thyroid	5th	Dampening effect on thyroid
Mercury	Thyroid	5th	Speed
Saturn	Anterior Pituitary	6th	Mechanical control, masculine traits, thought & reason
Mars	Adrenals	1st	Survival, fire, fight and flight
Jupiter	Post Pituitary	6th	Mechanical control, feminine, maternal traits
Uranus	Gonads	2nd	Higher moving center; can program deformities into the body
Neptune	Pineal	7th	Higher emotional center; can be artistic or dreamy

Like all the overleaves, the planetary types have positive and negative poles.

Diagram 5

Ordinal	Neutral	Exalted
Inspiration		
+ luminous		+ rugged
LUNAR ———————————————— SATURN		
- pallid		+ gaunt
Expression		
+ grandeur		+ agile
JUPITER ———————————————— MERCURY		
- overwhelming		- nervous
Action		
+ voluptuous		+ wiry
VENUS ———————————————— MARS		
- sloppy		- impulsive
	Assimilation	
	+ radiant	
	SOLAR	
	- ethereal	

Diagram 6

Maximum Attraction Between Planetary Types
Saturn ——————————— Lunar
Jovial ——————————— Mercurial
Martian ——————————— Venusian

The above table shows the planetary types that have maximum attraction for one another. Stable relationships are facilitated when bodytypes are one step apart. Glandular differences relate to the chemistry between people.

The Seven Major Bodytypes

Lunar

- Negative, passive, feminine
- Pancreas, lymphatic system, subject to lunar cycles
- Water

Physical Characteristics
Luminous, pale or pasty skin; fleshy, round, moon- faced; poor digestion (lower tract), constipation, immature build. Common among orientals.

Psychological Characteristics
+ calm, methodical, passive, patient, tenacious, maternal, sympathetic, receptive, detail- oriented, mathematical (often genius).

- moody, introspective, cold-hearted, incommunicative, willfull, stubborn, unforgiving, depressive, destructive.

Miscellaneous
May be accountants, librarians, programmers.
Tend to be less developed physically and more intellectually.
Like being up at night.
Can be alone; don't like fame - meek, timid.
Are the mid-point of femininity; therefore tendencies of homosexuality among lunar men.
The watery element means flux and instability.
Often genius intellect.

Examples
Andy Warhol, Boy George (+Uranus), Woody Allen (+Mercury),
Truman Capote, Indrid Bergman, John Lennon,
Robert Redford (+Saturn, Mars) and Charlie Brown.

Venus

- Passive, positive, creative
- Parathyroids and adrenals (glands of passion)
- Earth

Physical Characteristics
Full-bodied, physical, voluptuous, soft, sensual, warm, hips wider than chest.   Thick hair, olive skin, eyes large and dark.   Broad bones, big feet and hands.

Psychological Characteristics
+ harmonious, socially warm, loving, gentle, non-judgemental, loyal, appreciate beauty, easy- going, friendly, good lovers.

- lazy, inert, vegetative, nonexistent, dependent, indecisive, careless, slovenly, gushy, sentimental, vacuous, sloppy.

Miscellaneous
Artistic, understanding of teenagers, good cooks, service-oriented, natural healers, good-looking; understand people in karma and are in a lot of karma; bring out strong emotional responses from others and feel strongly themselves.

Examples
Elizabeth Taylor,   Diana Ross,   John Travolta (+Mercury),
Marilyn Monroe,   Ted Kennedy,   Elvis Presley (+Mercury),
Warren Beatty and Queen of Sheba.

Mars

- Negative, active, focused
- Adrenals (fight & flight)
- Fire

Physical Characteristics
Solid; hair and skin can be red, pink, strawberry; freckles, swarthy, mottled complexion. Average or short height; muscular or action type;

Psychological Characteristics
+ vigorous, energetic, passionate, highly sexed, decisive, freedom-loving, brutally honest, forthright, feisty, live with a flair, defender of the weak & downtrodden.

- impulsive, easy to anger, sage, pugnacious, over- reacting, defensive, quarrelsome, brutal, rude, over- hasty, boisterous, lacking forethought, heart attacks, bad skin, high blood pressure.

Miscellaneous
Armed services, actors, firemen, animal magnetism, warriors, animal husbandry.

Examples
John Glenn, Paul Newman (+Neptune), Martin Luther King (+Jovial), James Dean (+Neptune, Mercury),   Shirley Maclaine (+Neptune), Farah Fawcett (+Saturn) and Robert Redford.

Saturn

- Positive, active, focused
- Anti-pituitary, skeletal, reason
- Earth, heavy metals.

Physical Characteristics
Rugged, gaunt, large tall frame, hollow eyes, square jaw, large forehead, broad nose, usually fair. Arthritic, chiropractic problems, migraines.

Psychological Characteristics
+ paternal, natural leaders, just, moderate, self- controlled, enduring, closed mouthed, secretive, calm, can handle crises, pioneering, survivalists.

- immutable, over-worked, inflexible, overly intellectual, despondent, severe, aloof, not forgiving weakness, political, feelingless.

Miscellaneous
Models, endurance activities, business, research, world leaders, TV personalities, carpenters, teamsters. Often in dominance.

Examples
Uncle Sam, Abe Lincoln, Jimmy Carter, Mick Jagger (+Mars), Meryl Streep (+Nept.), Princess of Wales, Cher (+Mercury) and Jacquelyn Smith (+Solar).

Solar

- Neutral
- Thymus, immune system & growth
- Fire

Physical Characteristics
Childlike, youthful, refined, delicate, frail, clear skin, slight figure, fairytale appearance, broad lips, poor digestion (upper tract).

Psychological Characteristics
+ radiant, creative, elegant, dignified, refined, innocent, fun-loving, childlike.

- airy, aloof, intolerant, naive, indiscriminate, greedy, androgynous behavior, juvenile, not wanting to grow up (Peter Pan), avoid reality (if they don't want to see it, they won't).

Miscellaneous
Like religious orders, good with children.
Often good voices and singers.

Examples
Judy Garland, Snow White, Peter Pan, Goldie Hawn (+Venus),
 Grace Kelly and Michael Jackson (+Nept)

Jupiter (Jovial)

- Positive, passive, focused
- Post pituitary, maternal
- Water, fog

Physical Characteristics
Ponderous, bulky, short, large, broad shoulders, fleshy, large breasts, light body hair, short-necks, sensitive ears, good hearing, poor sight, small teeth - in all, severe physical limitations. Soulful eyes.

Psychological Characteristics
+ Grand, generous, compassionate, kind, loyal, caring, affectionate, maternal, lucky, philosophical, arts, languages, well-directed mental powers, highly evolved appreciation for life, powerful presence, almost king-like.

- subject to periodicity, self-indulgent, extravagant, conceited, wasteful, craving attention, over-whelming.

Miscellaneous
Football players, wrestlers, benefactors, don't like being alone, like people around, Mars-Jovial is a common combination.

Examples
Santa Claus, Falstaff, Orson Welles, Einstein, Barbara Streisand, Pavarotti, Mr. Magoo, and Pope John Paul.

Mercury

- Active, negative, creative
- Thyroid, speed
- Communication, intellect
- Air

Physical Characteristics
Bright clean appearance, good grooming, dark hair & eyes, olive skin, figure is slender and agile, long lives, resonant voice, healthy large teeth, good eyesight.

Psychological Characteristics
+ Intellectually active, perceptive, witty, clever, versatile, sunny disposition, will not hold a grudge, clarity of expression.

- inconsistent, impulsive, explosive, nervous, jittery, argumentative, sarcastic, cynical, critical, frenetic, wired.

Miscellaneous
Latin races, Philippinos
Entertainers, debaters, politicians, many sages.

Examples
Johnny Carson, Sammy Davis Jr , Ronald Reagan,
Flip Wilson (+Mars), Elvis Presley (+Venus), Cher (+Saturn),
E.T. (+Jovial), Carly Simon.

Uranus

- Gonads, genetic manipulation
- Corresponds to higher moving center
- Masculine

Psychological Characteristics
+ independent, original, loathing restriction, strong-willed, humanitarian.

- eccentric, rebellious, deviant, particularly in sex, criminal genius.

Miscellaneous
Makes things different, has a drive toward fame.

Examples
Yul Brynner, Robert Duvol, "Lex Luthor", General Patton and King Henry VIII.

Neptune

- Pineal
- Higher emotional
- Hypothalmus
- Feminine

Physical Characteristics
Large saucer-like eyes, thin, dreamy quality

Psychological Characteristics
+ soulful, quiet, deeply emotional, idealistic, spiritual, imaginative, sensitive, artistically creative, graceful.

- impractical, unworldly, uncertain, melancholy, diffuse.

Miscellaneous
Artists, hypnotists, dancers.

Examples
Mia Farrow (+Solar), Anna Pavlova (+Lunar,Mercury),
David Bowie (+Solar),   Liza Minnelli (+Mercury, Venus),
Audrey Hepburn (+Solar,Lunar), Rommel and Mata Hari.

Pluto

They may do things in their lifetimes that have consequences for generations. Often, the significance of their lives is not recognized at the time.

Examples are Napoleon, Alexander the Great, Louis Pasteur.

Chapter Thirteen

Integration

This chapter has four parts:

1. The Overleaf Septant and Vignettes
2. Using the Overleaf Chart
3. Observing the Personality
4. The Value of the Teaching

The previous chapters have described the personality from a variety of viewpoints including seven distinct sets of overleaves and basic astrological influences. Now you can readily see the mechanism of the overleaves and how they work - in front of your very eyes, everyday.

> *When standing in a room at a party, you can see the people acting out of the whole system. On your left is an artisan in passion mode wheeling through idealism and impatience, on your right a quiet lunar man has just met your best friend and looks like the beginnings of karma they will both enjoy. The whole intricate machinery keeps spinning along in all its incredible complexity.*

This chapter is aimed at drawing the threads together and showing you what it means to have a personality. It sets out to answer the question, "So what?" So what that I have a personality? What am I meant to do about it? How do I get unstuck from false personality?

In this chapter we will recap all the overleaves in summary form and show how they form a septant. Every overleaf is used in a series of vignettes to illustrate how they work together to form the personality. Here also we review the significance of the axis, learn how to read overleaves, and discover how to stay in the positive poles. Finally, we have the opportunity to see how all this can be used to achieve greater awareness and operate more from essence.

Part 1: The Overleaf Septant

This section shows one of the ways that the overleaves relate to each other and interact with one another. They are not isolated features that pop up at random in your experience. There is a vast complex mechanism of energetic interrelationships that is touched on in one of its simplest forms as the septant. The septant principle applies to all the overleaves. The following example is one interactive pattern and there are many others:

A Sample of the Overleaf Septant (or Enneagram)

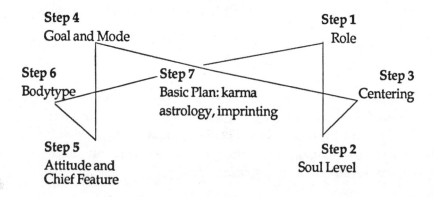

Step 4
Goal and Mode

Step 1
Role

Step 6
Bodytype

Step 7
Basic Plan: karma
astrology, imprinting

Step 3
Centering

Step 5
Attitude and
Chief Feature

Step 2
Soul Level

The Overleaves at Work

The following vignettes are examples of how the overleaves work together according to the septant just described.

For the sake of illustration all overleaves have been used in the seven vignettes that follow. These are simply examples of an infinite variety of combinations. Each role has been presented within a particular soul age and level and it is important to realize that all ages, levels, and overleaves are experienced by all roles over a variety of lifetimes. To give examples of each would require many volumes. Look around you at other people and you will see abundant variety.

Example Sets of Overleaves

Example 1: Warrior

Role:	Warrior
Soul Level:	Sixth Old
Centering:	Moving Part of Intellectual
Goal & Mode:	Acceptance & Caution
Attitude & Chief Feature:	Cynic & Impatience
Bodytype:	Mars & Lunar

Karma, Imprinting, Agreements - In this case karma and agreement dictate a meeting between a man and a particular woman which results in marriage.

Let's say that you come to the planet as a sixth level old warrior (Steps 1 & 2). This means you are an action-oriented, focused, solid role who leads a hectic life, from an old soul perspective. When you walk into a situation the first thing you use is your centering (Step 3). Using your intellectual center dictates how you are going to pursue your   goal, that is you will approach it through a thinking process.

So to set the scene, suppose you decide to go to a party. You are in intellectual center and looking around you from old soul perceptivity. You have a goal of acceptance so you walk through the door thinking about being acceptable, and being in caution mode you are   feeling cautious about that. You go into the party cautiously being acceptable, thinking it out (Steps 1 through 4).

Events begin to unfold and your attitude comes up. Somebody tells you just as you reach the punchbowl that there is none left. The negative pole of cynicism leads you to mutter that you knew you weren't going to enjoy this party (Step 5), and being in the negative pole throws you into your chief feature of impatience.

You start to think (still using intellectual center) that if things don't improve soon you'll go home (moving part of intellectual - acting on the thought; also action oriented warrior). However, you strongly desire to accept the situation (acceptance from old soul perspective) and when you catch the eye of a friendly woman you decide to stick around.

All the while you are responding out of your bodytype - both appearance-wise and emotionally. From across the room people respond to your looks without having spoken to you. One woman thinks (unconsciously perhaps), "I'm looking for a nice man with a martian bodytype (Step 6). Maybe this is him." She comes over to say hello.

In the meantime your basic plan comes up. You have set up certain experiences and karma to unfold this lifetime. Tonight, as usual, you have your imprinting, and astrology is causing you to feel more ˙cheerful and open than usual. You have an essence agreement to start a major experience from meeting someone tonight, and here she comes...your favorite bodytype too. (Step 7)

So there you go around the whole set of your overleaves, operating step by step through the septant, a dance of energies and interactions that is infinitely variable.

Example 2: Server

Role:	Server
Soul Level:	Seventh Mature
Centering:	Moving
Goal & Mode:	Dominance & Perseverance
Attitude & Chief Feature:	Stoic & Stubbornness
Bodytype:	Lunar

Karma, Imprinting, Aggreements - In this case karma pushes for repayment of an old debt owed to a person for having deprived them of shelter. Your imprinting makes you feel vulnerable to younger people.

You are a seventh level mature server who experiences life intensely. This means you are inspired by service to others from a heavily identified perspective. You are moving centered with a goal of dominance and this gives you an active life of leadership.

To set the scene, let's say you work for the Red Cross and travel frequently to disaster sites to set up shelters and assistance to those afflicted. In this case there has been a tornado and there are many homeless victims as well as people still trapped in the debris. Being in dominance you are in charge of a crew setting up meals for the victims. You are all over the place giving orders and pitching in to create food lines (moving centered) and you work relentlessly (perseverance) and without complaint (stoicism). Your Lunar body type gives you extraordinary intelligence that you use effectively in your work.

Although you are occupied you feel an intense urge to shift what you are doing (karma calling) and join a crew rescuing trapped victims, something you usually do not do. You quickly arrange for someone to take your place (the subtle control of the server) and join the rescue crew. You seem to know exactly where to go, stubbornly insisting on a particular direction. Being in dominance you get your way, and soon you hear the muffled cry of a trapped child. You identify intensely with the child's fear (mature soul) and work feverishly to free her. Just as you get her loose you slip and become trapped yourself in the debris (karmic debt and agreement to save her). You are trapped for hours and suffer intense fear and discomfort because you are moving centered and cannot move. However, again you do not complain and appear unscathed because you are a stoic. After some hours, you are freed and without delay you return to your post. You assist with meals once again, feeling lighter and more energetic now that a major karmic debt is complete.

Had you looked at your astrological chart for the day you would have seen a configuration of influences suggesting a high potential for heroics as well as accidents. (As well as natal chart showing certain types of accidents in certain places at given times.)

Here again you can see the dance of overleaves as they weave in and out to set the scene for lessons and provide an interesting stage for karma to play itself out.

Example 3: Artisan

Role:	Artisan
Soul Level:	Second Baby
Centering:	Emotional
Goal & Mode:	Re-evaluation and Reserved
Attitude & Chief Feature:	Spititualist & Self Destruction
Bodytype:	Mercurial

Karma, Imprinting, Agreements - You are heavily imprinted by restrictive and punitive parents with whom you have an agreement to live with for your life's duration. This also sets the stage for a karmic repayment in a later lifetime in which the roles are reversed.

You are a second level, baby artisan who has suffered genetic damage in-utero and you now live with your parents in a semi-retarded state. Your parents, also baby souls, are sternly religious and believe in many restrictions and punishments. This has caused a conflict within you because you are emotionally centered but are compelled to repress your feelings because of your fear of them (punished for expressing them).

Your entire life is dominated by your disability (reevaluation) and you are unable to provide for yourself. You spend your days carving religious figurines and statues for the local church (spiritualist artisan). This provides an outlet for your creativity as well as your emotional centering. Your work is surprisingly refined and delicate (reserved mode).

One day you are carving away trying to perfect a religious figurine (Mercury body type) and you are frustrated in your attempts. You become enraged (emotional centering), break through your reservation and throw a tantrum, breaking the figurine in the process (self-destruction). Your parents drag you to your room with severe admonitions and lock you in for hours. Feeling that your life is valueless you pound your head against the wall (self-destruction), until exhausted you turn to prayer for comfort (spiritualist).

Example 4: Scholar

Role:	Scholar
Soul Level:	Third Young
Centering:	Intellectual
Goal&Mode:	Discrimination & Observation
Attitude & Chief Feature:	Skeptic & Arrogance
Bodytype:	Saturn

Karma, Imprinting, Agreements - Your imprinting has caused you to be picky and hard to get along with. You have an agreement to teach but are highly introverted and this creates much self-karma for you.

You are a third level, young scholar who has a position as a professor and researcher in a major state university. This fits well with your intellectual centering and scholarly pursuits (assimilation of knowledge). Being third level, you are highly introverted and prefer research but are required to teach some courses that you dislike. You often alienate students in your classes and are considered an extremely difficult grader (discrimination). You prefer your research as a debunker of parapsychology and metaphysics, subjects you are positively scathing about (skeptic with discrimination). You have written many books on these matters, spinning your theories (negative pole of scholar) and compiling data to disprove other theories. You believe you are the ultimate authority on the subject and snub other professors rather than dialogue with them (arrogance).

One day you are called before a committee of your peers regarding a distressed student whom you had insulted with suspicious questions about his integrity (before an entire class). You try to analyze and figure out what reasons you will give them for what happened (intellectually centered). You arrive at the meeting scrutinizing the room and those present (observation mode) and put on a bold front (arrogance) by standing to your full height (Saturn body type) to appear impressive. Inside you are quaking because you are unsure of yourself and uncomfortable with the level of emotion you feel. You are quite skeptical of their motives and decide that they are not worth talking to (rejection, negative pole of discrimination).

The outcome of the meeting is that you are chastized heavily but not fired, because nobody wanted to be on your bad list for obvious reasons. You feel rejected, and since you live alone and have few friends, you pour yourself into writing a book - another scathing attack on your pet subject, parapsychology.

Example 5: Sage

Role:	Sage
Soul Level:	Fourth Old
Centering:	Emotional
Goal & Mode:	Stagnation & Passion
Attitude & Chief Feature:	Pragmatist & Greed
Bodytype:	Jupiter

Karma, Imprinting, Agreements - This is a rest life for you and thus you have planned little karma and few agreements. Your imprinting makes you easy-going with a flair for the dramatic.

In this scenario you are a fourth level old sage who is independently wealthy and doesn't have to work. You are the mother of four children who are cared for by yourself, assorted nannys, and the many relatives who like to hang around you for your wit and wisdom (jovial bodytype). You are, however, passionately interested in the study of metaphysics and philosophy. You have a spiritual teacher who provides you with great emotional satisfaction (emotional centering) and who you cannot seem to get enough time with (greed), although you are his chief informal entertainer (sage). You are an efficient and practical manager of your estate (pragmatist) now that your husband has died and left you with a vast inheritance.

One day you are feeling excited about doing something new in your life for fun (emotionally centered and passion mode). You hear about a local amateur theatre group and decide to try out for a part in the play. Amazingly, you are picked for the lead because of your great natural talent but this seems like too much work to you and you opt for a secondary role (pragmatist). The play is a great success and you have a wonderful time bringing amusement to the entire theatre group. Interestingly, at the same time you have interested a number of them in a spiritual teaching that you are involved in (sage in passion). You quickly pass them on to your spiritual teacher, leaving you free to play (stagnation).

Example 6: Priest

Role:	Priest
Soul Level:	First Mature
Centering:	Intellectual
Goal & Mode:	Submission & Power
Attitude & Chief Feature	Idealist & Self-Deprecation
Bodytype:	Solar

Karma, Imprinting, Agreements - You have been imprinted to put others' needs before your own and yet be outspoken as well. Although you are involved in the ministry, karma dictates a sexual relationship with a man.

You are a first level mature priest who is in the clergy of a large traditional church with much hierarchy. You have a goal of submission which causes you to follow the dictates of the church and to put the needs of the downtrodden and poor before your own. This creates a terrible conflict in you because as a mature soul you are identified with and concerned about the welfare of the needy and at the same time you are ordered to amass wealth for the church. Your idealism intensifies this struggle because you believe you ought to be able to do both. The desire for material wealth and power of the young soul still has an influence on you and you slip back and forth on the issue. All this causes you to feel terrible about yourself much of the time and you are constantly doing self-imposed penances to feel more worthwhile (self deprecation).

One day you are ordered to shift funds set aside for the poor to an expense account for a visiting dignitary. You are in great conflict and try to think through the problem over and over (intellectual center). Because of the struggle, you seek out the advice of a friend of many years, also in the clergy. You are in a vulnerable state and when your friend suggests intimacy with you, you give in to his sexual advances and become heavily involved (karma). You feel even more worthless because you have broken your vows (self-deprecation) and eventually this results in your ultimately leaving the clergy and setting up a non-profit corporation that provides food and shelter for the poor.

You are dedicated and highly successful at this endeavor and in a short time have reached many people as well as raised a vast amount of funds due to your radiant (solar) personality (priest in the power mode). You no longer feel conflicted in your work and your karmic affair has ended because your friend remained in the clergy. Now you devote yourself for the rest of your life to this project (submission).

Example 7: King

Role:	King
Soul Level:	Fifth Baby
Centering:	Moving
Goal & Mode:	Growth & Aggression
Attitude & Chief Feature:	Realist & Martyrdom
Bodytype:	Venusian

Karma, Imprinting, Agreements - You come from a poor broken family in a violent neighborhood that has caused you to fight for your survival. Being a baby soul you want to create some lessons and karma this lifetime and you have agreements for six children of your own.

You are a fifth level baby king who has grown up using your fists to settle differences on the streets. You have learned that it is better to attack first rather than be stabbed in the back (aggression mode). You have a good sense of how things are on the streets (realist) and because of your presence and ability to master your environment (king) you eventually run one of the most successful drug operations in the city (moving center). You have a taste for pleasures and women (venusian) and you run a pimping operation on the side (tyranny). You are known for your unusual and rather eccentric sexual practices (fifth level) and these border on the violent. Although you are ruthless and somewhat successful you often end up getting stung in shady deals (martyrdom).

Later in your life, after much womanizing, fighting, and brushes with the law, you settle down of sorts to a more traditional lifestyle (growth). You marry and have six children whom you exercise absolute tyranny over. You become a regular churchgoer and never allow your daughters to date until they painfully abandon you and break away from home in their late teens (martyrdom).

You now have a job as union organizer and are a constant ball of action (moving center) as you learn the tough political machinery of this work. Ultimately, you are deposed and end your days in disappointment and feeling a victim. Nevertheless, you have learned to be less violent and have developed some mastery in communicating with others (growth).

Working with the False Personality

The Overleaves

The overleaves make up the personality. They are the tools that we use to experience the physical plane. They are not bad as such, only limited in their scope. You need not be restricted by them. Learn to function out of their positive poles. Learn also to slide to the positive pole of the complementary one as needed to remove yourself from a stuck place. Here is a brief review of the main overleaf categories and their function.

Role

The aim is to act out of your role because it is your primary beingness.

Goal   *SUBMISSION*

As your essence purpose, it motivates you and guides you in your aspirations. Use it as your guiding star, for what to aim for in situations.

Attitude   *REALIST*

The easiest overleaf to change, it is how you see the world - positively, negatively, either enabling you or disabling you.

Chief Feature   *IMPATIENCE*

You can uncover ways it blocks you from achieving your goal. Coming to terms with the underlying fear is a life task, and the aim is to erase it completely.

Everyone's life has specific traps, where you bought into beliefs, attitudes and fears that in later life you find yourself confronted with.

Mode   *POWER OR AGGRESSION*

Act your life out of it, and play with acting out of its complement.

Centering

See how it governs your responses. Find a balance of the three centers: intellectual, emotional, and moving.   Observe the trap.

You can distract the trap appropriately to access the third, least used center to develop it. Those with the moving trap can get in touch with feelings by, say, going for a walk. The emotional trap can be engaged by, for example, listening to music, and so on. The aim is not to tie up your other centers, but only the habitual one that you wish to distract.

Bodytype

Recognize both emotional and physical attributes. Focus on appropriate bodycare, diet, exercise and sex.

Part 2 - Using the Overleaf Sheet

Stay in the Positive Poles

The negative poles generally relate to acting from fear and or illusion. The positive poles mostly describe a form of reality-checking. So, for an idealist, the negative pole of naivity means an overly-simple view of the world (therefore incorporating a measure of illusion) and the positive pole of coalescence relates to seeing how something would actually work.

For a cynic, the negative pole of denigration is essentially a projection of fear, and the positive pole of contradiction is putting one's world view out there for others to respond to - a form of reality check. When you slide from your usual overleaf to its complement, it is generally to the negative pole. So, someone who slides from growth will go to withdrawal, from acceptance to rejection, from impatience to victimization, and so on. Practice sliding to the positive pole instead.

Act from the Neutral Point

All the overleaves except the neutral axis have a pair. Let us take caution mode and power mode. Caution mode is disabling, a fear of doing it wrong, and power mode is enabling, a feeling of confidence and authority. The first creates the inner experience of self-karma. The second makes for karma out in the world.

The best place to be is a balance of both, the middle ground.

Caution mode is a triad with a positive and negative pole, and power mode is another triad. Together they form a septant, and the seventh element is the neutral point in the center of the pair. (Triads and septants are described in Volume Two.)

Being able to hold that neutral point for every overleaf is the best way to manifest one's personality. This could be fairly described as a step toward enlightenment as the burden of one's personality is lighter at this point.

Note the Significance of the Axis

Power mode is different from the goal of dominance. One of the differences is that power mode is on the expression axis. This means it is felt. Dominance is on the action axis and it is done. There is a distinct qualitative difference. Observation mode is assimilative whereas, a stoical attitude is inspirational. Notice how many of your overleaves fall within a certain axis. Do you have mostly inspirational overleaves or more action overleaves? more expression overleaves or a majority of neutral overleaves?

The configuration of overleaves according to axis can tell you much about your own or another's behavior.

Learn to Read the Overleaves

Anyone can learn to read other people's energy. You can practice looking at them and discerning the subtleties. You can start with dress, for example. A fifth level person may be quite eccentric with streaks of pink hair, and so on. His or her soul age can be easy to pick out--baby souls being fixed in their beliefs, young souls being determined to succeed, mature souls being consumed by the drama of their lives, and old souls with an air of "well - who cares?"

This is a skill that you can practice, and all the overleaves can be read with a measure of success.

Here is a clue. In order to determine someone's role, first determine whether they look ordinal, exalted, or neutral. Do they have an ordinary, everyday look? Ordinal: Artisan, Server, Warrior. Do they stand out somehow dramatically? Exalted: Sage, Priest, King. Do they appear neutral? Scholar.

Next determine their axis. Are they expressive? Artisan, Sage. Do they exude inspiration? Server, Priest. Do they look ready and built for action? Warrior, King. Do they look as if they are neutrally studying the situation? Scholar.

If you are in doubt, look into the eyes. The eyes tell a great deal about the person's soul age, role, and other overleaves. From looking into someone's eyes you can tell if they have had a lot of lifetimes or just a few. You may doubt your own skills but it's like learning the piano - it is constant practice.

At first follow this process for each of the overleaves. After awhile you will become adept at picking up the overleaves without thinking about them. This is like learning any skill. First you learn the structure and then you let it go.

Personality Influences not Covered by the Overleaves

The following are factors that shape and affect personality in addition to the basic overleaves. These however are never accidental and influence according to the master plan of each person. Paradoxically, they increase the possibilities for freedom of choice.

These influences include:

● past lives

● parallel or alternate universes (termed "aspects" of yourself)

● deep connections with others

● karma, agreements and monads

● resources of the planet - gems, herbs, spices, and animals, medicines, etc.

● dreams

● one's place in different configurations e.g., triads, quadrants etc.

Where this volume describes who you are, the next volume describes how you relate to everyone and everything, and includes all of the above.

A Review of Centers

Plane	Centers
Ordinal	
Physical	Moving (doing)
Astral	Emotional (feeling)
Causal	Intellectual (thinking)
Assimilative	
Akashic	Instinctive (awareness/review/neutral)
Exalted	
Mental	Higher intellectual (truth)
Messianic	Higher emotional (love)
Buddhaic	Higher moving (energy)

The lessons associated with the centers are related to seasonal activity. For example, Fall is the heat (reproduction) cycle and matches higher moving (sexual) center lessons, as does Spring. Winter characterizes the ordinal, closed in lessons and Summer the outgoing exalted lessons.

The Lower Centers

The lower centers, instinctive, moving, emotional, and intellectual, are necessary for survival in the human body. They are the ones that we operate out of principally. Although each of us is well developed in one center, the object is to strive for balance among them all.

The lower centers have traps associated with them that cause disfunction, distress, and imbalanced behavior. While elimination of the trap is a worthy goal, we can still use the parts of centers to accomplish what we wish. The difference is that of being trapped and consciously choosing.

The Higher Centers

The origin of the term "high" as in high priest relates to perspective. From the top of a mountain you get a perspective on the plains, the farms and what people are doing. From high up you see all that is going on down there; you are far away and detached.

Higher centers are similar in this sense of being able to look down on your life and see the path that you are following. You can see where you are identified in your life, where your false personality might have gone rampant, and you can see where you would like to be. The higher centers are a place of fresh choices. Higher is not better, just different.

Everyone has their own way of going into higher centers and it is another means of taking charge of your life.

One of the consequences of time is that we fall asleep and forget. To stay awake it is necessary to practice being in the higher centers, or self-remembering, as it is called.

People like to gather once a week or every two weeks as a minimum to remind themselves of the principles that they like to live by. That is why people go to church, for example. They like to express their ideals in their daily lives, act on them and assimilate them. The key that prompts that chain of events is inspiration, which is why priests, literally and role-wise, are so important. They wake us up, to keep striving toward higher ways of being.

Creating Your Path to Greater Awareness

Greater awareness begins with detachment and the ability to look at your own false personality. At first this may be a tricky thing to do. False personality is much like a cloak, and because we each have one on we are unable to see it under normal circumstances. In other words, the overleaves overlay our perceptions very effectively just as a cloak would overlay the body.

There are techniques whereby you can gain glimpses of your false personality - such as zazen or vipassana meditation. With these methods you intensely observe your thought processes until eventually you perceive that they are nothing but a construct of the mind and that all "reality" is merely a construct also.

This system teaches that false personality is based on two pillars - illusion and fear. The negative poles are a manifestation of them. Thus, when you are upset about anything, you can trace it to either or both of those two demons.

Fear is the emotion attached to separateness - for example being afraid of death is the fear that you will be even more separate from the Tao. Love of course is the sense of oneness.

As an example, people are so used to living with high stress that they don't know how to live without it. Even if you alleviated the cause of stress, they still wouldn't be able to be happy. They would commonly feel empty, and express it as boredom.

Part 3 - Observing the Personality

It will be apparent to the accomplished student that we are our own "self-delusional systems." This is one of the purposes of the false personality, to make the game of forgetting more real. To observe the false personality is to subdue it.

Let us look at this in another way.

1. The universe is in a constant state of imbalance and therefore growth. It is always evolving to higher and higher levels of consciousness by seeking balance.

2. You have false personality to keep you in imbalance and therefore growth. You exactly replicate the universe in this evolutionary process toward higher consciousness.

This chapter has been directed toward enabling you to sense imbalance and be responsive to it. You are then more in charge. The mechanism to sense imbalance is tricky and the skill of observation is elusive. The practice was refined and developed by Gurdjieff.

The steps are as follows: 1. Experience, 2. Observe, 3. Discuss. Simply repeat this process over and over. Let us look at an example.

> *A man comes home from work, as does his wife, and they prepare dinner together and eat it. Afterward they are washing the dishes by hand when they have an altercation. She insists that the spoons should be put "upside-down" or concave on the dishrack, and he says this is the wrong way up for spoons. She says that way they collect water - and so on. That, then, is their experience.*

Now, if each party is identified with their position the fight may escalate and false personality reigns supreme. The result is greater separateness and forgetfulness of at-oneness. However ,they can stop, detach for a moment, and observe their actions. If they sit down and discuss their observations they may come to an understanding of what occurred. This is an actual case, and the conclusion the couple reached was that she felt territorial about the kitchen, that it was her domain and that he should learn from her as she felt she knew more.

This example brings out an important principle. The very first inkling you get that things are not going the way you want them to comes from *unconscious behavior.*

The moment you start to smell a mouse you have a clue. This is the observation part. Then look at it and sense the feelings involved. These can lead to further clues such as key memories that show you your imprinting. If you know what is happening it enables you to change the way you do things. There is always a rationale. Human beings always do something for a reason, even if the reason died thirty years ago and the behavior continues.

The quicker you can catch yourself in inappropriate behavior and change it, the more conscious you are becoming. This is a process of become more aware of your subconscious (intellectual part of instinctive center). Consequently your behavior becomes more conscious and deliberate, and less unconscious.

This is a practice you can do daily, in all your waking time. It is profoundly challenging and rewarding. This system gives you the tools to work out why any given situation has occurred and what you can do to transform it to your greater satisfaction.

In a society that is largely unconscious, this is a radical and effective way of being.

In summary, the principles are:

1. *Experience*
2. *Observe*
3. *Discuss*

The purpose of this is of course to derive what is **true** and then to resolve it in the context that we all really care for each other and it's all okay (i.e. **love**).

Essence sets up opportunities for you to learn and grow many times each day. Your richness and wisdom as a human being is reflected in how well you understand yourself and the world around you. Your "lessons" will always stretch and test you to exactly the right degree.

The greatest single power in the universe is consciousness, and working toward higher consciousness is the greatest thing you can do with your life.

Part 4. The Value of the Teaching

The bottom line purpose of this system of knowledge is as follows:

1. Recognize false personality.

You have a false personality each lifetime in the form of cultural and parental imprinting and programming. If you do not recognize it and are not aware of it, the nature of the beast is such that you are constantly at the effect of it. This is all very well for creating karma and leading an intense and exhausting life but the message is that you don't have to do that. You have choice and the tools are here to live pleasurably from essence.

2. Master karma.

The purpose of your being here is solely to experience intensity. Intensity is emotion. Emotion is karma. By understanding karma, and self-karma, you can move through the intensity in your life.

3. Use support.

Share your life. Remember that we have set up separateness as a part of the physical plane. The point is to remember that we are all in the same bathtub together. In fact, we are one. Therefore trying to go it alone in life is an illusion. Support your friends and let them support you. Pull in your special support people and exploit the wealth of knowledge, loyalty, friendship and love.

> *The reason primitive man formed tribal groups was to be more powerful. Pull in the skills, knowledge, and strengths of others that you don't feel you have. Use them to achieve success, however you define it. You can extend your experience of living deeper than your false personality.*

4. Get what you want out of your life.

Note that you have chosen a body with intelligence, wit and beauty that contains every attribute you need to achieve your desires. If that wasn't the case, you wouldn't have chosen it. You can see yourself as having all the ingredients for success within you, and the challenge is to bring it out.

The purpose of being here on the physical plane is to master it. What holds most people back most of the time is a lack of inspiration, so that they feel motivated to strive. Finding the situation or the people to inspire you forward is a good move. If you resist doing that, notice your resistance and use this system to identify the cause.

This system is a potent approach to life. It firstly pulls to bits the component parts of how we go about our daily lives - how we set our goals and decide about attaining them. We get to see ourselves in great detail.

Having done that we are now in a position to grasp the bigger picture. Having seen how we are separate creates a context for sensing the original whole. Seeing the greater context is freeing because it provides perspective and choice.

Now you are able to step back and say, "Hey! - I am going to be a skeptic here and not my usual idealist." You are able to choose your overleaves and how you see the world. This is enriching because it prevents you from seeing yourself as a victim and puts you in the driver's seat.

> *In addition, you get to be more tolerant. You see what is happening when you are confronted with a person who is a Cynic in Discrimination with Power Mode and you get the opportunity to be truly tested as to how well you have mastered this teaching. Can you be even mildly tolerant of this difficult person? You may even succeed in enticing them into their positive poles.*

Sundry Principles

1.   To create new cycles in your life you must first end old ones. Ending old cycles creates a vacuum, and the universe abhors a vacuum.

2. If you resist a lesson it will take longer. It will take as long as it takes for you to experience what your essence is directing you to. Let come and go freely without desperation or need.

Essence seeks to give you your greatest lessons. What you fear the most will tend to happen, until you no longer fear it. Be neutral around pleasures and sorrows.

3. The vacuum principle means that every space is eventually filled. Therefore, one person who is growing fast will create a vacuum that will draw someone close to him to move fast in their life as well. And another person follows them - and so on like the flow of water when the plug is pulled in the bathtub. Similarly, for couples, groups, families, universities, countries, planets and so on. There is an evolutionary cycle with the elements progressing upward like steps on an escalator - and many forms of escalators!

4. Nothing is too slow or too trivial for the physical plane. There are no constraints on your life and who you can be.

5. Love yourself and all things are possible.

HAPPY TRAILS

Epilogue

(Jointly channeled by J.P. Van Hulle and Mark Thomas)

This teaching has been around for some time and the precepts are available to anyone and fairly readily grasped. They are basically the overleaves and the structure of the false personality.

Having mastered that, you can step beyond it to sense the integral nature of things - their essential wholeness, a theme that lies below the information you have.

The first book (*Messages from Michael*) and subsequent information was based on showing how people are different - how a sage differs from a scholar, how one goal differs from another. That is, of course, very useful because you have to understand who you are before you understand how you fit in.

The next step is about pulling it all together. Those distinctions, while they are significant and are the basis for seeing how the personality works and how you create your lessons and roll with them, don't always take you to the understanding of how you are connected to all things.

It is important to broaden your focus in a day-to-day kind of way, to back off and gain a longer perspective on your life. It is well nigh impossible to gain a sense of agape or self-agape beyond a mere intellectual appreciation unless you have a sense of how you ARE connected to all things.

One of the things that is readily left out of this teaching is to look at why you got involved with it in the first place. The reason was to learn about agape. You want to open up to being more tolerant and loving, you want more love in your life, you want more abundance, to have your life work better.

The real point of this teaching is to integrate your centers well so that you can be in higher centers a lot of the time. You can experience love, beauty and truth in all time frames - not exactly all at the same time but continuing to combine and come together.

The way to do that, the way to feel loving, and appreciating of beauty and being very much in truth is to integrate the lower centers. The way to do that is to have the physical world, have the emotional world, and have the intellectual world so that everything is having an equal amount of attention.

It is not going to work if it is always through struggle and always through pain and the emotional harassment of yourself that you attempt to live.

You work through all the seven centers, applying this information with emphasis on each center in its turn.

Once that is achieved you can let go, and start to seek tying it all together through enjoyment of the product of your work. You have come to terms with your major karmas, you have examined the truth in your life, you have weeded out the relationships you didn't want, you grasp how personality works and can take yourself into higher centers and so forth. This all leads you to enjoyment. Enjoyment of your life.

You are mastering how to do that. That leads to experiencing love.

So you can take holidays from this stuff, let your hair down and relax. It is easy to push and push in looking at truth, to examine it constantly for many years. You look at love and apply the truth to it and so on. Then let go and back-off.

Take deep breaths, gently look around you and BE. Sense how you fit in as a part of it all, and the wonderful pattern that is your life. You can marvel that you never did starve to death or go bankrupt because there was a plan and a purpose to all that you did and said. It was only that your opinionated mind might not have stopped opinionating long enough to fully grasp the beauty and complexity of it.

One can move into a wider scope of vision, that your life is wider and can have less pressure. This is harder for the solid roles, where the "do this" part of the information was easier. It is about relaxing, letting go, handling your life from "go with the flow." It is not wild and crazy or dull and boring.

Take more care of yourself and the ones you care for, and allow agape to come up.

The first place you can do that is around yourself. You can look at the positive parts of yourself, some self-appreciaiton - what it is you really like about yourself, what you think your talents really are.

When you think about what you want, think about how worthy you are of having it. Focus back on your self. "How is it I feel about me?" Don't shy away from what has been an overwhelming part of your existence for so long.

Most people don't like to appreciate themselves. Society, in general cuts people down to size to fit them into a larger group or structure. The well-oiled machine works better with less individuality.

Feel the cry of your own individuality and heed it. Find out more about it and how you are a wholesome worthwhile human.

Cast an eye also at what you don't like about yourself. You can think about whether or not you want to improve that. Just look at it. It doesn't mean doing anything about it - this is about being. How do you be? What IS about you?

While you live day to day, do you have to be those things you consider to be negative? Can you BE some other way when a certain situation shows up? Can you react more positively than before, not from pounding at the issue or forcing yourself but noticing that you weren't being what you wanted to be in the first place.

Give up on societal norms and ideals. No one interested in this information fits societal norms and ideals. They are not a very good guide anyway.

The highest criterion is what you expect of yourself. Only where you fall down and you aren't pleasing yourself should you look at "should I do something else here?" All it takes is noticing and being yourself - being awake.

So, when you are fully awake and aware of your unique individuality, you can recognize the essential oneness of all life. For what ties all life together is individuality and self-expression, essential attributes of the Tao.

Appendix

The Planetary Shift

Currently, the average soul age of the population of the earth is late young moving towards early mature. This shift started in the 1950's and is expected not to be completed until 2050. The shift is to some degree traumatic as it represents a change in values and perspective from a preoccupation with the material world to an intense focus on emotions and relationships.

Young soul qualities correspond with the astrological qualities of the age of Pisces and mature soul qualities correspond to Aquarian characteristics.

The shift will be characterized by events that compel people to look at life differently and these are often stressful. We have seen an increase in certain crises to date such as the quadrupling of oil prices followed by their collapse, local shortages of food, toxic chemical disasters and so forth.

This stress gives segments of the population an energetic shock and causes them to revise their values. An everyday example of this was the space shuttle (Challenger) disaster. This caused an intense re-evaluation, from the launch decision-making process to a review by the whole nation of the importance of the space program.

We could see an economic contraction start during the next five years resulting from excessive debt nationally and world-wide. In order for people to let go of materialism and excessive competition, it has to no longer work.

The world economy and especially the U.S. economy is approaching a major turning point during the late 1980's. If the 1990's were a period of economic hardship and distress this would facilitate the change, albeit via suffering.

The purpose of this appendix is to clarify the choices, and as you, the reader, understand the situation, you can choose to act creatively and positively. You can exchange work with others and form bartering groups. Help others to adapt, rather than having them react in anger and frustration.

Essence arranges these kinds of experiences to thrust peoples' soul perceptivity forward. The letting go of an old way of being that worked and was trusted, and the wary and reluctant trying of a new way of being involves fear. Therefore the fear of the consequences of holding on to the old view must be greater than the fear of the new. In other words, a measure of trauma is a part of the recipe.

Note however it doesn't have to be this way. Difficulties can arise but we do not have to create suffering out of them. The more we share what we have and work in supportive circles the easier things will be.

We are already seeing the influence of increasing mature soul values. Traditional structures such as organizations and governments that rely heavily on a vertical authority can be seen to be on the decline. In the last two decades twelve dictatorships around the world have fallen and have become democracies.

Structures that invite and include a horizontal level of decision making are seen to thrive. This includes small businesses and group-managed enterprises.

This shift in perceptivity affects all soul stages and motivates each one to reach the next stage more quickly. Thus, there is now a powerful thrust around the planet for infant souls to push on to baby soul perceptivity and for baby souls to push on to young soul perceptivity. An example of the latter would be the South American countries pushing for more urbanization, more technology, and more productivity.

There is a push for the younger soul population to shift into the mature perceptivity level, and an urge for the mature soul population to shift into the old. The older soul population will find this radical transformation of consciousness on the earth easier to experience than the younger soul population for whom the shift is experienced most critically.

Since the majority of the Earth's population is late level young, a shift in their perceptivity to early mature will create a critical mass, moving the level of consciousness of the planet forward a quantum leap. Let us make the move safely together.

Channeled Aphorisms

These aphorisms are reproduced here with the permission of Aaron Christeaan (10 Muth Drive, Orinda, CA 94563 U.S.A.)

Work is play or you have fallen asleep.

People always place a value on truth. If it comes free, they will find it to be worthless or priceless depending on whether they are on a spiritual path.

It is fine to resist. It is good work to look at what you are resisting, however. It may be a lesson you are ready to crack through.

Truth is always more compassionate than ingratiation. No-one ever stopped growing from hearing the truth.

There is no true rejection available in the universe.

Work is striving at what you really don't want to do.

You can't stop your own growth. You can't even stop someone else's for long.

All relationships are really only you and your attitude toward the other person.

The Truth does not need to be defended. It withstands any attack.

If you are defending yourself, you are defending false personality.

What is already ultimately decided. When is the only issue. All possibilities are available through your use of when. That is why time is such a valuable illusion.

Everyone can heal through love. You cannot heal someone without his permission, however.

Most threatening to the false personality are truth, love and the acknowledgement of Oneness. The irony is that "pleasure" is resisted much more than "pain". That is why more of your lessons are "painful".

In order to truly experience Truth, Love and Energy you must be willing to sacrifice boredom.

Boredom is the pillow that cushions you from being awake. It is a potent tool and terrifying to set aside.

The only reason you ever do anything is because you want to. All other "reasons" are part of the game.

Most of you use "privacy" as a way of maintaining loneliness and the illusion of separation. Privacy breeds masks and gossip.

You *cannot* hurt someone else. Whether or not he or she is hurt is *their* decision.

Once you know the physical game is an illusion you can truly enjoy the game.

Most of you would suffer gladly to grow, but what if the instructions were to play and enjoy your life? That is why so many grow slowly.

People can and will make their own decisions about this information. People hear what they want to hear and what they have decided to hear. This system cannot be misrepresented.

Honesty with one's self is crucial. Self-delusion is the blindest state there is and nothing could be further from growth.

There are different schools and teachings that lead one to truth and growth. This teaching is the path of love. The school of obedience is the most appropriate for baby souls. The school of "hard knocks" is the most appropriate for young souls. The school of intellectual pursuit and non-identification is most appropriate for mature souls. The school of love is always appropriate and the only school consistently attractive to old souls.

You are *not* a victim of circumstance.

Teaching is merely reminding others of what they already know. You've only remembered it first this time around.

It is appropriate when on a path of spiritual awareness to choose not to associate with those not on a similar path.

On the crucifixion of Christ: He was in agape. The four points were energy flows to and from the body to the four quadrant positions in the cosmos. His teaching was love and the heart wound indicated that.

True humility is for the strong.

Life is art and should be respected. Berating oneself is inappropriate. It means you have decided to refuse a lesson.

You teach what you most want to learn. Learning is remembering what you already know.

There is no such thing as a mistake. There are no accidents in the universe. There are no secrets in the universe.

Every event has its own significance.

All the planes of existence are competitive and play.

The teacher has the greater intent.

Groups operate at different speeds and levels. Be with a group you are comfortable with, this system of knowledge is not strenuous.

Don't guess - perceive!

The most powerful member of a family is the youngest.

The Law of Mob Intelligence: The more people in a group the lower the collective I.Q. or intelligence. That is why T.V. advertisements and programs are pitched at such a low level.

The larger your power, the slower and simpler you must be.

Glossary

The system of knowledge outlined in this book is more than a collection of concepts, it is a way of seeing the world. Certain words and phrases take on specific meanings. The definitions offered here are selective and partial, designed to educate the reader rather than offer dictionary accuracy.

abasement	Worthlessness, low (self) esteem.
abstraction	Generalized, unfocussed.
acceptance	To be in agreement with.
agape	Brotherly or spiritual love; unconditional love.
agreement	Simple unbinding arrangement to carry out a plan.
amoral	Indifferent to moral standards, principles or ethics.
anatomic	Machine-like, automatic, acting from instinct rather than thought.

appetite	Keen appreciation, develop a taste for.
arrogance	Superior manner, (indicating low self esteem), covers shyness.
aspect	A spin-off universe containing a spin-off of oneself.
astrology	Configuration of planets at birth and throughout life influencing the life plan.
atavism	Return to a simple, child-like state.
atomic	Instinct directed by essence.
attitude	Overleaf determining one's primary perspective.
audacity	Boldness or daring; radical initiative with a brave disregard for a negative outcome.
authority	Having or taking power to command; conviction stemming from superior knowledge or skills.
basic plan	General design for a lifetime, includes all overleaves.
beauty	Combination of qualities evoking awe and inspiration.
a being	Unit of intelligent consciousness sparked from the Tao.
belief	Placing trust in some person or fact without verification.

belligerence   Physically threatening, hostile, unfriendly.

bodytype   Configuration and appearance of one's body based on the influence of planets at conception and birth.

bondage   Slavery; involuntary service; controlled by another.

cadence   The group of seven in your entity that you arrived on the planet with; position 1 to 7 says something about your nature and style of lifetimes chosen.

cadre   Group of seven entities with whom you do most of your karma. About 7,000 people.

caution   Acting to minimize risk; fear of wrong move.

center   Overleaf that orders and organizes experience in seven ways that influence perception; communication channel between essence and personality.

-higher   Direct perception of the Tao.

-lower   Filtered perception of the Tao.

chakra   Energy vortex along spinal column organizing experience; communication channel and filter for movement of selected forms of energy.

channel   To communicate information and energy consciously from the non-physical planes.

chief feature	Main obstacle to achieving one's goal in a lifetime.
circuit	A completed set of cycles.
clarity	Free from ambiguity; distinct; focused; resolution.
coalescence	Translating thought into action; coming together.
coercion	Using force to gain compliance.
compassion	Deep empathy for another's sorrow or misfortune, with the desire to see it alleviated.
-ruthless	Telling the truth to another who wants help but who doesn't want to hear what is true.
comprehension	Intellectual grasp of a concept; knowing.
confusion	Disorder; bewilderment; chaos; embarrassing lack of clarity.
contingent	7,000 cadres or 49 million fragments, approximately; 1% of the earth's population.
contradiction	Speak-up against; make public contrary perceptions or beliefs.
cording	Energy connection between two people's chakras in order to communicate or draw energy.
creation	Bringing something new into existence; drawing from cosmos to the physical plane.

cycle	Completion of all stages from infant to old from vantage point of a particular role.
cynic	Focuses on what is negative or potentially negative.
death	Change of frequency from physical to non-physical.
daring	Bold move that is unexpected and non-conformist.
deception	Delusion; RE-creating of reality around others but especially around oneself.
deliberation	Careful consideration before decision; formal, slow approach.
denigration	To bad-mouth, defame, rubbish, pour scorn on, deride.
determination	Resolute, fixed purpose or intent.
deva	A fragment/essence/entity or cadre that inhabits a mountain range, a redwood tree or a duck etc. for experience; exists on the astral but is sensed and senses the physical.
devotion	Committed in service or dedicated to a person, or situation.
dictatorship	Overbearing, bullying, coercive, misuse of power.
discrimination	Ability to make fine distinctions. Discernment.
dissemination	Sharing, teaching, publishing (information etc.)

dogmatic   Requiring belief without validation.

dominance   Leadership or resulting from presence, outstanding attributes. Desire to win.

dynamism   Vigorous, energetic, hectic.

ego   False personality. Restricted to finite physical body.

egotism   Self-centered, preoccupation with self.

empathy   Vicariously experiencing feelings of another.

enduring   Long-suffering, stamina in face of hardship.

energy   The action component of the universe; includes matter, evolution, and growth. Space & time are derivatives.

energetic   (1) A quality of movement, growth or process. (2) Intense or protracted activity.

enlightenment   An experience of knowing the truth, love and energy of the Tao.

entity   A sentient being or oversoul comprised of 800 to 1000 fragments.

-fragment   A single part of the entity, a person.

erotic   Stimulating physical sexual desire; Lust.

essence   Soul, fragment, higher self, inner being, spirit.

-twin	Soulmate; fragment paralleling one's lifetimes, special intense relationship; he or she acts as traveling companion and reality check.
-mate	Former essence twin from a past cycle in another essence role.
ethereal	Unworldly, unconcerned with practicalities.
evolution	Growing or unfolding into a higher way of being or doing.
exalted	Wide focus, visionary.
expression	Disseminating a quality of life; outer manifesting of an inner intensity.
exploited	To be taken advantage of.
faith	Belief without proof; unverified stance.
false -personality	Comprises imprinting, negative poles of over- leaves and chief feature; illusion of sepa- rateness. Reality is a construct of the person- ality.
fear	Alarm or sense of danger; emotion around illusory separation from the Tao e.g. fear of death because "When I'm dead I'll be totally lost (separate)."
flow	Being congruent with events.

free-flowing	Not holding onto one's schedule or expectations in the face of changes.
frequency	Vibration rate of an essence or role.
frenetic	Intense and unproductive activity.
gems	Minerals energetically influencing the overleaves and deemed valuable.
goal	Overleaf determining primary motivation in a lifetime.
God	Tao, Atman, Supreme Being, Great Spirit, all that is.
greed	Excessive acquisitiveness for things, experiences.
growth	Seeking new experiences that expand one's sense of self or the universe.
Gurdjieff,G.	Armenian-born teacher who laid foundations for Michael Teaching.
heart link	Special loving relationship between two fragments spanning many lifetimes of experience.
herbs	Plants with medicinal qualities influencing overleaves.
humility	Modest sense of one's own importance.
idealist	Aspires to high standards of perfection, excellence.

identification	A process wherein a person takes on the emotions, qualities or characteristics of another. There is a loss of sense of separateness, without insight or understanding.
illusion	Of misleading or deceptive appearance.
immolation	Inappropriate sacrifice of one's life or wellbeing.
immutable	Fixed, unchanging.
impatience	Fear of missing out.
imprinting	Taking on how someone else handles a situation or life in one area.
inertia	The inability to change; inactivity; sluggishness.
ingratiation	Selling out one's own integrity to gain the good graces of others.
inhibition	Held in, reserved, repressed.
instinctive	Reactions that maintain the integrity of organism.
-center	That part of you that looks after your survival; behaving with an absence of thought, feeling or action, from doodling to illness.
-review	Looking at past experiences as a guide to next step.
integration	The organization of the components of self (essence & personality) into coordinated harmonious whole.

intolerance	Disapproving of or denigrating opinions, situations, people that do not conform to one's desired form of them. Can manifest physically as allergies etc.
intuition	Knowledge gained without an apparent source and independent of the reasoning process.
investigation	Searching enquiry to ascertain facts, especially where complex or hidden.
karma	Universal law of consequences or balance; emotional payback; can be caused by interfering with another's free choice.
knowledge	Clear and certain grasp of fact or truth.
leadership	Guide, direct, head-up or take initiative with a group.
love	The sense of oneness.
luminous	Glowing.
mastery	Perfection of expertise; command or control.
maya	Illusion; in its broadest sense, the entire physical plane.
Michael	Causal plane entity who disseminates this teaching.
mode	Overleaf determining primary method of operating.

monad	Achievement of a unit of life experience of a type e.g. husband-wife monad.
mortification	Humiliation, embarrassment, wounding of pride or self-respect.
naivety	Assuming too simple a view.
obstinacy	Adhering firmly or perversely in one's purpose; unyielding; fear of loss of integrity if one gives in.
order of casting	The order that you arrived on the planet in your entity.
oppression	Bossy, abuse of power, unfair imposition of demands.
ordinal	Narrow-focused.
Ouspensky,P.	Student and essence twin of Gurdjieff who put his teachings into writing.
overleaves	Specific traits and characteristics that make up false personality each lifetime.
pallid	Pale.
passion	Intense emotions intensely expressed.
perception	Immediate or intuitive recognition; knowing.
perseverance	Persist despite opposition or discouragement.
persistence	Stick-to-itiveness; continued efforts.

personality	That part of us that constructs our reality for us.
persuasion	To prevail upon a person to do something.
phobia	Irrational fear, obsessive dread.
plane	Seven relative levels of experience created by Tao for evolutionary purposes.
-physical	Most solid and slow level, of most forgetting and separateness.
pole	Extremes of overleaves, either positive or negative.
-positive	Essence oriented function of the overleaf.
-negative	False personality oriented function of the overleaf.
power	Influence or authority over self and others.
power animal	Source of guidance and information to an individual.
pragmatist	Mindful of results, pros and cons of a course of action, sensible, practical.
prejudice	Preconceived opinion without due consideration of facts or in the absence of reasonable inquiry.
pride	Self-respect, self-esteem.
prosperity	Experience of abundance in health, spirituality love, truth, etc.

rejection	Dismiss person or thing, often based on prejudice.
reason	Use of logic; explanation, rationalization.
re-evaluation	Review, reconsider, process with detachment.
reservation	Repression, held-in, restrained, focussed.
resignation	Unresisting acquiescence; mildly feeling a victim.
restraint	Keeping within limits as to action, space or choice.
role	Primary beingness through which a fragment experiences all of life.
sacrifice	To give over something of very high value for sake of something considered even more important.
self -deprecation	Lower esteem of self than held by other's estimations.
self -actualise	Completeness of individuality; fullness of experience.
self-karma	Lessons given to oneself that involve a polarity of experience eg. wealth-poverty, health-illness. Or attribute of yourself that you either like or dislike, and feel anything but neutral about.
selflessness	Having little or no concern for oneself, or a reward.
sensibility	A feeling or emotion; aware of the senses.
sentient	Ensouled; have intellectual part of intellectual center; have intellectual knowledge that they exist.

sentimentality	Excessive indulgence in feelings.
septant	1) Octave; eight steps that comprise a cycle of growth. 2) Group of seven people.
service	Assistance, nurturing; particularly pure as cause as in "cause and effect".
sexual	Combining male and female energies, can be physical, or energetic as in the case of the higher planes.
soul age	Development of perceptivity on continuum from infant soul to old soul.
-level	There are seven levels within each soul age.
sophistication	Refined, cultured, knowledgable.
spirit	Overguiding force above your essence and personality. You comprise all three.
spiritualist	1) Concerned with non-material, higher values. 2) Seeing manifold opportunities.
spirit guide	Assistant, guide, healer from non-physical planes, usually a member of one's own entity.
stagnation	Rest, flowing, riding the horse in the direction he is going.
stoic	Mask-like quality.
stubbornness	Insistence, fear of loss of integrity or change.

submission Serve or support a person or cause. Putting others ahead of oneself.

subservience Obsequious servility, may be due to fear of reprisal.

support circle Twelve specific positions of assistance filled by family and friends.

supposition Assuming as true regardless of fact.

surveillance Suspicious observation, spying?

suspension Separation of self from issue at hand to obtain rest, objectivity.

suspicion Doubt, mistrust, belief that what one is examining is probably negative in character.

sympathy Pity; Belief that subject of sympathy is a victim as opposed to compassion that encourages self-help.

Tao All that is, Atman, Great Spirit, God.

task companion Someone chosen at the beginning of the cycle, like an essence twin, with whom you frequently share life tasks.

teaching Description of a spiritual path that has the potential to guide one closer to the Tao or oneself.

telepathy Communication between minds by means other than five senses.

theory	Proposed explanation, rationale, guess.
thought	Direct intellectualizing on the physical plane.
time	Prevents everything from happening at once yet ensures each person eventually experiences all things; For adv. students - has three dimensions, linear, parallel, and simultaneous.
tranquility	Peace of mind, quiet, serene.
triad	Unit of learning; threesome; the "modus operandi" of karma; sub-division of a septant; Law of Three.
truth	What is.
tyranny	Gaining control by terror or nastiness or abuse of a situation.
universe	A sequence, complete in its entirety of all the stars, planets, structures and beings of one of the Tao's creations.
-parallel	A new universe is created for every significant possible outcome of a given event.
vanity	Attaching undue importance to one's appearance, qualities or achievements, due to low self-esteem.
verbosity	Talking with absence of meaning or purpose.
verification	Act of confirming the truth of; authenticity.
victimization	False belief that being at the effect of events is beyond one's control.

voracity   Insatiable appetite to possess or consume life.

walk-in   One essence agrees to take over the body that
                 another essence is leaving. Note that the sense of
                 "I" is the same as before but subject to different
                 influences. A walk-in is NOT a TOTALLY
                 different person although he or she may evolve
                 faster than they were formerly, giving a sense of
                 strangeness.

withdrawal   To retreat, retire or move back from involvement.

zeal   Excessive fervor for a person cause or object.

OVERLEAF CHART

	EXPRESSION		INSPIRATION		ACTION		ASSIMILATION
	Ordinal	Exalted	Ordinal	Exalted	Ordinal	Exalted	Neutral
ROLE	+ Creation ARTISAN - Self-Deception	+ Dissemination SAGE - Verbosity	+ Service SERVER - Bondage	+ Compassion PRIEST - Zeal	+ Persuasion WARRIOR - Coercion	+ Mastery KING - Tyranny	+ Knowledge SCHOLAR - Theory
GOAL	+ Sophistication DISCRIMINATION - Rejection	+ Agape ACCEPTANCE - Ingratiation	+ Simplicity RE-EVALUATION - Withdrawl	+ Evolution GROWTH - Confusion	+ Devotion SUBMISSION - Exploited	+ Leadership DOMINANCE - Dictatorship	+ Free-Flowing STAGNATION - Inertia
ATTITUDE	+ Investigation SKEPTIC - Suspicion	+ Coalescence IDEALIST - Naivety	+ Tranquility STOIC - Resignation	+ Verification SPIRITUALIST - Beliefs	+ Contradiction CYNIC - Denigration	+ Objective REALIST - Subjective	+ Practical PRAGMATIST - Dogmatic
CHIEF FEATURE	+ Sacrifice SELF-DESTRUCTION - Suicidal	+ Appetite GREED - Voracity	+ Humility SELF-DEPRECATION - Abasement	+ Pride ARROGANCE - Vanity	+ Selflessness MARTYRDOM - Victimization	+ Daring IMPATIENCE - Intolerance	+ Determination STUBBORNNESS - Obstinancy
MODE	+ Deliberation CAUTION - Phobia	+ Authority POWER - Oppression	+ Restraint RESERVED - Inhibition	+ Self-Actualization PASSION - Identification	+ Persistence PERSEVERANCE - Unchanging	+ Dynamism AGGRESSION - Belligerence	+ Clarity OBSERVATION - Surveillance
CENTER	+ Insight INTELLECTUAL - Reasoning	+ Truth HIGHER INTELLECTUAL - Telepathy	+ Perception EMOTIONAL - Sentimentality	+ Love HIGHER EMOTIONAL - Intuition	+ Productive MOVING - Frenetic	+ Integration HIGHER MOVING - Desire	+ Aware INSTINCTIVE - Mechanical
BODY TYPES	+ Grandeur JUPITER - Overwhelming	+ Agile MERCURY - Nervous	+ Luminous LUNAR - Pallid	+ Rugged SATURN - Gaunt	+ Voluptuous VENUS - Sloppy	+ Wiry MARS - Impulsive	+ Radiant SOLAR - Ethereal

Overleaves for _____

Role _____
Soul Age _____
Soul Level _____
Goal _____
Mode _____
Attitude _____
Chief Feature _____
Center _____
Part of Center _____
Bodytype _____

Overleaves for _____

Role _____
Soul Age _____
Soul Level _____
Goal _____
Mode _____
Attitude _____
Chief Feature _____
Center _____
Part of Center _____
Bodytype _____

Overleaves for _____

Role _____
Soul Age _____
Soul Level _____
Goal _____
Mode _____
Attitude _____
Chief Feature _____
Center _____
Part of Center _____
Bodytype _____

Overleaves for _____

Role _____
Soul Age _____
Soul Level _____
Goal _____
Mode _____
Attitude _____
Chief Feature _____
Center _____
Part of Center _____
Bodytype _____

Overleaves for _____

Role _____
Soul Age _____
Soul Level _____
Goal _____
Mode _____
Attitude _____
Chief Feature _____
Center _____
Part of Center _____
Bodytype _____

Overleaves for _____

Role _____
Soul Age _____
Soul Level _____
Goal _____
Mode _____
Attitude _____
Chief Feature _____
Center _____
Part of Center _____
Bodytype _____

Overleaves for _____

Role _____
Soul Age _____
Soul Level _____
Goal _____
Mode _____
Attitude _____
Chief Feature _____
Center _____
Part of Center _____
Bodytype _____

Overleaves for _____

Role _____
Soul Age _____
Soul Level _____
Goal _____
Mode _____
Attitude _____
Chief Feature _____
Center _____
Part of Center _____
Bodytype _____

Overleaves for _____

Role _____
Soul Age _____
Soul Level _____
Goal _____
Mode _____
Attitude _____
Chief Feature _____
Center _____
Part of Center _____
Bodytype _____

Workshops and Seminars

Jose Stevens, in addition to writing sequels to *The Michael Handbook*, has developed a handbook for counselors using the Michael system as well as an essence and personality profile. He is currently lecturing, consulting, and giving workshops on the Michael teaching, Shamanism, and prosperity for older souls. Workshops may be scheduled in your area by arrangement. You may contact him for consultation, classes, workshops and channeling at P.O. Box 5314 Berkeley, CA 94705.

Simon Warwick-Smith is well-known as a speaker, teacher and channel. He has been holding seminars on the Michael system throughout the San Francisco Bay Area since 1984. Simon has regularly scheduled seminars and is available to speak or teach in you area by special arrangement. For information regarding personal channeling appointments or class registration write to: P.O. Box 2023 Orinda, CA 94563.

More Books

The Michael Handbook
Jose Stevens, Ph.D. & Simon Warwick-Smith
A must for all serious Michael students! The authors cover soul ages, roles and overleaves in detail. An excellent reference book to the Michael system and easy reading. Illustrations, diagrams, glossary. **$11.95 Warwick Press**

The Michael Game *The Michael Digest Group*
A collection of articles by dedicated Michael students. Fascinating topics include 101 questions to ask a channel, the state of the planet, planes of existence, AIDS, whales and dolphins as sentient beings and more! **$7.95 Warwick Press**

Michael's Gemstone Dictionary
Judithann David, Ph.D. & JP Van Hulle
The most comprehensive collection of channeled material on the uses and healing properties of gems and minerals available today. Over 400 gems and minerals are covered. An essential guide! **$8.95 Affinity Press & Touchstone**

The World According to Michael *Joya Pope*
Provocative and engrossing, this book will be enjoyed by anyone with a curiosity about the universe we live in. Michael's ideas come to life as they are applied to public figures. An unforgettable book. **$8.95 Sage Publications**

Send ___ copies of *The Michael Handbook* - $11.95
Send ___ copies of *The Michael Game* - $7.95
Send ___ copies of *Michael's Gemsone Dictionary* - $8.95
Send ___ copies of *The World According to Michael* - $8.95
Please add $1.25 per book for postage and handling.
California residents include 6.5% sales tax.

Name_____
Address_____
City_____ State _____ Zip _____

Send orders to: Warwick Press P.O. Box 2023 Orinda, CA 94563

Professionally Produced Michael Tapes

Bring the energy and clarity of Michael into your life with cassette tapes of channeled material distributed by The Michael Educational Foundation.

Tape topics include:

> Michael Speaks Events
> Utilizing Your Support Group
> The Harmonic Convergence
> Essence Twins and Task Companions
> The Origins of Michael's Teachings
> Your Cadre and Entity
> Cosmology According to Michael
> And Many More...

> *Channeled by*
> *JP Van Hulle and Aaron Christeaan*

Also available taped series on the value and uses of crystals and minerals by Larry Byram.

Call or write for a complete catalog for all available tapes.

> **Michael Educational Foundation**
> 10 Muth Drive
> Orinda, CA 94563
> (415) 254-4730